MANAGEMENT 4.0

HANDBOOK FOR AGILE PRACTICES

Release 3

This handbook is created under the direction of the "Agile Management" professional group of the GPM German Association of Project Management e.V.

The book is published under the Creative Common License:
www.creativecommons.org

Alfred Oswald, Wolfram Müller (editors)

Management 4.0

Handbook for Agile Practices

Release 3

All authors have ensured that they have been granted all copyrights and that they alone are fully responsible for any copyright issues with respect to their contributions in this handbook.

Bibliografische Information der Deutschen Nationalbibliothek:

Die Deutsche Nationalbibliothek verzeichnet diese Publikation in der Deutschen Nationalbibliografie; detaillierte bibliografische Daten sind im Internet über http://dnb.dnb.de abrufbar.

English proofreading by Jeannie Graham.

   Alfred Oswald, Wolfram Müller

Herstellung und Verlag: BoD – Books on Demand, Norderstedt

ISBN: 978-3-7494-3097-0

CONTENTS

CONTENTS 5
THE AUTHORS 8
PREFACE 13
PRODUCT BACKLOG 18
CHANGES from RELEASE 2 to RELEASE 3 19
PART I – FOUNDATION 20
1   Agile Management – Traditional Management has reached its Limit 21
2   Management Models over the Course of Time 36
3   Theoretical Foundation 39
    3.1   Positioning: Models, Theoretical Approaches, Definitions 39
    3.2   Mindset of Agile Management 4.0 42
    3.3   Complexity, Agility and Agile Management 52
    3.4   Self-organization 55
    3.5   Principles of Scrum and Kanban Agile Frameworks 59
4   Agile Leadership 4.0 67
    4.1   Principles of Agile Leadership 4.0 67
    4.2   Agile Leadership 4.0 – Digital Network Intelligence 80
5   Cybernetics and Organization 111
    5.1   Agile Enterprise Structures from a Cybernetic Perspective 111
    5.2   Agile and Fluid Organization 131
6   Reference Model Agile Organizations 143
PART II – BECOME AGILE AND STAY AGILE 159

7	The Impact of Working Agile on Human Resources	160
8	Reliable and Ultimate Scrum	180
9	Agile PMO 4.0	196
10	Agile Scaling	212
10.1	Scaled Agile Management 4.0 - new	212
10.2	Scaling Agile by using Critical Chain Project Management	233
11	Agile Transformation 4.0 - new	240
PART III Agile Management in Practice		257
12	Learnings and Guidance for the Implementation of Agility - new	258
13	Interaction Patterns for the Digital Transformation - new	288
Notes		312

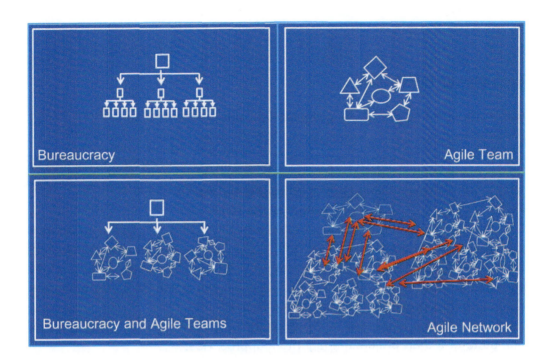

(Figure based on http://www.forbes.com/sites/stevedenning/2016/09/08/explaining-agile/#727a73c12ef7, accessed 15/12/2016)

With a systemic leadership approach, Management 4.0 provides the guiding competence for viable learning organizations in complex situations and environments.

Management 4.0 integrates an Agile Mindset, the universal principle of self-organization as a governance guideline, and relevant work techniques, for sustainable working models of the future.

THE AUTHORS

Prof. Dr.-Ing. Patrick Balve

Heilbronn University, Faculty for Industrial and Process Engineering, 74081 Heilbronn

holds a master's degree in Mechanical Engineering with specialization in International Project Management. After graduating, Dr. Balve spent five years in the field of consulting and research at the renowned Fraunhofer-Institute for Manufacturing Engineering and Automation. Since then, he has held various management positions in logistics and quality in the automotive industry. In 2009, Dr. Balve was appointed professor at Heilbronn University in the Faculty of Industrial and Process Engineering. He is director of the "Manufacturing and Operations Management" bachelor's program and head of the Heilbronn Learning Factory. His fields of research include lean manufacturing systems and state-of-the-art project management approaches.

Dr. Frank Edelkraut

Mentus GmbH, 22359 Hamburg

is Managing Director and a well-versed Human Resources manager. As a Technical Chemist he started his career in Project Management and subsequently became a Human Resources Manager. In the last 15 years he has worked as an Interim Manager in a variety of industries and as a trainer in Leadership Development Programs. He is a member of the professional group for Agile Management of the GPM (German Association for Project Management e.V.). His field of work is Organizational Development and Leadership Development and the consequences of agile methods on organizational design and developmental matters.

Dr. Jens Köhler

BASF SE, 67056 Ludwigshafen

received his Diploma in Physics from Bonn University and already began tackling the subject of complexity in his doctorate. He focuses on the Digitization in research and development. His specialty is the regulation of social complexity to lever the efficiency and effectiveness of project teams, being inevitable for successfully forming the digital transformation.

Wolfram Müller

VISTEM GmbH & Co.KG., 64646 Heppenheim

Founder & Principal Consultant at Speed4Projects.net and VISTEM, Wolfram brings 25 years of experience as a Consulting Executive, IT Project Portfolio and Project Manager, Process Engineer, and Software Engineer. As head of the PMO at 1&1 Internet AG, he led 40 project managers in the delivery of 500 projects, innovating industry-leading methods, to drive unprecedented improvements in speed and reliability across the portfolio. He has published over 20 articles and books on 'Critical Chain', 'Agile', and 'Lean' and is a well-known speaker in Europe on how to achieve hyper-productive IT project portfolios.

Dr. Helge F. R. Nuhn

PwC AG, 60329 Frankfurt

studied Information Systems at the Technical University, Darmstadt and obtained his PhD (Dr. rer. pol.) from the European Business School University, Wiesbaden. His areas of research lie in the realm of organizational theory and temporary forms of organizing. A Certified Scrum Master and Certified LeSS

Practitioner, he seeks to enhance the ways in which teams work in every conceivable project and environment. In his job as a manager and consultant, he is part of an internal Agile Community of Interest.

Dr. Alfred Oswald

IFST - Institute for Social Technologies GmbH, 52223 Stolberg

earned his doctorate in Theoretical Physics at RWTH Aachen University. He is Managing Director at IFST-Institute for Social Technologies GmbH, a Consulting Institute for Agile and Fluid Organizations. He is head of the professional group for Agile Management at GPM (German Association for Project Management e.V.). His field of work is the efficiency and effectiveness of organizations through innovative social technologies. He has many years of experience in the management of innovative and complex projects, as well as in the transformation of project-oriented organizations into high-performance organizations.

Steve Raue

Accenture, 10117 Berlin

is an expert for strategic change and project management. He uses his expertise in communications, culture and behavior analysis for an innovative approach to changing organizations in projects and team development. He is a Scrum Master and founding member of the professional group on Agile Management of the GPM (German Associations for Project Management e.V.). Steve is currently working on his doctorate in Cross-Cultural Complex Project Management, exploring implications for future project management based on systemic integration of conventional and agile project practices.

Norbert Schaffitzel

DB Systel GmbH, 60329 Frankfurt

studied economics in Freiburg and Berlin with specialization in Business Informatics and marketing of investment goods. Since 1988 he has been working in enterprise IT, initially as a software developer and subsequently as project manager on different projects at DB Systel GmbH, the IT service provider for Deutsche Bahn AG. Since 2012 his special interest has been the implementation of Agile Management techniques in projects of large organizations and the transformation of project teams by using agile practices. To extend his knowledge of agile experiences and management of the future, in 2014 he joined the Agile Management GPM professional group.

Marcel Schwarzenberger

projektimpulse GmbH, 20354 Hamburg

works as a consultant and trainer at projektimpulse GmbH. Between 2004 to 2016 he was responsible for organizational and public administration investment projects in the security and defense industry. As a former federal armed forces officer, he is particularly interested in changing the methodology for leadership, and organizational development of Agile Project Management practices. He has been a member of the Agile Management professional group at GPM since 2017 and applies his knowledge and experience in management and strategic development of organizations to Agile Management. His research interests are leadership and organizational development practices for value creating organizations of the future.

Prof. Dr. Hubertus C. Tuczek

University of Applied Sciences Landshut, 84036 Landshut
TCC-Management – Strategy Consulting, 81247 Munich

received his doctorate in Engineering from the Technical University in Munich (TUM) (Prof. Milberg). He has accumulated over 30 years of management experience in the machinery and equipment, aerospace and automotive industries. For 17 years he held the position of group vice president on the board of the Dräxlmaier Group, an internationally operating automotive supplier, with responsibility for international business development, quality and project management, as well as global procurement. At the beginning of 2015 he was appointed Professor for Management and Leadership at the University of Applied Sciences in Landshut, near Munich. His research is focused on the changing requirements for leadership in the digital age.

PREFACE

Perhaps you are familiar with the phrase: "Are you just residing or have you started to live? (Wohnst du noch oder lebst du schon?)" If we interpret the message in this slogan within the context of "Agility", it could be more freely interpreted as "Are you still just plodding on, or are you making sense of your life?"

The buzzwords "Agility, Agile or Agile Management" are often interpreted as miracle-workers.

But the number of different meanings attributed to these terms is immense: There are thousands of experts and tens of thousands of books and articles on what agile work actually is. And on the subject of agility, everyone is an expert — everyone knows how to do it best. But out of the thousands of experts and books, which ones are right? Or are all of the experts right? What is of importance? What do we need to know, so we can assess what is right in our own context?

There are those that suggest "unless you are sprinting all the time, you are too slow, and you are not agile". Then there are others who argue that "if you are unsure of your product vision, then this is a sure way to make lots of mistakes". Others place trusty old Lean and Kanban on a pedestal. And then there are those who assume complexity is responsible for everything. And if all else fails — it is a question of attitude as to whether one is agile or not. Last but not least, there are the pragmatists who have introduced the hybrid of - 'do not throw away the old, but include something new'.

The "Agile Management" professional group of the GPM (German Association for Project Management e.V.) was founded to offer a deeper understanding of agility: our aim is to understand the need for a new kind of management, grounded on basic principles and free from pigeonholing.

Our vision "together with users, to establish cross-sectoral agile working models to deliver added value for the future" flows into an integral theory-practice framework: We believe that this framework includes a new mindset of agility, systemic thinking, an openness to welcome the 'new' as a friend, and the capability of retaining proven management tools.

When one starts to deal with the important things in life like love, truth or agility, then the picture tends to have as many facets as there are people. In discussing this topic, it becomes increasingly clear that it is not possible to give an operational definition of agility without including a context. – Hence this book has no chapter on "definition". What emerges though, are principles of agility (like natural laws) that hold concepts together. These principles are explainable and help in understanding the practice. They also help assess which expert ideas are useful and which are only useful in a particular context.

This book was conceived as a manual or "handbook" and ended up as a "brain book". It is full of concepts and principles – some rough and coarse – some fine polished. But all help to understand and put into practice the agile movement, and to ride this great wave without sinking!

Who should read this Book?

This book is written for anyone who is interested in agility or needs to be agile. It is for those who seek deeper knowledge about what keeps the agile world together. You can read it from the perspective of a top manager or decision maker who feels the urge to be more agile. But you can also take the book and just follow it from the perspective of a user.

What do you get?

- A systemic picture of agility – to enable you to analyze your system (your team, your department, your company or your business network) and identify fields of agile application and the specific need for agility.
- The ingredients of an Agile Mindset – this allows you to transform your organization and develop an agile culture for your organization.

- The theoretical foundation of agile principles – so that you can really understand and assess the value of all the expert ideas for you and your organization. You will get the necessary skills to tailor organization specific agile frameworks without losing essential ingredients.
- Input for your own reflections – you will be capable of innovating agility and be ahead of the main stream.

The Principles behind the Book?

We illustrate the big picture of the concept of the book by roughly outlining the content of this book. This book is Release 3 of the Management 4.0 Handbook. In Release 3 we have omitted some of the content present in Release 2 and introduced new content. The new content is indicated by "new" in the header.

PART 1 FOUNDATION

In Part I FOUNDATION we start with an outline of one of the main drivers of complexity, the megatrend "digitization", followed by a short analysis of the choice of the name "Management 4.0" for this book.

We then go on to explain the basic principles of Management 4.0:

- Management 4.0 as a new way of thinking
- the key principles of an Agile Mindset and the link to Management 4.0
- the relationship between agility and complexity
- the "definition" of hybrid (project) management
- the basics of self-organization
- the key principles of Scrum and Kanban agile frameworks from the perspective of Management 4.0
- the principles of Leadership 4.0
- Leadership 4.0 in digital networks - updated
- the relationship between cybernetics and agility and how guidelines for the design of agile and fluid organizations are derived

- a reference model for Agile Organizations

PART II BECOME AGILE AND STAY AGILE

In Part II BECOME AGILE AND STAY AGILE we start by describing the impact of agile working on human resource issues.

We outline the "Reliable and Ultimate Scrum" agile frameworks as examples of how agile principles can be applied, and give input to the discussion on agility and fixed price contracts.

In the chapter "Agile PMO 4.0" we outline the concept of an agile Project Management Office.

In the chapter "Agile Scaling" we derived a Scaled Agile Management 4.0 from first principles and describe "Scaling Agile by using Critical Chain Project Management".

In the chapter "Agile Transformation 4.0" we outline a model and an example for transforming a conventional organization to an appropriated Agile Organization.

PART III AGILE MANAGEMENT IN PRACTICE

Part III AGILE MANAGEMENT IN PRACTICE is devoted to practical examples of Management 4.0.

Chapter "Learnings and guidance for implementation of agility" gives strategies and hints to pitfalls in introducing and using Agile Techniques.

In the chapter "Interaction Patterns for the Digital Transformation" we use the Dilts Pyramid to describe communication patterns and to derive some consequences for the Digital Transformation.

The Management 4.0 Handbook – Release 3: A Minimal Viable Product

One of the most important agile principles is to get feedback from customers as quickly as possible!

The book is not yet finished, and we still have enough material remaining for further releases – there is so much more to write and say. So much so, that it would be easy to keep working on the book for an infinite amount of time.

However, we believe that this release - again - contains enough to be of value for you as reader. Your feedback is of great importance to us - it will help us to improve quickly!

We have created a product backlog on the next page, which contains the topics we have planned for the next release of the handbook. We intend to change the content and priorities of the topics depending on the feedback we receive from you.

So feel free - after reading the book – to discuss your ideas with us. You can contact us at: agile-management@gpm-ipma.de.

Nürnberg, February 2019

Alfred Oswald and Wolfram Müller

PRODUCT BACKLOG

Megatrends (e.g New Work, New Learning) and Management 4.0

Aspects of Digitization (e.g. Fab Lab)

People Analytics

Digital Agile Competences

Collective Intelligence, Collective Mind

DevOps: Continuous Integration to Continuous Delivery

Viable System Model and "Off-the-Shelf" Agile Frameworks

Common Language to describe Agile Frameworks

Controlling and Management 4.0

Agile Modeling

Agile Management for safety critical domains

CHANGES from RELEASE 2 to RELEASE 3

Omitted

Lean Management

Agile fixed priced projects with hybrid software development

SAFe – Scaled Agile Framework

Example Wire Swiss

Example Agile Transformation - From Acting Agile to Being Agile

New

Scaled Agile Management 4.0

Agile Transformation 4.0

Learnings and guidance for implementation of agility

Interaction patterns for the Digital Transformation

PART I – FOUNDATION

1 Agile Management – Traditional Management has reached its Limit

Author: Hubertus C. Tuczek

Summary: Digitization is changing the environmental conditions for management in a radical way. Increasing change dynamics combined with new business models cannot be handled using traditional management concepts. Common enterprise structures, which have been successful so far, are not flexible enough for these new challenges and have to undergo a fundamental transformation process. New approaches need to be designed according to Agile Management principles and individual solutions developed for every branch or company.

Key terms: Digitization, Changing Environmental Conditions, Disruptive Business Models, Traditional Management vs. Agile Management, Increasing Change Dynamics, Transformation Management

Digitization – a Game Changing Force

It is currently the number one topic: DIGITIZATION. We are living at the beginning of the next Kondratieff-cycle and everything around us is influenced by this new development. We are in the middle of a technological revolution, accompanied by economic, social and cultural change. What is happening?

After the major technical innovations of mechanization, electrification and automation, the Internet has initiated a development, characterized by rapid paradigm changes with uncertain outcome. The Internet is actually nothing new anymore, given that 25 years have passed since we started to surf the World Wide Web and connect with each other around the world. But today's technology has reached a level of maturity, with its dynamics capturing our private and business life with breath-taking velocity. While in those early days, only IT-geeks would have placed orders on the Internet, today shopping online is commonplace. This has changed the structure of business trading dramatically. On the book market for example, there is no getting away from the Internet giant Amazon. Assisted by digital technology, such disruptive business changes do not happen over longer time frames, but gain momentum in an exponential manner. This poses great danger to companies from a strategical point of view, as business environments and conditions may change suddenly from day to day. The short response time required does not match the time frame, which is typically anticipated for the strategy process within companies.

What does this mean for the economy? The market capitalization of DAX-30 companies does not even add up to half of the stock-exchange price of the 30 most valuable companies in Silicon Valley - a tectonic shift of values. Additionally, studies carried out on the further value development of DAX-Companies do not generate confidence. Most companies in Germany, especially medium-sized businesses, were identified as having missed out on new trends. This is not a surprise, as such companies are typically led by "digital immigrants" who have written their success stories before the age of digital technology.

Is there a need for change in every industry or company? Or are there islands of consistency where the traditional way of doing business can continue into the next decades, retaining a successful share of the market?

In fact, the picture is not so black and white. As a business leader, you need to determine how your markets will develop, and therefore, subsequently, also your business model. There are companies like Kodak, which – an erstwhile dominant market leader in photographic supplies - was erased by the development of Digitization. Another example in the mobile phone sector is Nokia, which – despite being a market leader in its field – failed to understand and effectively react to the challenge of smartphones and their embedded App-logic. These dramatic examples show the need for top management to be able to foresee such disruptive changes, which in hindsight seem obvious, yet were not anticipated using traditional strategic corporate development processes.

A model has been developed to help identify potential drivers for exponential change dynamics. This model classifies businesses and companies according to 2 dimensions. One is the technical complexity of the products involved and the other is the social complexity of the organization and its customer relations.

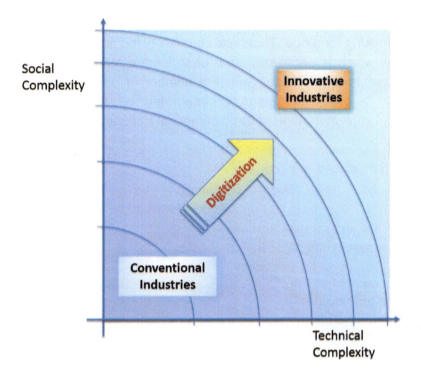

Figure 1-1: Industry Dynamics Classification matrix (IDC)

The industry dynamics classification as shown in Figure 1-1, suggests that a company positioned in the lower left corner of the matrix is characterized by low social complexity and products with low technical complexity. This can be referred to as a conventional industry. The more a company is exposed to social and technical complexity, the further the position of the company moves to the upper right corner of the matrix. Digitization is a driver for such increased complexity.

For example, if you look at a taxi company, you could call this a rather "conventional" business (see also Figure 1-2). You require a license and a certain number of available cars and drivers who are coordinated by telephone operators, who then book journey requests from passengers. With digitization the game changes. Uber Technology Inc. has become a ride-hailing giant with billions of dollars of revenue, by offering an Internet platform, which connects drivers and people looking for a ride. Technical complexity increases due to IT-platform technology, which is necessary as a base for this kind of business approach. Social complexity increases with the number of passengers and drivers, who need to be brought together and integrated with their individual needs, for successful implementation of the commercial transaction.

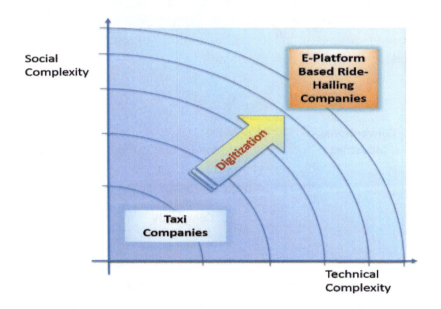

Figure 1-2: Game changing dynamics for the taxi business

The worldwide growth potential of Uber's business model is staggering. In 2015 they doubled their revenue every six months, according to Uber's Chief Executive Travis Kalanick. After only 7 years of existence on the market, the company is valued by investors at more than $ 50 billion. These figures indicate the game changing dimensions of this new business model, which was made possible by the opportunities created by digitization. In the market of smaller local enterprises, a global player, the size of a large international corporation has suddenly emerged within just a few years.

Does this same logic apply to industries, where big global players dominate the market? Are they facing similar potentially disruptive changes in their business? Or is size a protective shield?

An apt illustrative example in this context is the automotive industry. A massive consolidation process over the past few years has resulted in a small number of globally relevant enterprises. Now digital technology is coming into play and is changing the industry focus from mechanical to one with more and more digital know-how. One force for this development is the concept of autonomous driving. The necessary hardware, such as sensors and control units, is currently available. The further maturation of the technology is controlled by smart software algorithms, which enable the vehicle to safely find its way in all traffic conditions, without driver interaction. Traditional car companies are finding themselves at a digital cross-roads, where they need to invest intensively in new digital competences, in order to manage the paradigm, change they are facing. This transformation not only refers to technical challenges, but to a change in leadership style, which is also required. The high level of dynamics in this new environment cannot be accommodated using traditional functional hierarchies, but requires agile structures, which are already familiar in innovative software companies.

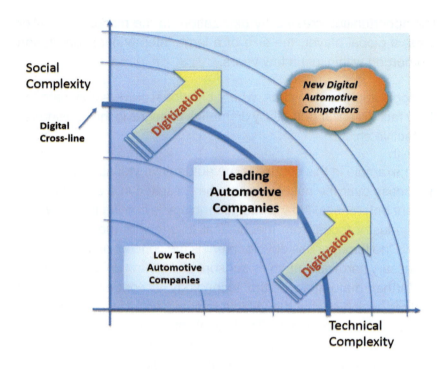

Figure 1-3: Game changing dynamics for the automotive industry

On the one hand, there are low-tech automotive companies, fulfilling the need for basic transportation and focus on developing countries. On the other hand, there are leading automotive companies, working on a variety of concepts to explore the potential of new business models. They are experimenting with car sharing enterprises, offer new emission-free powertrain options and are attempting to shape a new world of digital services around the vehicle industry. Meanwhile, new competitors have emerged in the automotive market whose core business is in the digital segment. Google is one example. They are developing the Google self-driving car, which can already be seen on the road as a prototype. They intend to bypass the hurdle of automotive market entry - the large sales and service organization, which has been necessary up until now - by having no intention of selling the car, but leasing it to customers for the time required. If a car develops a technical problem, it will simply be replaced by another car, with its repair being neither customer, nor time critical, for Google. This approach is also attractive for companies like Uber, who have already announced their intention to use self-driving cars for their ride-hailing business in the near future. It is not yet clear, who will win the race. But, it is a huge challenge for traditional car manufacturers, to transform their mechanically-based business into a digitally-integrated high-tech company.

The next stage of technological development in the automotive industry is already visible with prototype applications: 3D-Printing. With this, customers would purchase the design for a specific car and then have their individual car printed on demand.

Consequences for Management – What does the New Management Look Like?

In this environment of increasing dynamics with newly emerging business models, traditional management concepts are unable to react in a quick and flexible manner. Based on the division of labor, functional structures and optimizations, it creates a hurdle to exploring new potentials and shifting resources to innovative departures. If you take a close look at how projects often struggle to fight their way through the jungle of functional organizations, then you will understand the deficit of an approach built on technical expertise in more or less separated entities within a company. The managers of these units have been successful in their careers, as a result of strengthening the profile of their department, but not necessarily because they acted in the best interests of the business as a whole. It is often quite astonishing to see how seldom, operative problems seem to attract management attention in today's large corporations, unless they impact on the tactical strategies of the manager involved. A more integrated approach is needed, to encourage management to focus on the total throughput of the company, rather than on the individual interests of single departments.

This is where Agile Management principles come into play. Agility stands for speed and flexibility. These characteristics are required from managers and their enterprises in a disruptive digital environment and its corresponding business models. But what exactly does this mean for operational management?

In the world of software development companies, in 2001, a guideline called the "Agile Manifesto" (see Figure 1-4) was written and distributed. It describes software development principles, which lead to more flexible and leaner software creation, in contrast to the traditional – and rather bureaucratic - software development process. The concept is based on the delegation of responsibilities, self-organization and incremental development steps, which allow a flexible response to customer needs. These principles can also be transferred to general management tasks. Their benefit lies in the fact, that there is already a great deal of experience available of using these principles with large software projects with many teams involved. This know-how can be transferred to management activities. In addition to having better quality of results and achieving defined goals more quickly, Agile Management has social benefits, as it subsequently increases job satisfaction. Values such as self-responsibility and self-organization result in individual fulfilment of employees and as a consequence lead to intrinsic motivation.

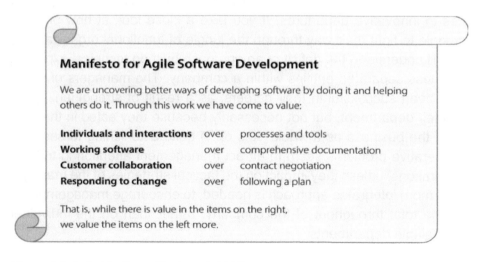

Figure 1-4: Agile Manifesto (Beck et al. 2001)

So what can be done? How can large groups of people, who are supposed to achieve common goals, be best organized to become more effective overall?

In this context, what is extremely important is the difference between effectivity and efficiency. Today's management concepts are mostly based on using organizations to their full capacity – or in other words making them efficient. A very different logic is applied, if the focus is on the throughput of an organization. As a consequence, employees are given more leeway to organize themselves and to define and achieve their goals. This fulfils a basic human need, increases motivation, fosters creativity and on top of that, provides more scope for individual development. The upshot for the company is that unused energy is freed up and the overall performance of the organization is boosted for better effectivity.

This is supported by social communication platform technology, which represents a new way of information exchange within a company, in addition to writing e-mails. All necessary information can be shared on a common platform between communities or virtual project teams. Activity streams collect relevant data for each individual user, so that there is quick and easy access. The embedded work flow is visible for everyone involved, which supports a transparent process. Status information can be commented on or enhanced online. Wikis, blogs and forums enable central availability of knowledge. Social platforms enable the introduction of a new way of entrepreneurial collaboration. The managers themselves are forced to give their input on these platforms too. This procedure enables teams in an organization to work autonomously, with the boss as a coach, rather than a manager who gives directions in the day-to-day business. Thus, smart and effective collaboration of all those who are able to contribute to successful realization of a specific objective, is introduced in a natural way.

It would be a fatal misunderstanding though, to see such an approach as an IT project. To achieve an effective transformation, using this type of smart collaboration, the company needs to bring about nothing less than a complete culture change. Management has to relinquish its monopoly on information ownership, which may be perceived as loss of power. In fact, if an operational base is more or less self-organized, then less hierarchical intervention is required. Of course management still retains responsibility for steering the company as a whole in the right direction, yet its role has changed. As coaches to cross-functional teams, they need to cooperate closely with management colleagues. It is necessary for management to collaborate, in order to eliminate bottlenecks for the teams, by focusing on the total throughput. There is no longer room for individual power play between departments, as all teams have cross-functional tasks.

On a strategic level, it is important that as much of the total knowledge of the company as possible is brought into the process of shaping the future of the enterprise. This leads away from the traditional top down approach and adds a bottom up dimension, which brings employees into play. By doing so, the operational experience of various facets of the business can be integrated to determine the way forward. Misinterpretation of business drivers can be reduced and new options can be generated. The use of social media enables the systematic collection of customer input and underlines the strategic direction.

Strategies can no longer be determined for 5 years and more. A variety of possible scenarios for strategies need to be defined. These are verified by indicators identified during the strategy process and which make a scenario more or less probable over the time. The direction determined upon needs to be followed consistently, yet according to the principles of agility, and sufficient checkpoints should be established, to question the validity of the chosen route in light of changing environmental conditions.

One critical core competence in enterprises is symbolized by the decision making process. In a digital mode, speed of decisions is the key to good performance. In Agile Project Management, where iterative tasks have a duration of four to six weeks, the decisions necessary for the team to be able to continue their work, need to be made within a day. If these decisions cannot be made on an operational level, then top management must be available for such decisions via a quick escalation mode. This is hard to envisage in today´s large, traditional corporations. It can sometimes take weeks, or even months, to obtain a slot in a board meeting for a decision, and even then it may be postponed due to other priorities. And there are many examples, where the decision-making authority in large corporations has been reduced to a few, or even one person, and has led to severe problems. An increase in speed for decision-making can only be achieved by delegating responsibilities.

In conclusion, the change or transformation of a company into becoming a leader in its field, in the new digital age, requires a new management approach (see Figure 1-5), which is described in the context of this book as Management 4.0.

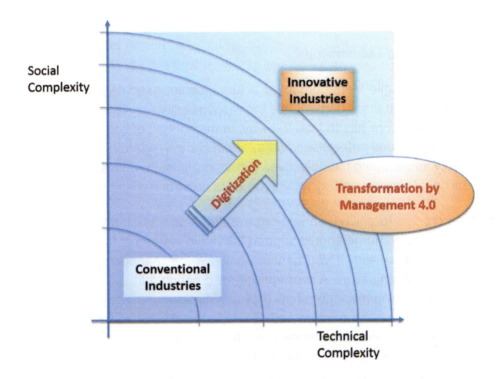

Figure 1-5: Transformation to the digital age by Management 4.0

The various chapters provide the reader with detailed information on how to implement agile and forward-orientated concepts to cope with future requirements in a digital world. It has to be understood, that as a first step, the culture of the company needs always to be addressed. The success of the transformation depends on a successful and enduring transformation of the company culture.

The way in which agile principles should be transferred to a corresponding enterprise has to be chosen individually, case by case, and should be verified in steps – according to the agile philosophy.

But for successful businesses in the future, there is no avoiding a transformation process geared to agility!

Challenge for Agile Leadership

In discussions on Agile Management structures, senior executives often bring up the argument that management has the responsibility for the success of the company and therefore has to lead the way. In the context of self-organisation, managers of traditional enterprises feel a loss of control regarding their impact, responsibility and shaping the objectives of their organisation. This makes them very sceptical of change or they may even build up strong resistance.

To make a change to agility and self-organisation successful, the question as to why managers in charge should support the move instead of fighting against it needs to be addressed. If you cannot convince the managers, you cannot create an agile organisation. A prerequisite for creating intrinsic motivation to change lies in showing managers how they can discover their new role. Strong managers want to shape the future and use their power to make things happen. A mere role as a coach to their employees does not seem to provide adequate satisfaction. Nevertheless, in today's dynamic markets, managers cannot ascertain the right way to move forward by themselves, but need to organize the answers found within their enterprise. This makes them number one networkers in the company.

A concept needs to be developed that gives management a clear perspective as to how they can set up a management system which supports self-organisation and, at the same time, still gives them control over the direction of activities. Working with the system as a paradigm, instead of working in the system, includes permanent readjustment of the system parameters to adopt to change in the market, the organisation itself or its environment.

Working with systemic order and control parameters is the first step in establishing a system that supports self-organisation.

Literature

Appelo J (2010) Management 3.0: Leading Agile Developers, Developing Agile Leaders, Addison-Wesley, Munich

Beck K et al. (2001) Manifesto for Agile Software Development, agilemanifesto.org

Becker T et al. (2015) Digitales Neuland, Springer Gaber, Wiesbaden

Cole T (2015) Digitale Transformation, Vahlen, Munich

Drucker P (2009) Management, Campus Verlag GmbH

Eberspächer J, Holtel S (eds.) (2010) Enterprise 2.0, Springer, Berlin Heidelberg

Gloger B, Rösner D (2014) Selbstorganisation braucht Führung – Die einfachen Geheimnisse agilen Managements, Hanser, Munich, 2014

Lehky M (2011) Leadership 2.0: Wie Führungskräfte die neuen Herausforderungen im Zeitalter von Smartphone, Burn-out & Co managen, Campus Verlag, Frankfurt am Main

Petry T (2016) Digital Leadership - Erfolgreiches Führen in Zeiten der Digital Economy, Haufe, Freiburg

Rossmann A, Stei, G, Besch M (eds.) (2016) Enterprise Social Networks, Springer, Wiesbaden

Schütt P (2015) Der Weg zum Digitalen Unternehmen, Springer Gabler, Berlin Heidelberg

Sprenger B, Novotny T (2016) Der Weg aus dem Leadership Dilemma – Team-Exzellenz an der Spitze, Springer, Berlin; Heidelberg

Sutherland J (2015) Scrum: The Art of Doing Twice the Work in Half the Time, Crown Business, New York

Tuczek H (2005) C4P - Die 4 C des Projektmanagements bei der Dräxlmaier Group, PMaktuell - Heft 3/2005

Tuczek H, Frank J (2016) Managing of Partners in Programmes, in: Lock, D, Wagner, R (eds.), Gower Handbook of Programme Management, Routledge, Abingdon, New York

Tuczek H (ed.) (2016) Landshut Leadership Band 1: Führung im Zeitalter der Digitalisierung, Shaker Verlag, Aachen

2 Management Models over the Course of Time

Author: Alfred Oswald

Summary: This chapter outlines the evolution of management mindsets.

Key terms: Management 1.0, Management 2.0, Management 3.0, Management 4.0

The essential purpose and benefits of Management 4.0 are to ensure that projects progress efficiently and effectively and with appropriate agility for a given business. Agility - as an expression of speed and flexibility – guarantees the level of adaptability required and is a response to the increasingly complex environments in which companies operate today. The drivers of these complex environments may be environmental requirements, globalization, digitization, disruptive innovations or the interaction of cultures. In the previous chapter, we outlined the impact of digitization as an example.

We speak of "fluid organizations" when teams, departments or companies are able to adjust to these complex environments by assembling and disassembling quickly and flexibly according to agile structures and processes. The use of agile and traditional project management (PM) techniques falls short here. Management 4.0, therefore, is not identical to agile techniques or agile frameworks, such as Scrum. Instead, we stress that Management 4.0 is an attitude, a mindset. Self-reflection, appreciation of human needs, systems thinking and the self-organization of social systems have predominant importance. Both agile and traditional PM techniques contribute to agility, only if they are able to incorporate this mindset. Leadership also plays a prominent role. This has its roots in the relationship between mindset and self-leadership and is due to the fact that self-organization cannot be obtained without leadership.

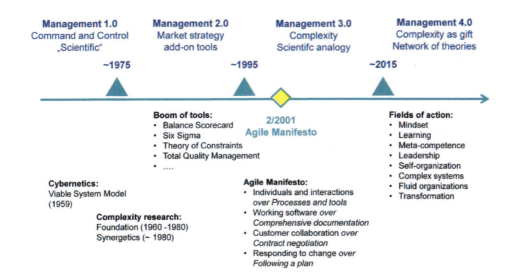

Figure 2-1: Evolution of management mindsets

Figure 2-1 shows the evolution of management mindsets. This process started with the Taylorism mindset, which we have called Management 1.0. This was followed by a boom in management tools, a period which was the golden age of global consulting companies and we have called Management 2.0. The Agile Mindset arose during the late 1990s. Its birth is often associated with the advent of the Agile Manifesto, which was followed by agile frameworks such as eXtreme Programming, Scrum and Feature Driven Development. Appelo (Appelo 2011) was one of the first agile practitioners to recognize drawbacks in the practice of agile techniques. He suggested that these techniques needed a theoretical foundation to promote an understanding of which values, basic assumptions or techniques bring which added value, and under which circumstances. He named his approach Management 3.0. This designation - along with the fact that the GPM professional group likes to emphasize the relationship with Industry 4.0 - led us to coin the term Management 4.0 about four years ago. As with Industry 4.0, interconnection is the dominant characteristic of Management 4.0, interconnecting humans, teams or any social organization. Interconnection is a key characteristic of complexity, and therefore, organizational complexity is seen as gift. To regulate complexity, this handbook offers a network of theories and practices. For a deeper understanding of the relationship between agility and complexity, we refer to Oswald (Oswald 2016).

Literature

Appelo J (2011) Management 3.0: Leading Agile Developers, Developing Agile Leaders. Pearson Education Inc., Boston

Oswald A, Köhler J, Schmitt R (2016) Projektmanagement am Rande des Chaos, Springer Vieweg, Heidelberg. This book is avalaible in English: Oswald A, Köhler J, Schmitt R (2018) Project Management at the Edge of Chaos, Springer Verlag, Heidelberg

3 Theoretical Foundation

3.1 Positioning: Models, Theoretical Approaches, Definitions

Author: Alfred Oswald

Summary: This chapter defines agility and Management 4.0.

Key Terms: Agility, Management 4.0

Agility stands for maneuverability, alertness, flexibility, and adaptability, but also for speed and creativity. Agility includes skills and values that people or organizations have, or consider to be important. Very often agility is seen in the context of competences, which in times of change and uncertainty enable people and organizations to act adequately. Agile people and agile organizations are those that show energy in their actions and use this energy effectively. Agile people and agile organizations are distinguished by their ease of value creation.

Agile people and agile organizations are not hindered in thought and action by conditions. They show the necessary mental flexibility and openness to see, permit and absorb new things. Agility reflects the belief that the values of maneuverability, alertness, flexibility, adaptability, openness, speed and creativity are central components for a business benefit creation process. These values are necessary conditions to perceive situations and be attentive and vigilant, and to have the freedom to then be able to act. However, this is not sufficient to permit and carry out agile behavior. This is where Agile Management begins. We understand Agile Management as a leadership and management practice, to be able to act in an agile and proactive way in a complex environment characterized by uncertainty. It is described as an Agile Mindset with a focus on:

- leadership for which self-leadership is the basis
- leadership, which is based on a respect for basic human needs
- leadership, which demands an understanding of complex systems and promotes their regulation through iterative procedures
- people who self-organize in teams
- fluid organizations, which promote adaptable and fast delivery of useful results and create innovative customer solutions through proactive dealing with changes

Figure 3-1 outlines a semantic network covered by the cornerstones of (Agile) Management 4.0:

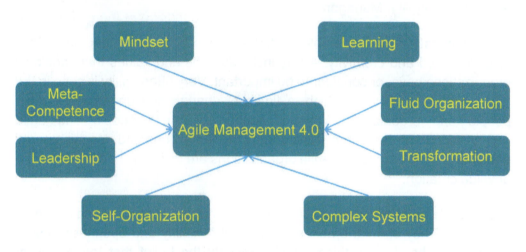

Figure 3-1: Cornerstones of Agile Management 4.0

In this Management 4.0 Handbook we will illuminate the following cornerstones: Mindset and Learning, Meta-Competence and Leadership, Self-Organization and Complex Systems and Fluid Organization and Transformation.

We will show that selection of these conceptual fields is not arbitrary, but arises naturally. Management 4.0 is a tool to create agility in a complex system. The central anchor for all other considerations is the conceptual field "Mindset"; here Agile Mindset. With this term we describe a personal attitude or an organizational attitude. The mindset is the basis for the ability to learn and develop meta-competence to act within complex systems. Self-Organization is a specific type of organizational complexity and regulates system complexity to create new system structures. It is, inter alia, the basis of so-called high-performance teams. With the term "Fluid Organizations", we describe organizations that behave in an agile manner as a whole and are capable of building and breaking down structures and processes, depending on their needs, to create business value in a complex environment. Systems interventions in complex systems are carried out via Leadership. Therefore, Leadership requires consideration of the interaction of system and intervening leader, perception of systemic patterns, and an agile adaptation of interventions. Leadership is the prominent active role in Management 4.0 (Oswald 2016). All these accumulate as Transformation, the need for permanent adaptation of complex systems to complex environments.

Management 4.0, as described in this handbook, integrates existing frameworks, such as Scrum or Kanban, but also extends far beyond these, based on a theoretical background and the described principles of Agile Management. The presented theories and practices are not industry-specific, although the examples are from specific domains of industry. However, it is our aim to show underlying general agile concepts in industry-specific examples.

We will use Agile Management and Agile Project Management often synonymously, as we believe that in a complex system and environment, these differences are increasingly losing ground.

(Agile Project) Management 4.0 supports and promotes the integration of traditional project management techniques: Accordingly, we define Hybrid Project Management as project management, based on an Agile Mindset, which applies Agile Management 4.0 and supplements this where appropriate by models and methods of traditional project management. As we will see later, we integrate traditional PM tools in the Mindset of Management 4.0 and not vice versa: So traditional PM tools do not prevent agility per se, it is a person's mindset that prevents agility. Therefore, agile tools may be at home within a traditional mindset, but agility is not.

Literature

Oswald A, Köhler J, Schmitt R (2016) Projektmanagement am Rande des Chaos, Springer Vieweg, Heidelberg. This book is avalaible in English: Oswald A, Köhler J, Schmitt R (2018) Project Management at the Edge of Chaos, Springer Verlag, Heidelberg

3.2 Mindset of Agile Management 4.0

Author: Alfred Oswald

Summary: This chapter defines the term "mindset", gives stereotypical examples for agile and lean mindsets, and describes the basic idea of learning and its relation to agility and Agile Management 4.0. It also defines hybrid project management according to a mindset model.

Key Terms: Mindset, Dilts Pyramid, Level of Learning, Meta-Competence, Agility, Agile Management 4.0, Hybrid Project Management

The English Wikipedia page offers the following definition of the term "Mindset" (Wikipedia Mindset 2016):

"In decision theory and general systems theory, a **mindset** is a set of assumptions, methods, or notations held by one or more people or groups of people that is so established that it creates a powerful incentive within these people or groups to continue to adopt or accept prior behaviors, choices, or tools. This phenomenon is also sometimes described as *mental inertia*, "groupthink", or a "paradigm", and it is often difficult to counteract its effects upon analysis and decision making processes.

A mindset can also be seen as incident of a person's Weltanschauung or philosophy of life. For example there has been quite some interest in the typical mindset of an entrepreneur."

A mindset is therefore a cluster (a "set") of thought snippets that belong thematically together. These thought snippets are also called memes. Please also see "meme theory" (Wikipedia Mem 2016) and the cultural and consciousness theory "Spiral Dynamics" (Wikipedia Spiral Dynamics 2016).

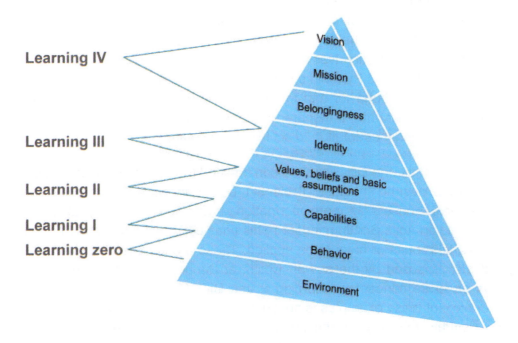

Figure 3-2: Dilts Pyramid and Learning Levels (Oswald 2016)

In short, the elements of a mindset describe an inner attitude, which in turn results in external behavior. The Dilts Pyramid, known from NLP (NeuroLinguistic Programming) is a simple, but very effective model for a mindset (Oswald 2016). The Dilts Pyramid represents an extension of the Maslow Pyramid of needs and is used in NLP as a key model for individual and organizational change work. As can be seen from the above Figure 3-2, the Dilts pyramid consists of the elements: environment or context, behavior, capabilities, values, beliefs and basic assumptions, identity, belongingness, mission and vision, and arranges these elements in a hierarchical order. This hierarchical order is referred to as the hierarchy of neurological levels:

We humans, as well as organizations, display behavior, or processes and methods in a particular environment. This behavior is generated by specific capabilities. Values, beliefs and basic assumptions affect and control this behavior according to capabilities. The understanding we have of ourselves (our identity) acts on our values, beliefs and basic assumptions. With our identity, we feel that we belong to a group or an organization. We give our life an orientation, asking ourselves why we are there (mission) and where we want to go (vision). The Dilts Pyramid can be used to analyze and change individual and organizational behavior and to make visible and resolve communication blockages. This will bring transparency in management and leadership styles and allow situational adaptation to act in an agile manner.

In order to do this, the Dilts Pyramid can be used to make a mindset visible or to specify a desired mindset. Table 3-1 below shows an example of two stereotypical mindsets (for more information we refer to Oswald (Oswald 2016): a Lean and an Agile Scrum mindset.) This does not imply that these mindsets are the „right" ones or have to be applied. These are stereotypical, imaginary mindsets, proposed by the author, which, at the time of writing, express his views on these mindsets, according to the Dilts Pyramid format. Thus, the importance of these examples is not so much in their actual manifestation, but they illustrate the value of the transparency that arises when individuals or organizational mindsets are revealed.

	Agile Scrum mindset	**Lean mindset**
Vision	Our working world is more human.	Our working world is better.
Mission	In the team, we solve every complex task with "empiricism". *Or in other words: We find a solution and create an effect.*	We impress our customers with our products and at the same time increase business value. *Or in other words: We increase efficiency and effectiveness*
Belongingness	We are members of a community that solves a complex task by delivering early and frequently.	We are members of a community that creates efficient, customer-oriented products.
Identity	We are problem-solvers who respect our customers and expect respect from our customers.	We are entrepreneurs who create benefit for our customers and thus earn money.
Values, belief systems	Values: Transparency, focus, courage, openness, commitment, respect Principles: Early and frequent deliveries are possible thanks to iterative checking and adaptation. "Self-organized" teams make the working world human and create added business value.	Values: Quality, customer orientation, reliability, standards Principles: Waste must be avoided. The added value for the customer is crucial.

	Agile Scrum mindset	**Lean mindset**
Capabilities	Using Agile Scrum framework: Work in a team, execute an iterative operational framework with discipline, understand and implement a product vision, demonstrate solution competence as service provider.	Using Lean framework: Understand and continuously question own system of processes, see and implement the added value for the customer.
Behavior	Execute the Scrum operational framework: Iterative search for a solution.	Execute Lean operational framework: Continuous optimization of the system.
Environment	A complex task must be solved in the context of an agent-principal relation and the solution is assessed based on the satisfaction principal.	A known product is to be produced (lean production) or a new product is to be developed (lean development). Continuous improvement is accepted and results in better products for the customer.

Table 3-1: Agile Scrum mindset and Lean mindset (Oswald 2016)

The structure expressed in the pyramidal hierarchy of levels, is an expression of a much more general principle: The neurological levels of the pyramid represent levels of abstraction through which complexity is absorbed or regulated. In different contexts, humans display millions of different behaviors. These behaviors are determined by significantly fewer capabilities and are regulated by even fewer beliefs and values. A human, for whom value order is important, will display corresponding behavior and preferences: Their desk is perhaps tidy, they love structure in their daily routine or considers it important to maintain an approved project plan.

In an organization, where order is considered to be an important cultural element, particular importance will be placed on the conduct of meetings, for example, in complying with an agenda, and there will be the belief that business value is increased by standardizing processes. On the one hand, values and beliefs can act like viruses, infecting the minds of people, groups or organizations, closing them to new ideas. On the other hand, they can act as openers, revealing a world of new ideas and supporting their development. The value of trust is an example of an opener that absorbs complexity, freeing people from mutual control at the level of behavior and thus creating space for action.

In addition to the importance of neurological levels as absorbers and regulators of complexity, in the context of Agile Management, the Dilts Pyramid is the perfect model for explaining the formation of experience and to illustrate types of learning. The system theorist Bateson, identified four different types of learning, which he referred to as Levels of Learning (0, I-IV). Dilts linked these Levels of Learning to the Dilts Pyramid (Oswald 2016).

The following is useful for illustrating the Levels of Learning (0, I-IV) according to the example "Learning in Project Management":

Level of Learning	Description	Example
0	"Always" the same patterns of behavior	Project leader Paul Little repeatedly uses the same method (Scrum or Waterfall) to carry out different projects. Paul Little believes in the power of "best practices".
I	The adaptation or enrichment of our behavior as a result of a refinement of our internal mental model. An existing pattern of behavior is changed a little.	Project leader Paul Little has heard of agile methods, and enriches Waterfall process model with agile ideas.
II	The context is newly interpreted and behavior is adjusted accordingly by means of acquired capabilities. A behavior pattern derived from another situation is applied in a new situation.	Project leader Paul Little realizes that in one context the Waterfall approach method results in a better project outcome, but in another context in a poorer result. In future Paul Little checks the project context and selects his approach method accordingly.
III	The system of beliefs and values has either changed greatly or has been completely exchanged. It is possible that a completely new behavior pattern has been modelled, possibly based on another person or organization pattern.	Project leader Paul recognizes the values and beliefs that have led him to use his approach method(s). He checks what principles in which project context are meaningful and chooses the appropriate project methodology accordingly.

Level of Learning	Description	Example
IV	One can exit the system and enter a comprehensive system of systems: A state of openness and connectedness with the system of systems, the „whole world" is reached.	Senior project manager Paul recognizes that in the context of suspense and uncertainty, even the use of a portfolio of project methods can lead to poor project results. He raises the question "Which completely new approach is needed to deal appropriately with suspense and uncertainty?" Through a synthesis of theoretical considerations, hypotheses, experimental actions and corresponding correction of his actions he creates a new type of project management.

Table 3-2: Levels of Learning in a project management example (Oswald 2016)

This example shows how, by ascending the levels of learning, the agility of Paul, the project manager, increases significantly. He is agile - faster and more flexible, and adapts his behavior to the context - all of these being properties associated with agility.

This insight allows us "to define" agility and Agile Management based on the Dilts Pyramid:

Agility is generated when the upper neurological levels (from vision down to values and beliefs) are designed so that individual or organizational capabilities and behavior are adapted in an agile, quick and flexible manner, reflecting the context.

Therefore, Agile Management is a meta-competence used to cultivate agility in an organization. We speak of meta-competence, because an individual or an organization is capable of "going up or down", mastering each of the neurological levels, and if necessary "looking in at each level from the outside", in order to analyze and possibly reshape them.

With the Dilts Pyramid we are now able to define Hybrid Project Management: Hybrid Project Management is based on the mindset of (Agile) Management 4.0 using agile and traditional PM techniques where appropriate.

Logical Level	Management 4.0	Traditional PM
Identity	The organization, the project is a complex, "living" system	The organization, the project is a "mechanical" system
Values, beliefs and basic assumptions	Work is oriented on human basic needs. Self-organization creates efficiency and effectiveness.	Processes, structures, rules and process models are the basis of the work and generate efficiency and effectiveness
Capabilities	Meta-competence, self-reflection, leadership for self-organization, agile techniques	PM techniques
Behavior	Behavior on the basis of techniques that support agility	Behavior corresponding to processes, structures and process models
Environment	Vast and unpredictable environment	Stable environment

Table 3-3: Hybrid Project Management mindset

In Table 3-3, the Hybrid Project Management mindset is framed in black. We emphasize that Hybrid Project Management does not suggest merely including some agile techniques in a traditional mindset, but that it is necessary to shift the higher levels of the Dilts Pyramid to an Agile Mindset, using traditional PM techniques where appropriated.

Literature

Oswald A, Köhler J, Schmitt R (2016) Projektmanagement am Rande des Chaos, Springer Vieweg, Heidelberg. This book is avalaible in English: Oswald A, Köhler J, Schmitt R (2018) Project Management at the Edge of Chaos, Springer Verlag, Heidelberg

Wikipedia Meme (2016) https://en.wikipedia.org/wiki/Meme, accessed on 22/10/2016

Wikipedia Mindset (2016) https://en.wikipedia.org/wiki/Mindset, accessed on 22/10/2016

Wikipedia Spiral Dynamics (2016) https://en.wikipedia.org/wiki/Don_Edward_Beck, accessed on 22/10/2016

3.3 Complexity, Agility and Agile Management

Author: Alfred Oswald

Summary: Complexity, understood as characteristic of a system, leads to a perception of incomprehensibility and unpredictability. Complexity is the result of recurrent self-referential interaction of (many) system elements. To be effective, an agile manager has to monitor complexity drivers, identify complex social and technical interaction patterns, and adapt their actions based on PDCA-cycles.

Key Terms: Complexity, Complexity Driver, Systemic Patterns, Social Interventions, PDCA-Cycle

In Chapter 1 "Agile Management – Why Tradititional Management has Reached its Limit", we outline one of the main current drivers of social and technical complexity: Digitization. Other drivers, especially on the societal level, are disruptive innovations, ecological requirements or cultural interactions of different societies. In the context of a project, the scope of the project, the stakeholders and their respective organizations are the main drivers for complexity (Oswald 2016).

We speak of complexity if the social interactions or technical interactions of a system are, to a large extent, vast and unpredictable. We understand complexity as a system characteristic, which a system displays under specific conditions: A system shows complexity if all system elements interact coincidently, resulting in nonlinear interactions. For example, a system of two communicating human individuals mostly shows complexity, because the resulting systemic communication pattern is based on reciprocal adjustment and alignment of individual behavior patterns. The characteristics of the systemic communication pattern, are in fact based on individual behavior patterns, but also have other aspects: e.g. creativity is released or communication is trapped in a blocking pattern. Sometimes, to an external observer, the communication pattern looks simple, if only one-way information is transferred. Or it looks complicated, if the transfer of information shows many, yet straightforward facets. And at other times, communication is extremely unfocused and unpredictable. In this case, no stable systemic communication pattern is recognizable and we speak of chaotic communication. So the same communication system can show simple, complicated, complex or chaotic behavior. If more and more people are involved in a social system, as for example, in a project, the likelihood grows that the system will display only complex or chaotic system behavior: The simultaneous, self-referential behavior of all system elements results in systemic behavior of the system as a whole.

Digitization, disruptive innovations, ecological requirements or cultural interactions of different societies are environmental complexity drivers, which reinforce project inherent complexity drivers, such as project scope or stakeholder structure. Very often, the environmental complexity drivers act only through inherent complexity drivers: For example, in a project, the compulsion or desire to digitize business processes leads to a high(er) degree of innovation and/or degree of novelty, which in turn, fires technical and social complexity.

A manager and leader can remain effective in a complex environment if they introduce, in addition to long-term planning, a short-term horizon, allowing them:

- to monitor all complexity drivers carefully and continuously,
- to design and recognize systemic (social and technical) characteristic patterns,
- to act in an agile manner using systemic interventions and to learn to adapt actions, respectively.

Based on this insight, Oswald (Oswald 2016) describes in detail, the different models required to stay effective in a complex context:

- Complexity drivers are analysed by the diamond project type model
- The Dilts Pyramid, together with several psychological and social models, allows the analysis of systemic patterns. Recognized social

patterns are used as input for the building of hypothesis for social interventions.
- The design of systemic patterns is supported by the model of self-organization.
- Agility is supported by continuous application of one or several interrelated Plan-Do-Check-Act-Cycles (PDCA-Cycle). Depending on context, each "phase" in a PDCA-Cycle is supported by different agile techniques. The chosen collection of agile techniques for a specific context is referred to as an agile framework. Scrum or Kanban are examples of agile frameworks.

In the following chapters we will outline some of these issues.

Literature

Oswald A, Köhler J, Schmitt R (2016) Projektmanagement am Rande des Chaos, Springer Vieweg, Heidelberg. This book is avalaible in English: Oswald A, Köhler J, Schmitt R (2018) Project Management at the Edge of Chaos, Springer Verlag, Heidelberg

3.4 Self-organization

Author: Alfred Oswald

Summary: Self-organization is a universal phenomenon which regulates complexity and leads to emergent systemic behavior of systems. Self-organization can be used to build high-performance teams or high-performance multi-project organizations.

Key Terms: Complexity, Self-Organization, Setting Parameter, Control Parameter, Order Parameter, High-Performance Team, Multi-Project Organization

Self-organization is one of the buzzwords in the agile community. Very often, the meaning is self-management or the right of someone to define their own way of life. In the context of agile frameworks like Scrum, in particular, it means that the team members of a Scrum team have the "right" to define how they solve a problem, not what problem they solve.

When we speak of self-organization in this book, we are not only implying self-management, or that a team gives itself rules, processes or structures, instead we perceive self-organization as a universal phenomenon. Current scientific knowledge views the principles of self-organization as being responsible for many (or perhaps all) cooperative natural, social or technical phenomena: The formation of swarms of birds or schools of fish, many autocatalytic chemical reactions, the behavior of societies and LASER systems, are all self-organized systems. Self-organized systems are based on complexity and display newly emerging systemic patterns. In the case of LASER systems, a totally new system quality emerges. Oswald (Oswald 2016) shows that the principles of self-organization can also be used to regulate complex social systems, creating high-performance organizations: High-performance organizations are examples of the implementation of the slogan "The whole is more than the sum of its parts".

Self-organized systems are regulated by three types of parameters (Oswald 2016): Setting parameters, control parameters and order parameters. Figure 3-3 outlines these parameter types.

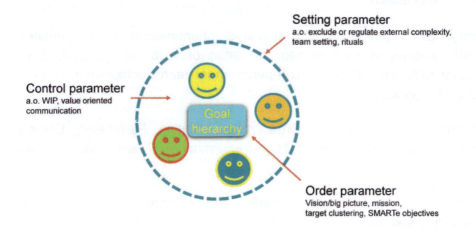

Figure 3-3: Leadership parameter of team self-organization

With the setting of parameters, value-destroying complexity is excluded and stability is introduced. For example, the exclusion of value-destroying complexity can be fulfilled by separating a team in a special team room to prevent interference with the environment and to build up team focus. Additional stability is brought into the team by introducing rituals, which support the human need for control and order.

The control parameters allow team member to reveal their personal strengths. The first control parameter guarantees that individual strengths and respective workload are in balance. This condition results in two issues: Individual strength should match individual tasks and ideally the so-called Work-in-Progress (WIP) should be no more than 1: At one time, a team member should only process one task. The second control parameter ensures that communication is supported by mutual appreciation. This results in the condition where each team member perceives their own beliefs and values, as well as those of other team members, and is capable of adapting their personal behavior accordingly, in the context of the project. If these control parameters match task, strength,

WIP and value-oriented communication, the team can enter into a team flow state.

The order parameter(s) introduces team goal-orientation and fulfils two purposes: The order parameter aligns team member activities and gives these activities a team goal. Oswald (Oswald 2016) shows that the order parameter has to have a three-tier structure from the big picture, via target clustering, to detailed SMART objectives. This order parameter structure is called a Collective Mind goal hierarchy.

The task of a leader is to ensure that these three different system parameters are able to develop. Therefore, we also speak of leadership parameters. In the next chapter, we will demonstrate that self-organization is also the basis of agile team frameworks.

Because self-organization is a universal principle, it can also be used to lead a multi-project organization. In the case of team self-organization, the system elements are humans. In the case of the multi-project management organization, the system elements are projects.

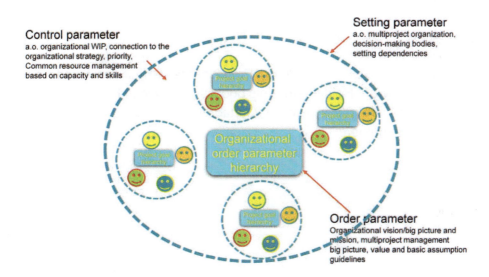

Figure 3-4: Leadership parameters of self-organization for a multi-project organization

Figure 3-4 outlines the characteristics of setting, control and order parameters for a system consisting of projects. Here, the setting parameters are once again, parameters which bring system stability: For example, special decision-making bodies define which new projects are brought into the system and which rules (rituals) need to be fulfilled, before new projects are introduced into the system. A Project Management Office (PMO) is an example of such a body, which controls the flow of complexity in the system.

Control parameters ensure that the interference in projects is as low as possible and to enable them to achieve high performance levels. Again, the multi-project WIP is the key for high level performance.

The order parameter in a multi-project context is a transparent visualization of ongoing projects, their dependencies and their performances. For example, a continuously maintained, multi-project management board is an example of an order parameter implementation.

In the following chapters, we introduce and use Critical Chain Project Management, which is based on self-organization principles in a system of projects.

Literature

Oswald A, Köhler J, Schmitt R (2016) Projektmanagement am Rande des Chaos, Springer Vieweg, Heidelberg. This book is avalaible in English: Oswald A, Köhler J, Schmitt R (2018) Project Management at the Edge of Chaos, Springer Verlag, Heidelberg

3.5 Principles of Scrum and Kanban Agile Frameworks

It is not the goal of this chapter to describe every aspect of Scrum and Kanban agile frameworks. For an in-depth description of all aspects, we refer to the literature ((Schwaber 2016), (Rubin 2012), (Foegen 2016), (Anderson 2013), (Pröpper 2012), (Appelo 2011), (Gloger 2014), (Mathis 2016) and (Oswald 2016)).

We will focus our description on the relationship of complexity, agility and self-organization.

We start with the description of an experience, which we have all probably had: We all know what we have to do to solve a complex problem or find an innovative solution, or if, as agent in a principal-agent relation, we need to get a task done under time pressure.

If we are smart (in such a context),…

- we shut ourselves away,
- we limit the amount of concurrent activities,
- we focus and draw up an activity plan,
- we communicate a lot with the principal and visualize our results,
- we want fast feedback from the principal,
- and we permanently adjust our activities according to feedback.

Figure 3-5 illustrates the structure of these "work parameters".

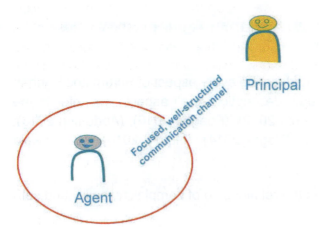

Figure 3-5: Agent under pressure

Figure 3-6 describes the arrangement of the above mentioned "work parameters" according to the continuous improvement process of the Plan-Do-Check-Act-Cycle ((GPM 2009), (Oswald 2016)).

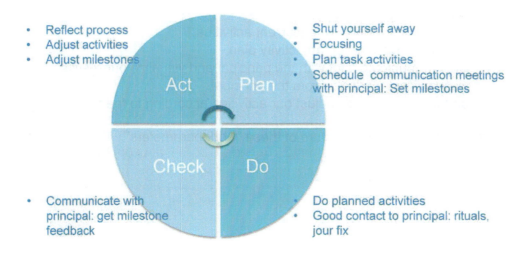

Figure 3-6: Agent using PDCA

Both figures together illustrate the main relationship between complexity and agility: To become agile, it is necessary to initially exclude unnecessary "external" complexity. If this is to be achieved, a lean process is required, which supports velocity and flexibility. The PDCA-cycle is a proto-version of a lean process of adaption to the environment.

Excluding "external" complexity and continuous improvement are two of the key principles of the Scrum agile framework: The third principle, which Scrum follows, is the principle of self-organization. According to Chapter 3.4 "Self-organization", we define self-organization by the manifestation of the system parameters of self-organization: setting parameters, control parameters and order parameters:

Setting parameters

Ideally the Scrum team should be co-located in one room, or at least all team meetings carried out with a co-located team. Virtual teams are possible, but are only second choice. System boundaries are "closed" and the Product Owner acts as a "guardian" of external complexity.

Rituals like daily meetings, to plan, check and adjust team activities, help control the internal team and task complexity. Furthermore, stability in the team composition supports the coherence of the team. Figure 3-7 illustrates the setting parameters.

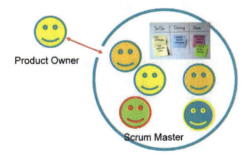

Figure 3-7: Scrum and Complexity

Control parameter

Scrum is an iterative and incremental process, and with this process, supports the main control parameters. Figure 3-8 illustrates this. There are two main control parameters:

The limitation of Work-in-Progress and of mutual appreciation within the team.

The limitation of Work-in-Progress can be twofold: Initially, there is limitation of work, which is forwarded from the Product Owner to the team. With the product backlog, the Product Owner controls the flow of requirements from the "external" world to the team world. During the so-called sprint planning phase, the team selects the amount of work it is capable of handling in one sprint (i.e. one iteration). Scrum iteration follows the PDCA-cycle: Sprint planning defines user stories, which can be probably done during one iteration. All user stories in a sprint define together a product increment. If the increment is done, it will be checked by a review by the Product Owner and the users of the product. If the Product Owner and the users accept the increment, the sprint is finished with a retrospective, i.e. a sprint lessons learned. The PDCA-cycle of the whole iteration is supported by daily team meetings, which also follow the PDCA-cycle for this specific day.

Mutual appreciation is based on a team-agreed set of values and these values are the basis of communication and conflict resolution. - The Scrum Guide (Schwaber 2016) defines a set of values – see also the agile Scrum mindset in Chapter 3.2 above – but these values should not be forced upon the team, instead they should arise as team values from the team. One key task of the role of Scrum Master is to monitor control parameters and bring the team, if necessary, back to a context where control parameters enable high level performance. Just as the Product Owner is a guardian of external complexity, the Scrum Master is a guardian of team-internal complexity.

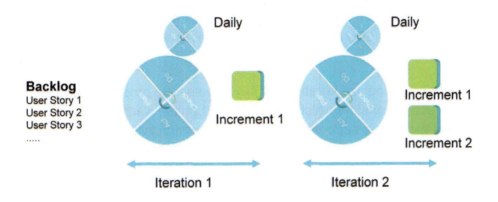

Figure 3-8: Scrum: an iterative and incremental procedure

Order parameter

The order parameter is designed as a threefold goal hierarchy, consisting of Product Vision, Product Backlog and Sprint Backlog. Transparency is one of the key values, which on the one hand supports this goal hierarchy, and on the other hand, acts as control parameter, supporting mutual appreciation. Transparency in the goal hierarchy is supported by several visualization tools: Product Backlog visualization, Sprint planning visualization, team velocity (team performance) diagram, etc. The key task of the Product Owner is to guarantee coherence of the goal hierarchy and ensure that the team grasps the whole goal hierarchy.

Kanban has its roots in production and related continuous improvement of the production process. The exclusion of external complexity to create a team focus is not a key issue of Kanban. (In contrast, Scrum was initially created in the context of complex software development projects, where external complexity is the main reason for bad project performance.) Nevertheless, it is necessary to limit internal complexity. Therefore, Kanban introduced the idea of Work-in-Progress limitation for each production step, depending on the number of available resources in each production step. Figure 3-9 illustrates the key aspects of Kanban. A flow of tasks, here a flow of user stories, enter the Kanban process flow. In the figure, we used a flow consisting of three stages, with each stage having its own WIP limit. A team member in a Kanban team is free to pull up the next task if they have finished the previous task and the WIP limit is respected.

Kanban does not recognize iterations or increments. The product continuously evolves with each user story which has gone through the Kanban pipeline. The monitoring of the task is supported by visualization of activities with a Kanban board. A Kanban board visualizes the status of activities per Kanban work stage.

Continuous improvement of the process flow through the Kanban pipeline is a key principle of Kanban and is organized as a PDCA-cycle. The goal of continuous improvement is to push the pipeline throughput to higher and higher levels of velocity (measured by the key performance indicators "cycle time" and "lead time", see (Anderson 2013)) and focusing more and more on customer added product value.

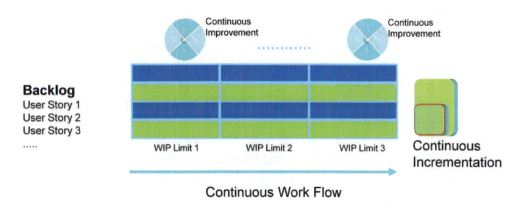

Figure 3-9: Kanban a continuous work flow procedure

The original Kanban framework is a very simple process model and therefore much harder to identify self-organization system parameters: With respect to setting parameters, only continuous meetings of Continuous Improvement are identified. There is no explicit system boundary or team structure with different roles. Kanban introduced WIP as a control parameter (Scrum implementations have borrowed the WIP principle from Kanban: The Scrum Guide does not recognize the WIP principle.) With respect to order parameters, the focus on performance improvements and on added customer value, includes some order parameter "aspects", but cannot be seen as full order parameter implementation.

"Continuous incrementation" of the product requires significantly improved continuous integration and delivery in the Development and Operation interface (DevOps interface (Gruver 2015)) than in the framework Scrum. In summary, Kanban appears simpler than the already simple Scrum framework, but needs deeper internalization of agile values and techniques.

Literature

Anderson D J (2010) Kanban: Successful Evolutionary Change for Your Technology Business. Blue Hole Press, Sequim WA

Appelo J (2011) Management 3.0: Leading Agile Developers, Developing Agile Leaders. Pearson Eduction Inc., Boston

Foegen M, Kaczmarek C (2016) Organisation in einer digitalen Zeit. wibas GmbH, Darmstadt

Gloger B, Margetich J (2014) Das Scrum Prinzip: Agile Organisationen aufbauen und gestalten. Schäfer-Poeschel Verlag, Stuttgart

GPM (2009) Kompetenzbasiertes Projektmanagement (PM3), Band 1.GPM Deutsche Gesellschaft für Projektmanagement e.V., Nürnberg

Gruver G, Mouser T (2015) Leading the Transformation, Applying Agile and DevOps Principles at Scale. eBook, IT Revolution, Portland, OR

Mathis C (2016) SAFe Das Scaled Agile Framework. dpunkt.verlag, Heidelberg

Pröpper N (2012) Agile Techniken für klassisches Projektmanagement (Qualifizierung zum PMI-ACP). mitp, Heidelberg

Oswald A, Köhler J, Schmitt R (2016) Projektmanagement am Rande des Chaos, Springer Vieweg, Heidelberg. This book is avalaible in English: Oswald A, Köhler J, Schmitt R (2018) Project Management at the Edge of Chaos, Springer Verlag, Heidelberg

Rubin K S (2012) Essential Scrum. Addison-Wesley, Upper Saddle River, NJ

Schwaber K, Sutherland J (2016) The Scrum Guide. Scrum.org and ScrumInc.

4 Agile Leadership 4.0

4.1 Principles of Agile Leadership 4.0

Authors: Alfred Oswald, Hubertus Tuczek

Summary: The understanding and the need that agility is a key corporate success factor has never been more urgent than it is today. Many companies are failing to implement true agile organizations. Why is this? What are the leadership drivers behind a sustainable transformation? A holistic approach for the total enterprise, starting with the mindset of the management and related government structures is the only way forward.

Key terms: Complexity, Agile Mindset, Neuro-Leadership, Macro-tier, Micro-tier, Intervention, Values, Objectives and Key Results (OKRs), Self-organization, Setting Parameter, Control Parameter, Order Parameter, Goal-hierarchy, Micro-tier, Macro-tier, Governance

Agility regulates Complexity

Management 4.0 is concerned with the adapted agility of teams and organizations in a complex environment. The main prerequisite of adapted agility is the systemic perception and understanding of complexity in a natural, social and technical context. This means that a leader has to have the volition to understand these complexity domains, and in particular, their interactions (see Figure 4-1).

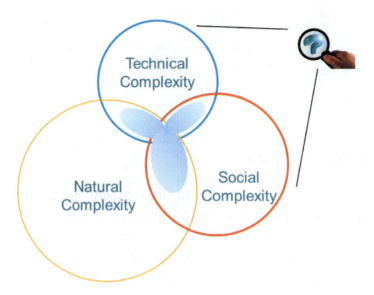

Figure 4-1: Complexity Domains

As an example of global importance for this interaction of complexity domains, we cite a 2017 press release [ntv 2017, translated by the authors]: "Old drill holes release methane: Methane is a climate killer. To date, methane emissions from cattle have been critically observed. But today, it is the North Sea that is spewing out this greenhouse gas - not naturally, but in places where the ground has been previously drilled." The natural domain has been disturbed by technical, i.e. human intervention, which sooner or later, will result in an interaction of the three complexity areas which create the potential for critical self-organization, with unforeseeable consequences for mankind and the planet.

Agility requires Fluid Networks

As a consequence of the fact that Management 4.0 has to cope with natural, social and technical complexity, there is a radical shift in leadership: As stated in (Oswald 2016), complex systems or organization can not be directed by simple linear cause-effect intervention patterns, because complex systems do not follow simple-cause-effect relations. They are essentially non-linear the effect an intervention (cause) will have in a complex system cannot be predicted: Ashby's law (Oswald 2016) states that a (mental) model requires a higher level of complexity than the environment, in order to regulate environmental complexity. This means that an individual, a team or an organization needs an appropriate degree of complexity to perceive, understand and regulate environmental complexity. Leadership in a complex world means using the complexity of a team or an organization to regulate environmental complexity. Therefore, Leadership 4.0 means a shift from "dominating and managing" to "networking and coaching", to construct a high level of organizational complexity for regulating high level environmental complexity (see Figure 4-2).

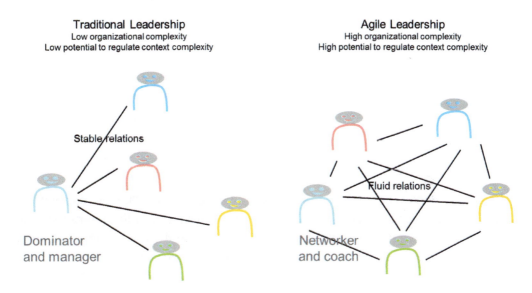

Figure 4-2: Traditional Leadership versus Agile Leadership 4.0

Agility requires Systemic Interventions

For a team or an organization to be capable of building up value-creating complexity to regulate external complexity, Leader 4.0 can intervene at two different levels in a team or organization: the macro-tier and the micro-tier. This also mitigates the consequences of Ashby's law, because on a macro-tier, a system shows fewer degrees of freedom than on a micro-tier.

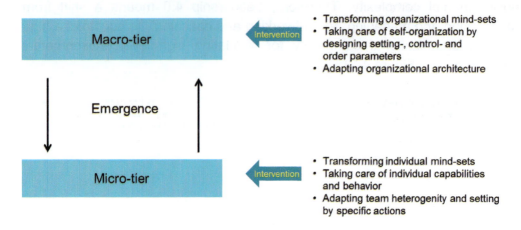

Figure 4-3: Types of interventions

Therefore, it can be stated that Leader 4.0 requires systemic capabilities (macro-tier) combined with the ability to switch from micro-tier intervention to macro-tier interventions, and vice versa (see Figure 4-3). In addition, Leader 4.0 has to be able to adapt interventions continuously and agilely using well-trained intuition based on systemic models, combined with a PDCA cycle, for continuous adaption and learning (Oswald 2016).

This has tremendous consequences for the self-concept of a leader:

In a fluid network of equal individuals, leadership can move around depending on respective leader capabilities and environment. Responsibility and commitment is no longer the domain of one person, but belongs to the team or the organization. Legally, it makes sense to have one, or several, legally responsible persons, but on the level of interaction, everyone communicate at the same eye level, i.e. are equal. The acceptance of complexity in the organization, to regulate complexity, encases equality within the network. Nevertheless, during the transformation phase from a traditional organization to an Agile Organization, some people may emerge as forerunners, or demonstrate forerunner capabilities during the first steps of transformation i.e. they have adopted an Agile Leadership style and the related Agile Mindset to serve as an inspiring example to others.

The nonlinearity of complexity can result in a feeling of loss of control. Not everyone has the capability or personality to handle this feeling of loss of control. But also, for those who have the appropriate personality, a lot of training is necessary to acquire the required ability to act proactively in a complex environment (Oswald 2016). Please see also (Tuczek 2017) for other perspectives and aspects.

An Agile Mindset is the Basis of Agility

In chapter 3.1 we defined Management 4.0 by the cornerstones self-leadership and Agile Mindset, respect for basic human needs, understanding of complex systems and meta-competence, continuous learning and adaption, and taking care of self-organization of teams and organizations to create customer value by agility.

Figure 4-4 describes a generic Agile Mindset with help of the Dilts Pyramid. A Leader 4.0 has to take care of the implementation of the Agile Mindset in their organization. By keeping the relevant context or environment in mind, appropriate agile behavior will result. This might also mean that the entire Agile Mindset accepts a low level of behavior agility if such behavior is required by the perceived situation. Appropriate agility behavior is supported by agile technical principles, such as visualisation or time-boxing, and appropriate agile techniques, such as daily stand up, as well as traditional management methods like stakeholder management or earned value analysis. The Agile Manifesto with related Agile Values and Agile Principles, represents the "values, beliefs and basic assumptions" level of the Dilts Pyramid. A Collective Mind is created as a team or organizational identity on the basis of self-organization. Self-organization is the pivotal point of Leadership 4.0: It means working on design, and continuous adaptation of the setting, control and order parameters of self-organization. This is a governance process, which is enabled by interventions on the macro-tier. The setting, control and order parameters are different for different system types, such as teams, multi-project organizations, product organizations or any other Agile Organization (see chapter 3.4 and (Oswald 2016)). Agile technical principles often act as setting parameters (time-boxing for the setting of time boundaries or team collocation as setting for space conditions), values act as control parameters and goal hierarchies (vision, epics/objectives, key results (sprint goal and user stories) act as order parameters (please see chapter 3.3). Figure 4-4 shows the implementation of the higher levels of the Dilts Pyramid by the goal hierarchy for the operational part of an organization (Vision-OKRs) mapped to the goal hierarchy of a product development or project-oriented part of an organization (Vision-Epics, Features, User Stories). A Leader 4.0, with their interventions, works towards the emergence of self-organization: In particular, this means that the order parameters (Vision-OKRs and Vision-Epics, Features, User Stories) and the related emergent macro-structure will emerge from the team and the organization and will not be predetermined by the leader. A leader is only allowed to contribute to the system via careful intervention propositions of order parameters, and in such cases they have to accept the emergence of order parameters.

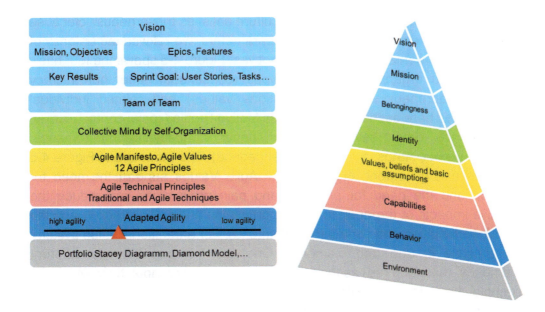

Figure 4-4: Generic Agile Mindset

In a team or an organization, Agile Values should act as organizational control parameters. In rare cases they can be used as order parameters, because such usage can result in a dictatorship of Agile Values. The respect for each personality e.g. temperament, motives and values, are key control parameters and should never be under the dictatorship of Agile Values. Neuro-Leadership is a part of Leadership 4.0 and is based on the observation that our motivation is at its highest if we can live according to our basic needs. Basic needs have their source in our neuro-system. Our neuro-system is composed of four basic needs. In coaching practice these needs are represented in a simplified manner by motives or values (Oswald 2016).

Neuroleadership supports Agility

Figure 4-5 shows the Neuroleadership consistency model. Neuroleadership analyses an individual's basic needs and tries to agree team or organizational setting, control and order parameters with the individual's basic needs. For agility to grow, it is essential for a leader to be aware of individual needs and the degree to which the organizational culture satisfies these needs. Because values and motives act as pivot control parameters, we refer to consistency of individual and organizational values or motives. Figure 4-5 shows the four basic needs, related organizational value types (consensus value, bureaucracy values, entrepreneur values, competitions values) and related individual motives, listed here as the so called Reiss Motive Profile (social contact, family, independence, order, saving, idealism, honor, curiosity, eating, romance, activities, power, status, acceptance, vengeance). The message of Figure 4-5 is that to a large extent, organizational Agile Values support the need for affection and the need for pleasure and pain prevention, and reduce the negative impacts of the need for self-appreciation and self-protection and the need for orientation and control (blue diamond). For a traditional value system, the opposite is true (red diamond). One can interpret the two different "diamonds" (blue and red) as the value systems of two organizations which, for example, have to cooperate, or as the value system of an individual (for example with the blue "diamond") who has to work in a traditional organization (red "diamond"). In both cases, a great deal to a large extent of friction will result.

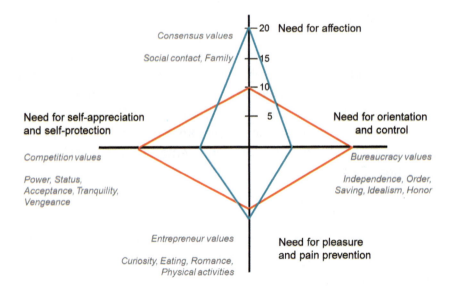

Figure 4-5: Neuroleadership: Traditional values (red), Agile values (blau)

A Leader 4.0 supports organizational Agile Values by respecting the individual values (motives) of each staff member, by designing organizational governance which supports self-organization, and by incorporating the "Personality-oriented Communication" essential control parameter in their daily communication (Oswald 2016).

Transformation to Agility

The key responsibility of a Leadership 4.0 is to take care of the self-organisation of a team or organization. Related interventions are carried out on both the macro-tier and the micro-tier. Macro-tier interventions are systemic Governance interventions and micro-tier interventions are necessary to support staff members in adapting and supporting the transformation. Because there are no simple cause-effect relations, it is necessary to monitor the transformation by feedback loops. These feedback loops follow a Plan-Do-Check-Act loop pattern: "Plan" in this case, means creating a hypothesis on appropriate self-organization parameters with the help of known theories, models, social techniques and agile frameworks. "Do" means letting the self-organization emerge in an evolutionary fashion. "Check" does not imply checking or inspecting, but more sensing, based on awareness and mindfulness. "Act" or "Adapt" is careful modification of the intervention strategy on both the macro-tier and the micro-tier, to be able to respond in an appropriate manner, based on sensed organizational patterns. At the beginning of a transformation, the number and strength of interventions may be high, but with the evolution of the organization, management interventions are reduced and transformed to interventions of the organization itself: In all sub-organizations, the organization acts as a self-organized whole (please see (Laloux 2014), (Rüther 2017)). The Leader 4.0 acts like a coach with the goal being the emergence of an agile corporate mindset. Leadership 4.0 is a type of Integral Leadership (Kuhlmann 2016). In (Oswald 2016) an integral repertoire of theories, models and tools for Integral Leadership and for handling related transformations is described.

For this Agile Mindset to emerge throughout the whole organization, interventions must be carried out at all levels, and in all parts of the organization. We say that interventions must be self-similar. Figure 4-6 outlines this process for an organization with an agile architecture, consisting of self-organized teams, two self-organized multi-project management organizations and a team organized for product development for example, based on the LeSS or SAFe scaled agile frameworks (see (Larman 2016), (Mathis 2016)).

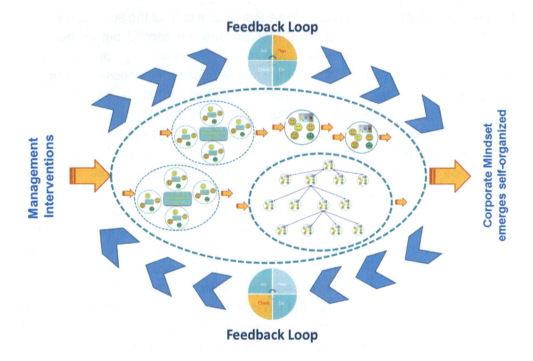

Figure 4-6: Transformation to self-organization

Figure 4-6 contains organizations based on agile principles. If at least some agile principles are implemented, we speak of an organization with agile architecture. But, we emphasise that nearly all published frameworks are not self-organized in the synergistic manner we adopted. Therefore, as an overall principle, we say that the goal of a transformation is to fulfil self-organization and not to fulfil the design rules of any published best-practices of an agile framework.

The "Big Picture"

All this results in a "Big Picture" of Management 4.0. With the help of intuition, a Leader 4.0 has to bring this complicated "Big Picture" into complex practice (Figure 4-7).

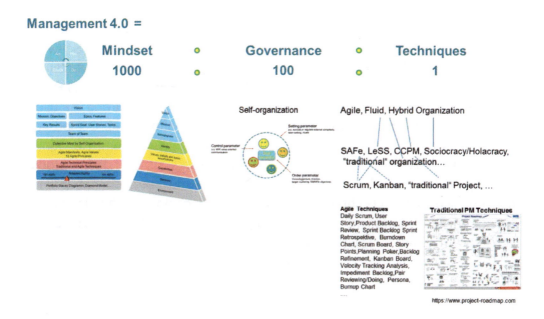

Figure 4-7: "Big Picture" Management 4.0 (as an example, we outlined only a few relations between the different scales of organizations).

Figure 4-7 represents a rule of thumb for Management 4.0 and the related Leadership 4.0. In a continuous feedback loop (a PDCA-cycle), Leader 4.0 uses three types of levers with three leverage factors and three different scales: Techniques are necessary, because they provide a process context for our behavior, so we need them to manifest agile behavior. But, from experience, we know that techniques have the lowest impact on agility. By comparing techniques with the mindset, we state that the leverage factors of both are related as 1:1000. In comparison, the leverage factor of governance is 100. The meaning that we associate with these relations is not number correctness, but the basic assumption that belief in the efficacy of techniques is a misbelief. This misbelief is actually the source of failure of many Agile Management initiatives. Figure 4-7 outlines the main models we use in Management 4.0: The Dilts Pyramid, here in a generic Agile Mindset version (see Figure 4-4 and the Dilts Pyramid described in (Oswald 2016) as master model for social technologies). The self-organization principle as pivot governance, in addition to a variety of techniques to support this governance principle. Techniques include agile basis techniques and all traditional basis techniques. Agile basis techniques are used in agile team organizations based on Scrum (Schwaber 2016) and Kanban (Anderson 2013) frameworks, as well as in hybrid/traditional project organizations. As we noted in chapter 3.2 with respect to Hybrid Project Management, a hybrid organization is built by an Agile Mindset and the use of agile or traditional techniques, and not by a traditional mindset. Scaled agile frameworks are built, based on agile organizations (like Scrum, Kanban, or "traditional" projects). This scaled agile frameworks uses a team product development concept, like SAFe or LeSS, or a multi-project management concept, like CCPM (Techt 2015). The range of techniques may also include frameworks for operational or parent organizations, such as Sociocracy or Holacracy ((Rüther 2017), (Laloux 2014)).

Literature

Anderson D J (2010) Kanban: Successful Evolutionary Change for Your Technology Business. Blue Hole Press, Sequim WA

Kuhlmann H, Horn S, Scharping C (2016) Integrale Führung: Neue Perspektiven und Tools für Führung, Management, Persönlichkeitsentwicklung, Springer Gabler

Laloux F (2014) Reinventing Organizations: A Guide to Creating

Organizations Inspired by the Next Stage of Human Consciousness, Nelson Parker

Larman C, Vodde B (2016) Large-Scale Scrum: More with LeSS, Addison-Wesley

Mathis C (2016) SAFe - Das Scaled Agile Framework: Lean und Agile in großen Unternehmen skalieren, dpunkt.verlag GmbH

Oswald A, Köhler J, Schmitt R (2016) Projektmanagement am Rande des Chaos, Springer Vieweg, Heidelberg. This book is avalaible in English: Oswald A, Köhler J, Schmitt R (2018) Project Management at the Edge of Chaos, Springer Verlag, Heidelberg

ntv (2017) https://www.n-tv.de/wissen/Alte-Bohrloecher-setzen-Methan-frei-article20006231.html

Rüther C (2017) Soziokratie, Holakratie, Lalouxs "Reinventing Organization" und ...: Ein Überblick über die gängigsten Ansätze zur Selbstorganisation und Partizipation, BoD, Norderstedt

Schwaber K, Sutherland J (2016) The Scrum Guide. Scrum.org and ScrumInc.

Techt U (2015) Projects That Flow: More Projects in Less Time (QuiStainable Business Solutions), ibidem

Tuczek C. Hubertus (2017) Management 4.0 und die Generation Y, Landshut Leadership Band 2, Shaker Verlag, Aachen

4.2 Agile Leadership 4.0 – Digital Network Intelligence

Authors: Hubertus C. Tuczek, Helge F. R. Nuhn, Steve Raue

Summary: Digital communication is a key driver for changing industry dynamics. Information can be shared and collaboration can be organised in a much quicker and more effective manner than in traditional analogue culture. However, digital tools have the potential to store information and actions indefinitely, resulting in ever-lasting accountability. In addition, digital environments do not currently address how to build trust and how to convey emotions. Communication and collaboration in this environment takes place within a horizontal network with a reduced or non-existent hierarchy. This necessitates a game-changing management approach. But what is it that really enables these digital networks? Why do they so often break apart before being established and sustained? And how do leaders position themselves in these new business environments with free flow of information and self-organization? One major prerequisite for success lies in the hands of the management, who can proactively create the right framework for self-organised communication. The conditions for an Agile Management System, which enables Digital Network Intelligence, need to be defined, those involved need to be committed via strategic exercises, and digital networks have to be lived and experienced accordingly.

Key Terms: Digital Networks, Horizontal Communication, Agile Management Systems, Corporate Mindset, Governance, Network Intelligence, Enterprise Social Networks (ESN)

Principles of Digital Social Networks

Collaboration and collectivity builds on connectivity. In a digital world, the potential for connectivity in a network does not compare to that in the analogue world - it opens up a completely new dimension of interaction between participants.

Demonstrators in Egypt, who met at Tahrir square in Cairo to protest against the regime, organized themselves by means of social media. This enabled them to gather in large numbers, which finally led to the dramatical political change referred to as the "Arab Spring". Without the connecting power of social media they would have had little opportunity to create a momentum of such immense power to force the end of a political regime. On the other hand, the attempted toppling of President Erdogan in Turkey in 2016 was prevented by the extensive use of social media channels and live streaming by the president himself. These examples demonstrate the enormous energy, which can be released using digital communication.

In a company context, you need to ensure that the potential of social media and corresponding networks is used to the benefit of the company and its customers and suppliers. Communication within a social media network follows the principles of self-organisation. Therefore, management needs to define rules for interaction in the network. A clear mission and vision for the desired company culture, from top management, is indispensable for effective digital communication. The architecture of social network software, as well as the specific use of technology and algorithms is only second to the mindset, which must support trust and transparency in the network.

Users of the communication system have additional requirements: the systems need to fulfill a very transparent form of communication to be accepted. Employees do not want their every activity in the network to be tracked or to be held accountable for comments, maybe even years after they were made. A certain level of privacy has to be guaranteed for participating groups, so that they are not stuck on a level of politically controlled communication, but instead, are able to interact in an open and effective manner.

Challenge for Agile Leadership

When discussing Agile Management structures, senior executives often put forward the argument that management has the responsibility for the success of the company. Therefore, it needs to direct the way. In the context of self-organisation, managers of traditional companies often feel a loss of control with respect to their impact, responsibility and shaping the objectives of their organisation. This makes them very sceptical of change and sometimes results in strong resistance being built up toward new ways of working.

To successfully transition to agility and self-organisation, the question of why managers in charge should support the move instead of fighting against it needs to be addressed. If managers cannot be convinced, an Agile Organisation cannot be created. A prerequisite for creating intrinsic motivation to change lies in showing managers how to discover their new role. Strong managers want to shape the future and use their power to make things happen. Simply playing the role of a coach for their employees does not seem to provide adequate satisfaction. Nevertheless, in today's dynamic markets, managers cannot discover the right way forward solely by themselves, but instead need to organize how problems are solved collectively by everyone within the company. This makes the manager the number one networker in the company.

A concept needs to be developed that gives management a clear perspective of how they can set up a management system which supports self-organisation, yet at the same time, still gives them control over the direction of activities. They need to work with the system as a paradigm, instead of working within the system. This includes permanent readjustment of system parameters to adapt to change in the market, the organisation itself, or its environment. The aim of this permanent readjustment is to ensure an optimal "flow" of resources within the organization.

In order to establish or increase self-organization within a company, managers of such organizations should perceive themselves as coaches. They influence the corporate culture (or mindset) of the organisation on the level of belongingness, identity, values and beliefs. In order to maintain or transform a culture to the desired state of the system, management intervention is defined by adjusting the settings for each part of the organization and the organization as a whole. In addition, specific controls should be set up to measure the state, mindset, culture and constitution of the organization, all of which influence management effectiveness.

An essential part of this coaching approach is to set up appropriate digital communication systems for different situations, in terms of both structure and technology. The type of business, employee competences and business environment, all need to be considered in context. If management, customers, employees and the overall mindset in the company are not ready for open and fast digital communication, then the introduction of e.g. an enterprise social network system is sure to fail. The damage will be significant, as the basis for digital transformation will be ruined for years to come. Digital communication eliminates power distance and status to a large extent. Therefore, the aspects of any change need to be thoroughly understood.

Agile Digital Network Intelligence

In order for managers to set guidelines for Agile Digital Network Intelligence, it is necessary to have a clear concept of what exactly is required to make these networks intelligent. Unfortunately, research on human intelligence has already shown us that there is no simple, broadly accepted definition of intelligence. Yet, in modern neuro-biological research, links between intelligence and network organization have been successfully established (Li 2009).

Common-day usage of the word points to problem-solving capabilities with self-enhancing properties. We therefore propose a similar concept for digital network intelligence, as shown in Figure 4-8. It encompasses a process cycle of four major phases: perception, problem solving, acting, and self-reflection. We relate this cycle to organizations. Through organized and unorganized digital interaction, organizations naturally form networks of weak and strong bonds between individuals. Agility is added to the concept, as the ability of the whole organization to rapidly reorganize by means of digital network communication, in response to changing environments.

Agile Digital Network Intelligence will be perceived, if the following cycle is run through successfully: The network perceives the right problems with the right priorities and engages in the development of efficient, effective problem solving approaches. It self-organizes the subsequent course of action to actually solve the problem and ends with measures to reflect what has happened.

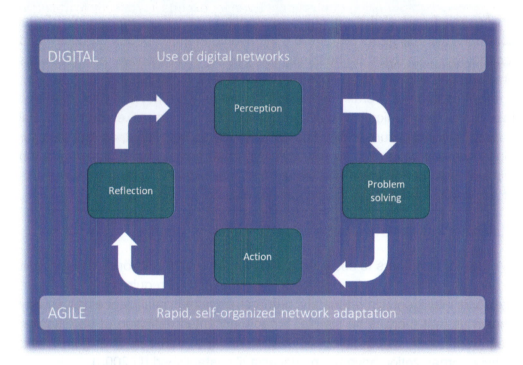

Figure 4-8: Conceptualization Agile Digital Network Intelligence

Imagine the following situation as a practical example. A new team of experts needs to be formed. It has been identified that different expert knowledge is required. The formation of this team takes place online during a digital social bar camp session. As a result of an organization mindset that fosters Agile Digital Network Intelligence, the initiator of the idea establishes a new messenger channel related to the defined business problem. The corresponding link for the bar camp session and membership to the communication channel is shared by every member of the initial discussion. In addition, anyone they think could help solve the problem is also invited to join the conversation. Yet, the team itself has chosen who should participate. The resulting discussion will bring all information relevant to the problem into one confined space, the messenger channel, thus enabling team members to access it and contribute knowledge via this newly formed sub-network. The team will engage in problem-solving and corresponding acts. Finally, throughout the communication process, the team and everyone who engages with the team, will decide in a self-organized way on the ongoing relevance of this consciously, newly formed sub-network, and also potentially disengage from it.

Such networked behavior is intelligent, in that its structures have been adapted in a self-organized and creative way. It is to be considered more or less intelligent as it reacts more or less effectively and creatively to differences in its environment, and it is to be considered more or less agile, depending on the promptness with which such changes take place.

However, so far, we have only looked at intelligence from a rather mechanistic perspective. The following sections will provide our theses and further insights into what we consider would be required to enhance Agile Digital Network Intelligence and how to elevate it to a truly social and cooperative network, based on the concept defined here. We will also discuss potential barriers to scaling Digital Network Intelligence in organizations relative to their size and the communication tools they employ.

Digital Corporate Mindset and Governance

The Traditional Mindset comes with an understanding of vertical hierarchy, which was developed in the industrial age. The dominant management approach can be described in terms of power and control. For digital networks to be a success, you first need trust and to be able to build on good, strong communication. Digital tools provide great potential for horizontal communication throughout the whole company, even if employees are spread out over the globe! But a Digital Agile Mindset also needs to be developed within the company. And this need to happen before the introduction of digital communication systems can even be thought of. Otherwise, the result will be chaos! To do this, the purpose of the change needs to be clearly identified and communicated. On the positive side, if you succeed in combining digital technology with the right mindset, you will succeed in pushing your company up to the next level of agile capability.

Decisions on digital communication and collaboration should take into account the effect and potential they have on building the right level of trust and trustful communication procesess within the organization. The design of digital networks in terms of structure, technology and algorithms has to follow the needs of the organization. This implies, wherever possible that access to the overall system should be granted to all employees. Individual access rights to specific information should be carefully negotiated. Confidentiality agreements need to be respected.

Management Intervention

Management has the task of defining and maintaining the overall direction and effectivity of the business as a whole. Delivering results and fulfilling corporate goals are the basic principles of every organization. On the other hand, enabling employees in their efforts to support company performance, reflects leadership effort, and will result in a crucial competitive advantage. Therefore, the purpose or meaning of digital transformation and digital networks, combined with a clear mission and vision will shape an environment where the belongingness and identification of individuals can flourish. This has to be understood as the indispensable basis for an ecosystem, where values and beliefs are shared to the benefit of a positive common digital mindset, which provides intrinsic motivation for everybody involved.

Trust as a corporate value, is an indispensable prerequisite for a digital network and describes the desired nature of interaction amongst those involved to form a lasting social digital network. As digital networks lack personal face to face contact, constant effort is necessary to maintain a required level of trust. Once people experience a deficit in this regard, they will either leave the network or only cooperate on a work-to-rule basis. Therefore, digital communication needs to be consciously handled with respect to its effect on other participants. Trust requires a great deal of personal exchange that respects the individual, in addition to openness and transparency. Thus, **Digital Agile Leadership should result in a constant feedback culture to ensure that the role model is understood by all employees.** The culture-forming potential of values is untapped if they are followed consistently and exemplified by management. Only then, will they be perceived as authentic and credible. This means that in a digital network, management needs to exemplify trustworthy and respectful communication based on empathy. A good indication of this can be seen in the philosophy of the generally binding culture at Netflix! Not many rules, but the defined values called for are without compromise.

Every organization will have a specific context, which sets out its particular circumstances, culture and structure and will result in different leadership styles, appropriate for the type of business (e.g. a more static or more dynamic environment), varying employee competencies, as well as an overall context of the enterprise as a whole.

Consequently, another important aspect for management **lies in adjusting the balance between hierarchical management and self-organization,** or in other words, supervision and trust (see Figure 4-9).

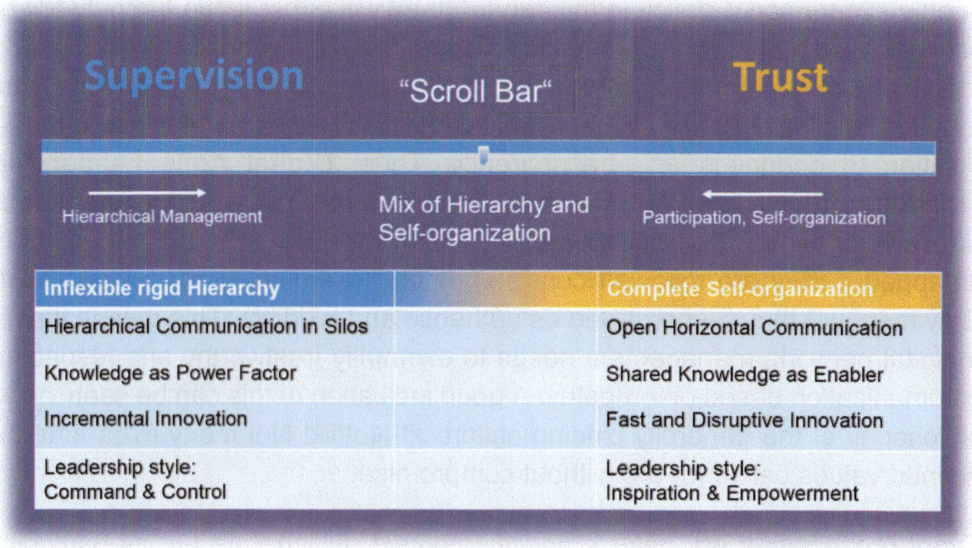

Supervision	"Scroll Bar"	Trust
Hierarchical Management →	Mix of Hierarchy and Self-organization	← Participation, Self-organization

Inflexible rigid Hierarchy	Complete Self-organization
Hierarchical Communication in Silos	Open Horizontal Communication
Knowledge as Power Factor	Shared Knowledge as Enabler
Incremental Innovation	Fast and Disruptive Innovation
Leadership style: Command & Control	Leadership style: Inspiration & Empowerment

Figure 4-9: Leadership between Supervision and Trust

The two extremes of an inflexible rigid hierarchy on the one hand, and complete self-organization on the other, will rarely be seen, and are also unlikely to contribute much to business success. The "Scroll Bar" needs to be adjusted and potentially shifted to a more Inspiration and Empowerment approach, rather than a traditional Command & Control approach. Participation of employees based on trust, in combination with self-organization, is ultimately the direction in which to develop your organization, in order to unfold the digital potential based on an Agile Mindset. Open horizontal communication, as provided by digital enterprise social networks (ESN) is a key enabler for such a setup. Knowledge needs to become a shared enabler, rather than a power factor. This belief will enhance your company and move from incremental innovation to fast and disruptive innovation. Overall, the capabilities and the maturity of the organisation need to be developed step by step, from left to right, to an all-embracing Digital Agile Mindset. We should not forget though, that there is also a need for certainty. This varies from individual to individual, but an organization can be de-stabilized by demanding a high level of self-organization without providing an appropriate level of guidance. In addition, the freedom of the individual ends where the freedom of others is restricted. It is therefore important to find the right balance to ensure an effective team.

The third aspect is **to secure the available content and information flow in the system.** The sharing of knowledge is crucial for the success of digital communication and can only be achieved by adhering to the values of openness and transparency. The manager needs to be the first to share their knowledge with the organisation using open and personal communication. Digital tools offer CEOs the opportunity to communicate to all of their employees at the same time. This has a great impact on the credibility of management actions.

Overall, the role of management becomes one which involves a great deal of sensitivity and empathy! Respect for the individual as a subject, not an object, is required! Feedback needs to be given to both the organization and to individuals, on their role within the company. At the same time, management needs to obtain feedback from the organization, to ensure that management interventions are leading the company in the right direction.

Moreover, it is always important to remember: Trust is hard to earn, but easy to lose! Therefore, every individual in a digital network needs to ensure that they act and communicate in a credible, authentic and reliable way. This needs to be maintained by continuous awareness and training.

Resulting Corporate Mindset

In an open Digital Agile Network, it is not possible to consistently follow goals, without trust exisiting as a commonly perceived value. The management of trust requires a great deal of communication. This is where digital communication offers a completely new dimension to interaction. Subsequently, the level of supervision needs to be reduced, to open an arena for dynamic self-organized structures, where free information flow can be developed (see Figure 4-10).

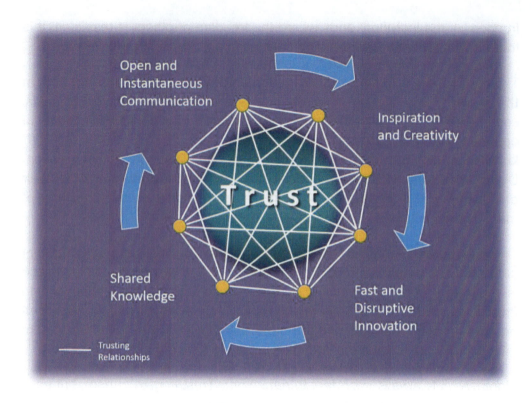

Figure 4-10: DNI-Cycle for Digital Network Intelligence (DNI)

The enormous speed and potential of digital networks leads to a cycle where individuals can cooperate in a way that is not possible in an analogue world.

It starts with the sharing of knowledge for the benefit of the company. Knowledge cannot be used without involvement of the owner of the knowledge! Openness means sharing your competences with those colleagues in the company who need it – and this is true for employees at every level in the hierarchy. Every individual in the network, therefore needs to have the personal desire to make their knowledge transparent in the company (e.g. via a digital competence finding tool). Being asked for support should be understood as appreciation and as giving something with a valued status in the network (see need for self-appreciation in Chapter 4.1).

Open and instantaneous digital communication leads to a high number of interactions between network participants. Employees can see what their colleagues are working on and can offer spontaneous advice and support based on their experience. On the other hand, everybody has the opportunity to receive input from different parts of the network, which subsequently provides varying perspectives. The resulting inspiration is taken to a new level and creativity is pushed further.

It must be emphasized again, that a company's value orientation correlates with the need for building individual confidence in what is said and done. Trust and open approval build self-confidence and a positive attitude, as a result of positive experiences overcoming difficult, stressful and uncertain situations. This forms the basis for creativity and a desire to shape the company's future. And it is not only about trusting one's own competences, but also trusting the competences of the organisation as a whole. Employees' inner concepts and their subsequent intrinsic motivations are boosted by a higher purpose, which gives meaning to their lives.

This momentum is destroyed by fear, stress or pressure. Too much supervision or micro management is the number one killer of the belief in inner strength and subsequent intrinsic motivation. As a result, the overall effectivity of the organization suffers. Emotions and feelings contribute have a vital role to play in the successful formation of a corporate Digital Agile Mindset that supports open communication and trust.

By taking into account the human aspects of the cycle dynamics, your company will be able to deliver innovations faster, and in addition, produce disruptive innovations.

Micro and Macro Level in a Network

While social research often focusses on the micro level of small group interaction, in the context of networks, connectivity on a macro level, which reflects the wider interrelation of an organisation as a whole, needs to be considered.

According to research by Marc Granovetter (Granovetter 1973), 75% of academics find a new job through their networks. Counterintuitively, however, they find them not through close friends, but with the help of people that they are only distantly, weakly connected within their network. This is what Granovetter calls "the strength of weak ties". The intensity of ties is described by the time people spend together, the degree of emotional intensity, the level of trust, and the amount of assistance individuals give each other.

Figure 4-11 shows different groups, which are characterized by strong ties between their members. These groups can be defined e.g. as a project team or a functional department. In a large organisation you will most likely find a mix of networked and hierarchical structures, which are interlinked in some way. Successful teams have the ability to amplify their performance by the use of combined competencies and their interrelating strong ties. On the other hand, over time, a form of group thinking will establish itself, which limits team members in the way they perceive and in their creativity for problem solving.

This is where random distant connections are crucial for the vitality of a network as a whole. So called weak ties between individuals of different groups build "bridges" between the various "spaces of experience" within an organisation.

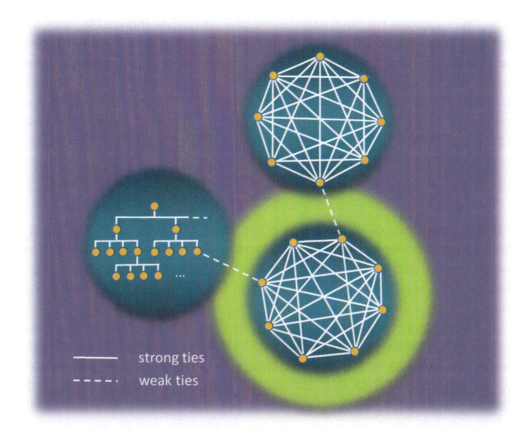

Figure 4-11: Strong and weak ties in a network

By means of weak ties, teams can widen their perspective and get new inspiration for their endeavour. The openness of this kind of unconventional interaction prevents groups from staying on an established path in their zone of comfort. A permanent mix of different perceptions, along with the questioning and renewal of exisiting solutions, will lead to the desired adaptability of the network as a whole. This corporate mindset of openness and agility needs to be exemplified and promoted by the management on a daily basis. The success of the network will be determined by ascertaining the right balance between the efficiency of proven concepts and the innovative potential of new approaches.

In previous sections we have established that previously, individuals were the dominant focus for governing organizations. In the digital age it is becoming clear that digital organizations need to consider the effectiveness and intelligence of their networks. In order to establish an environment for well-governed networks which display intelligent behavior, managers need to act as coaches who carefully support the forming and continuous emergence of organization networks with all their strong and weak ties. To facilitate this, we propose the concept of a Social Omninet.

Establishing a Social Omninet

With the emergence of digital technologies an important question has arisen. What should be done exclusively online and what should be done offline? The current response to the question is in the form of two diverging tendencies. On the one hand, we are experiencing a strong push toward bringing everything online. We are experiencing a massive increase of digital communication tools (e.g. Slack), organizers (e.g. Evernote), event planners and ticketing (e.g. EventBrite), project management (e.g. MS Project, Asana, Trello). Almost everything seems to be automated and digitized. Why? Because it eases how we communicate, collaborate, coordinate, document, process and crowd-source knowledge digitally. In particular, it is possible to do all this with colleagues over large distances using synchronous as well as asynchronous communication, when collaborating with colleagues in different time zones. It could be said, that these aspects are all necessary for organizations striving to establish digital work (see Figure 4-12). Yet, upon closer inspection we need to distinguish a second tendency. While the former seems mostly focussed on delivering business outcomes, organizations are also pushing creative formats, such as design thinking and daily standups using Agile. Essentially, this means bringing people together, leaving everything digital to one side, and taking pens and paper to brainstorm solutions offline. Most of the time, this is carried out for two reasons. First, because truly synchronized communication is associated with co-location in the same place with enhanced face-to-face communication. Second, because there are limitations on how information is shared on two-dimensional screens. Therefore, delivery and creation seem to take different routes. This begs a follow-on question: Should we and could we make a third push toward bringing both aspects together.

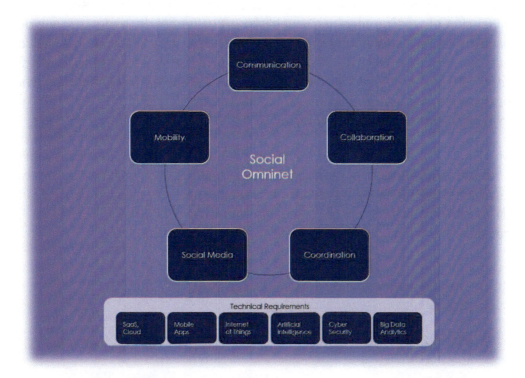

Figure 4-12: Aspects of a Social Omninet

Let us call this third push the establishment of a **Social Omninet**. So far, digital tools have consistently emerged around one or the other aspect of project work (see Figure 4-13). MS Project by and large provides the capability to visualize work breakdown structure, critical paths and organize work packages along timelines for delivery and reporting. It addresses how we govern, steer and coordinate projects. A second dimension of tools has emerged around how information is shared and documented, for example, through SharePoint, Dropbox and others. In the communicative dimension, tools like Slack integrate some of these aspects in a digital communication environment, by and large addressing the need for faster communication and coordination. Asana provides new approaches to agile collaboration. Yet, we should not stop there. Modern digital work needs to address the social dimension of project work even more. Beyond technical capabilities, it needs to look at the social and cultural dimension of working together, establishing trustful bonds, and subsequently enabling teams to funnel their individual capacities to achieve a new kind of effectiveness. We propose establishing a Social Omninet using tools which cover these socio-cultural dimensions, for example, by integrating the possibilities for creative thinking and crowdsourcing – just as we do in design thinking sessions with paper and pen.

The Social Omninet may be able to truly fulfil all project team functions within a digital environment – technical, social, cultural, communicative. In the following paragraphs we will outline in greater detail how this can be realized, by focussing not only on providing the technical capability, but on what is necessary to create a sense of identity and belongingness.

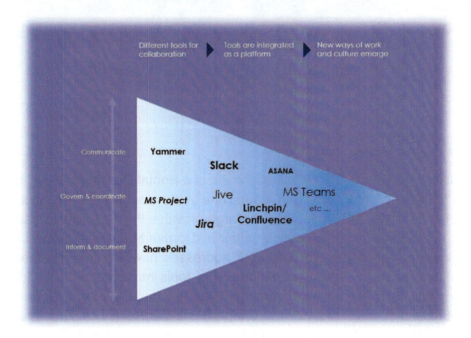

Figure 4-13: How new tools for collaboration emerge

Establishing Identity

Managers are far from being obsolete in digital, agile environments. Quite the contrary, their role is actually of much more critical importance. They lead the transformation, which means they need to ensure everyone in their workforce identifies with the goals and objectives of the company, resulting in engaged and high-performing teams. But whilst communicating identification with the organisation and its business objectives, it is also necessary to consider employee identity. The relation to both changes drastically in digital networks. The implications of working in digital networks need to be clear, as well as the limitations and potential to resistance. Firstly, not everyone is a digital native and the competences of those who take longer to adapt must not be neglected. It is claimed that to manage digital environments critically, an integration of various competencies is required, whether of digital natives or of others. Otherwise, the network will be unable to achieve its purpose and performance. This can be achieved by constantly developing and renewing available competencies. Secondly, it is essential to deal with the personal identity of all network participants as a driving factor for success. So what is the best way to transition effectively?

Management Intervention

When it comes to ensuring identification in Digital Agile Networks, a key hypothesis to start with is that every communication and action in the company's physical and digital space is political. From a systemic perspective, this is due to the fact that organisations assign tasks to particular, related roles and only then think about people as individuals to fulfil them. Each individual acts in many different roles, professionally and privately, identifying with these roles to greater or lesser degrees. We hardly ever witness a scenario where an individual identifies as a whole human being with their work, without having edited their behavior to the role. However, this does not restrict employees from engaging in their role in the team, as highly harmonized, high-performance individuals. It is essential to understand that digital workspaces amplify this setup, because initially, they create more distance between employees and significantly change the modes of interaction.

One of the success factors of efficient digital networks is the aim to ensure the congruence of network properties with a business purpose. The key to this is the ability to distinguish between what is possible and what is necessary. Digital collaboration includes a massive increase of complexity in communication and a means for realizing useful modes of collaboration. "Normal" organizational setups are driven by top-down workflows, communication and highly differentiated process landscapes.

Yet, intelligent digital networks are deliberately open agile, free-flowing processes of interaction and production. Different minds and different perspectives are directed and coordinated toward one goal. However, this can also lead to loss of effectiveness. The challenges associated with complexity are ambiguity, uncertainty and disconnectedness, due to information overload. It is like presenting people with infinite opportunities, but no guidance - identity is lost. With growing opportunities to communicate, to work and to interact, complexity reaches a level where choice becomes an impediment to action. In other words, while traditional forms of organisation focus on process design and structure guiding the production process, digital networks require orientation of a different kind. Even more so than in traditional work environments, they require orientation toward business objectives. This requires leaders to communicate, facilitate and engage employees in the vision of a meaningful business target. This enables employees to focus on the matter of carrying out their work, rather than the structures and processes for cooperation. The increased focus on output and outcome of a business endeavour, automatically gives digital networks the orientation to self-organize for meaningful collaboration. Ideally, complexity is managed in such a way that only those modes of interaction prevail, which the team deems beneficial for achieving its goal. On the other hand, if leadership applied traditional measures and provided a rigid structure, it would most certainly harm the benefits of digital collaboration by taking responsibility out of the employees' hands. The team would return to silo thinking or a call of duty mentality.

Secondly, self-guiding communication networks should share knowledge in an effective way and review required competencies. From the outset, digital communication and collaboration involve not only a social, but also a technical dimension, which requires the roles, competences and understandings of everyone in the value chain to be critically reviewed. Digital communication is not as rich as personal communication, which bears the risk of significant misunderstanding. It needs to be complementary. The ethnographer Annemarie Mol (2002) uses a fitting analogy to exemplify the challenge. She investigated the different perceptions various practitioners in the health sector employed to manage a disease, highlighting the importance of rich communication and the different realities individuals applied to understanding context. A layperson providing first aid has a limited understanding of disease, at a level relevant for their decision-making. The identificatio of symptoms and, at best, being highly aware of the psychological condition of the patient, is all that matters. Individuals with a strong awareness for the interpersonal dimension may easily outperform a rational scientist with deep medical knowledge in this situation. A general practitioner, on the other hand, bases success on their professional role and subsequent healing measures. Therefore, they need a deeper understanding of the functions of the human body and how they interact. On yet another level, there are laboratories with chemists who specialize in analyzing disease on a chemical level. For them, neither the psychological condition, nor the overall functionality of the human body are relevant. Their success is measured by the output of analysis. The challenge for leaders is be aware that those multiple realities also exist when it comes to how people engage with digital means of collaboration. And more importantly that a single measure is insufficient for digital proficiency. Digital natives may excel using new forms of collaboration, which directly affect their performance. Others, however may rightly consider digital environments as an additional means to their otherwise excellent performance in other areas (Grundén 2009; Leitner 2006). Those who consider digital collaboration and communication as a significant part of their performance, find value and enjoyment using online collaboration. Those who consider it only a means to an end, may be less interactive digitally, but are excellent communicators in face-to-face client interaction. The critical success factor is to realistically assess the roles and competences of digital communication for every participant. Secondly, you may conclude that those who are less proficient require more support and training. Yet, you may also come to the conclusion that certain employees do not need to be digital in every respect, as long as they perform well in other domains. The key question is: How should different competences be utilized?

Thirdly, it is essential to provide safe spaces. This originates from the fact that highly transparent digital networks generally lack specific private spaces where employees can interact without supervision and where there is room for error. It goes hand in hand with the right to forget, as a legitimate request. People change and are not perfect. What would have been forgotten in an analogous world, is now likely to affect performance, based on data-driven monitoring mechanisms and the ability to retrieve every bit of information. To some this represents an opportunity. Promoters of full digital transparency claim everything should be known about people we work with, to assess them correctly. The community should be allowed to make decisions based on all information about a person, to decide whether or not to form relationships. As much as this presents an opportunity for informed decision-making, there are significant challenges in the social dimension. Our ability to decide who has access to our work, who can collaborate with us and who we maintain relationships with, is of critical importance. Despite open and transparent collaboration, it is a given fact that we value certain levels of privacy, where we can think and act unrestricted from premature interpretation. The rules that apply to our behavior in different relationships are immensely contextual. What employees value and do in their private time, including with respect to social networks, for example, may be somewhat relevant to identifying skills and basic values for an employer. However, this is only true if the context of these behaviors is understood and evaluated correctly. The same applies to work environments. If companies want to engage employees in internal social networks in the hope of creating free flowing information and improved interpersonal contact, there needs to be a clear separation and contextualization as to what and how employees discuss in a private chat (informal) and what they discuss in a business meeting (formal). A differentiation between role and person is crucial. It is about relevance rather than accuracy. The individual capacity to change, develop, learn and adjust needs to be accounted for, to create a private space for the persona, and a public space for the role.

Resulting Corporate Mindset

These factors form the basis for keeping employees engaged and happy in highly creative Digital Agile Networks, which require the capacity of individuals to shape a high-performance environment. Yet, getting there also requires modern leaders to understand their ability to intervene, and to understand relevant additional mechanisms underlying Digital Agile Netowkr dynamics.

One success factor is the orientation around common business objectives. This is required to evaluate how the team fits the business purpose. It also enables the team to create a commonly shared identity. This means the leadership role changes from the classical management of structures and processes, to one of providing vision and guidance. It puts managers in the position to coach and engage, to reflect with the team, and to pose guiding questions, rather than simply giving solutions or managing by constraint. Similarly, it calls for a changing understanding of business processes by supporting individuals in their work and not predetermining workflows (Bauder 2012). This would be a waste of competence. These aspects of modern leadership are not new and have been discussed many times. Yet, while traditional organisations find it hard to live up to these innovative competences in daily, fast-paced operational practice, they become critical in digital networks. Managing classical performance parameters does not work. Teams who are required to establish self-organising practices can neither be monitored based on individual performance, nor micromanaged through each and every process KPI. Instead, they look for managers who provide and secure an environment for self-organised decision-making, along with relative freedom to try out new approaches. These environments are driven by monitoring output based on business objectives. Agile management practices are a good example of this mode of collaboration. Instead of monitoring every process, performance output is measured more frequently and through iterative cycles of production. In this way, team members receive more freedom to interact and contribute their individual value, without the risk of being evaluated every step of the way. It is the team that counts.

A second factor is to regularly check the competence-role-fit of team members to ensure knowledge sharing. As previously mentioned, not everyone in a team needs to be a highly competent digital native to create a winning team. It is the team and its output which should be the guiding performance measure in digital collaboration environments. Therefore, in the creation of digital teams the focus must lie on a continuous reflection of the overall harmony of the team and how it utilizes individual capacities. This means that more emphasis should be placed on regularly reviewing the fit of individuals and their competences in relation to the team output. It may very well be that a group of B performers can be brought to A performance level just by sheer effectiveness and the cultural communication and collaboration match. Similarly, it has been shown that even quite competitive individuals are able to create highly effective teams. Although this implies a clear understanding and regular reviews of those parameters by all team members. Unfortunately, there is no "one size fits all" solution and most team building measures which employ technical understanding underestimate underlying social self-organization mechanisms. A good start, however, is to look at two classic social indicators. One is the establishment of a strong awareness for weak signals in feedback and reflection workshops. These weak signals, for example, unconstructive critiques or weak engagement of individual team members, often develop into viable points of conflict if they are not responded to. A second indicator is the quality of a team's output, assessed with regard to how well its reflects the releant customers needs. It can be a good starting point to reflect whether the team spends enough time on figuring out a common perspective on customer demands. If it does not, the team might be too busy coping with internal conflicts or team-organization.

Finally, in order to ensure safe spaces, a regular review of team accessibility and "digital forgetting mechanisms" is necessary. This involves two kinds of safe spaces. From Scrum methodology (Sutherland 2014) we know that highly self-organising teams require a specific safe space in which they can act independently and without irritations from outside – even from management. These safe spaces are usually established in so-called sprints or iterations, lasting from a few days to several weeks. During these periods of time the team has clearly set tasks, but is self-responsible for establishing the processes and methodology to achieve them. This is only one example of where accessibility is restricted, but there are more forms whereby a team is able to limit its exposure to other influences, particularly intervention, during its self-organising processes (Luhmann 1984). A second form of safe space is that which allows the team to act and communicate freely, without fear of being supervised or monitored. As previously mentioned, this is critical for creating an atmosphere of creativity. Monitoring such "private" settings may lead to contextual misinterpretation by observers, and have a significant effect on how the team or team members are perceived in other contexts. Leaders are therefore required to continuously create regular opportunities where teams can engage freely. Similarly, they also need to ensure that the team is protected from potential intruders into these safe spaces and that agreed or promised forms of unrestricted interaction are not violated by others.

Establishing Belongingness

Another principal aim of managers in organizations setting up Social Omninets to enable a culture of Digital Network Intelligence, should be to influence the organizations' members into developing a feeling of belongingness and commitment towards the organization. The scope of this influence should not only be the respective employees, but staff of the organization/network as a whole. This is important, because digital communication cares little about organizational siloes. In addition, we theorize that such effects are more likely to increase than decrease in the future, as we already have a younger workforce entering the workspace that is more used to boundary-free communication.

We present three different types of intervention that managers can actively use to increase and / or review the belongingness and commitment of members of their organization to its respective digital communication networks. They help to critically question and reflect upon cause-and-effect mechanisms within the organization with regard to the forming of intelligent digital networks in the form of a Social Omninet and a feeling of belongingness to these networks.

Management Intervention

Throughout the past decade, digital communication within organizations has increased. Email communication in particular, has replaced personal meetings, discussions and telephone calls. This is unarguably beneficial in many cases. For example, large organizations are required to enable communication between employees over long distances and between far-spread business locations. Email communication efficiently decouples communication from waiting times. Specifically, when working across time zones, this form of asynchronous communication is of great importance. There are, however, specific shortcomings of this means of communication. First, asynchronous communication is not always the best choice when conveying complex information. It denies the recipient the opportunity to respond to it directly, pose questions and clarify unclear information or the specific context of the communication presented. Second, asynchronous communication hides organizational complexity. This means that the sender of the information is unable to assess whether the recipient is aware of the communication, has understood, rather than just received it, and if the recipient of the communication is able to respond to the communication in the way that the sender desires.

Despite these shortcomings, in many cases, the workforce employs email communication as their primary means of communication. Other forms of information dispersal like forums, messenger, (video) chats or even chatbots etc. are seen more commonly in young organizations, for example startups, or organizations that have successfully re-invented their business models in digital contexts (for example Klöckner, kloeckner-i.com).

Managers should carefully **review the use of digital communication** and understand that digital communication is only effective and efficient when the right level of maturity exists for the communication, as well as commitment of an organization's members towards their organization. In practical terms, casually providing increased modes of digital communication, such as implementing a chatroom or a chat-bot, to enable quicker communication, may not be appropriate in organizations that are not used to electronic, synchronous communication (Stendal 2013).

Taking this one step further, managers should **assess communication network abilities** and place special emphasis on the content of the communication where flow needs to be enabled. Voice, text, image, video, data/file communication, are typical categories considered for organizations today. This list, however is incomplete, as it excludes other aspects of human communication that are necessary for creating a feeling of belongingness. These include conveying emotion, feeling, atmosphere, context and values. It should always be remembered that communication is more than just content.

With this in mind, managers should constantly **review communication channel choices**. Again, simply providing all potential communication channels that can be thought of, may not be the appropriate answer to an organization's communication needs.

In an agile sense, managers should enable, oversee and review aspects of self-organized communication among the organization's members. A potential enabler for this would be providing an architectural overview of all digital communication channels. This could be further enhanced by a communication vision – such as the ultimate goal of customer-beneficial communication – and underlying values – such as mutual trust as a basis for communication, or respect as a guideline for communication channel content – for digital communication within the organization. Ideally, this managerial input would be a starting point for self-organized continuous development of a digital communication culture. In order to enable and drive behavioral change within the organization, the manager should lead primarily by example and employ the communication and network tactics that they would like to see mirrored within the organization.

Resulting Corporate Mindset

These three management interventions that we have outlined will result in three effects that are beneficial to forming belongingness to the (hopefully intelligent) digital network and its members.

By using efficient tools to review network communication, a manager can ensure the establishment of **sustainable communication networks**. Sustainable in this context, means that the networks are likely to last over time, are active, and act for the good of the organization's aims, without causing detrimental side-effects to real-world networks (Stendal 2013). Only if networks are likely to last a sufficient amount of time, will members start to use the respective digital networks. The degree of active usage of a network also needs to surpass a critical threshold, so that members do not experience ineffectiveness of the network e.g. answers to information requests via the network not provided in time, or an organization member who made a request forgets to access the network and only realizes later on that the information was in fact provided, but they did not obtain it due to their own lack of action.

Actions within analogue and digital networks are always political, and it can be argued that political actions may not be beneficial for the goal of the organization as a whole. Bu the main point is that such political actions are factually stored infinitely within the digital network and this information store within the network, may at a later point in time, be used "against" network members, to allege inconsistent or political behaviour. People's attitudes and convictions often change over time. It is therefore necessary to construct mechanisms within the network that acknowledge this. One way of doing this is to foster **forgetfulness of the digital network**, which prevents people being held accountable for actions and artefacts that have been historically recorded within the digital network. If this aim is not achieved, negative consequences with respect to forming a feeling of belongingness may ensue, and cause undesirable side-effects within an analogue organizational network.

Knowledge of **effective conveyance of emotions** within the digital network is a second effect of the proposed interventions. If, in a similar way to information, emotions can also flow freely within the network, and if they are also not subject to misinterpretation, members will begin to behave in a digital network, just as they would within an analogue network. This will eventually lead to greater consistency between the analogue and digital parts of the network.

Unfortunately, current standards of digital communication lack efficient methods to **support flow of emotion**. Therefore, organizations need to emphasize the development and extended use of technology that remedy this negative aspect. In order to do so, several technologies / approaches are available. Augmented reality appears to be a promising approach to this problem. But this type of solution is still rarely found to be standard office equipment within organizations. Video calls and regular telephone conferences are a good intermediate way of conveying more context during a conversation. But, other approaches that are commonly used in private contexts are still yet to be found within business contexts. For example, Facebook's range of emoticons, in addition to the simple like/don't like choice, which can be used to interact with posts on a timeline, is a low-level, but effective, way of conveying additional contextual and emotional information (Rosatelli 2011).

Even if digital networks exist in a sustainable way, and even if flow of emotion-related content is balanced with the flow of information-related content, managers still need to be concerned about the **appropriate use of digital and analogue channels**. Some channels may not be suitable for the informational or emotional content that users feed into the network (Picard 1997). It is the managers' responsibility to review and actively influence the routing of such information, in order to prevent negative side-effects of communication. For example, informal decisions that have been taken, may benefit the organization's overall goal, but documenting them via a digital channel may, without adding (potentially a lot of) additional context, send irritating signals into the network. In such cases, the manager could set up corresponding policies (written down or produced as part of the organizational culture) to guide all networks into the appropriate channel to be used. By doing so, managers would "gently guide" their staff into certain communication channels that ultimately support the forming of belongingness to the type of organization that the manager has in mind.

Conclusions on Agile Digital Network Intelligence

To unfold digital network potentials within your company, you need to make a move towards self-organisation, to enable free information flow to take place. The values of trust, as well as identiy and belongingness, are crucial for this and are an indispensable prerequisite for the success of the massive changes necessary for digital transformation.

Only the right balance between management expectations, and users' technical and social requirements, will enable the successful and sustainable use of enterprise social networks. Companies that are able to crosslink existing competences in an optimal way, are able to create a significant competitive benefit. The resulting collective intelligence becomes an organization's emergent phenomenon. Communication and specific actions by individuals, enable intelligent behavior of the super organism (social community) – or in other words, an intelligent system response. With regards to the concepts included in this book, it could be said that the dimensions "agility" and "digitization" are super-parameters for the adjustment of an intelligent (digital) network.

Literature

Bauder B and Weiland C (2013) Breaking habits: A co-creative approach to organizational processes. Berlin: The Systemic Excellence Group.

Foucault M (2010) Die Ordnung des Diskurses. Frankfurt/Main: Fischer Taschenbuch Verlag.

Foucault M (2012) The Archaeology of Knowledge. Knopf Doubleday Publishing Group.

Granovetter M (1973) The Strength of Weak Ties. In: American Journal of Sociology 78, S. 1360–1380.

Grundén K (2009) A Social Perspective on Implementation of e-Government - a Longitudinal Study at the County Administration of Sweden. Electronic Journal of e-Government 7, 1: 65 – 76. Academic Conferences Ltd. Retrieved from http://web.ebscohost.com.ludwig.lub.lu.se/ehost/pdf?vid=4&hid=5&sid=1137c904-d4c6-473c-ac0a-f287b9773f19%40sessionmgr10

Leitner C (2006) eGovernment: People and Skills in Europe's Administrations. Proceedings of the 39th Hawaii International Conference on System Sciences. Retrieved from ieeexplore.ieee.org/iel5/10548/33364/01579444.pdf

Li Y, Liu Y, Li J, Qin W, Li K, Yu C, et al. (2009). Brain Anatomical Network and intelligence. *PLoS Comput Biol 5(5): e1000395.* https://doi.org/10.1371/journal.pcbi.1000395

Luhmann N (1984) Soziale Systeme: Grundriß einer Allgemeinen Theorie. 15th edition. Suhrkamp.

Mol A (2002) The Body Multiple: Ontology in Medical Practice. Durham: Duke University Press.

Raue S (2010) How E Can Government Be? – The Digitization of State Services. Lund: Lund University Publications. URL http://lup.lub.lu.se/student-papers/record/1744421.

Picard R W (1997) Affective computing. Cambridge, MA. MIT Press.

Rosatelli M (2011) A Framework for Digital Emotions. Dissertation, Virginia Commonwealth University, VCU Scholars Compass. URL http://scholarscompass.vcu.edu/etd/239?utm_source=scholarscompass.vcu.edu%2Fetd%2F239&utm_medium=PDF&utm_campaign=PDFCoverPages.

Stendal K and Molka-Danielsen J (2013) Capabilities and Affordances of Virtual Worlds for People with Lifelong Disability. In: Linger et al., Building Sustainable Information Systems. Springer Science & Business Media.

Sutherland J and Schwaber K (2014) The Scrum Guide - The Definitive Guide to Scrum. Scrum.Org/Scrum Inc.

Tichy N (1983) Managing Strategic Change: Technical, Political, and Cultural Dynamics. New York: Wiley & Sons.

Tuczek C H (2017) Management 4.0 und die Generation Y, Landshut Leadership Band 2, Shaker Verlag, Aachen

Tuczek C H (2018) Neuroleadership und Künstliche Intelligenz, Landshut Leadership Band 4, Shaker Verlag, Aachen

5 Cybernetics and Organization

5.1 Agile Enterprise Structures from a Cybernetic Perspective

Authors: Patrick Balve, Norbert Schaffitzel

Summary: Reflecting on the characteristics of agile organizations, even practitioners are often concerned about the seeming lack of theoretical foundation of suggested agile tools, techniques, and methods. Therefore, we have investigated the validity of the most common agile concepts: Scrum, Kanban, and CCPM, from a cybernetic management perspective. This will help the reader understand that we are in fact dealing with practices, principles, and structures that can be well understood and justified from a theoretical standpoint. Based on this, we will argue that an Agile Mindset is an indispensable prerequisite for all agile practices and contributes to the implementation of cybernetic management functions.

Key terms: Management Cybernetics, Viable System Model, Neuro-logical Levels, Agile Mindset, Kanban, Scrum, CCPM

Background of Management Cybernetics

The short, but fast-paced history of cybernetics started in the 1940s, mainly with mathematician Norbert Wiener, neurophysiologist Warren McCulloch, and Jay Forrester, an early computer engineer. Along with neurophysiologist Arturo Rosenblueth and the young Stafford Beer, a lot of effort was put into exploring the conditions of self-regulating systems in a completely interdisciplinary, holistic way (Beer 1991). It was within this framework that in 1948, Wiener defined cybernetics as "the scientific study of control and communication in the animal and the machine" (Wiener 1948). This ambitious scientific movement was complemented by the founder of general systems theory, Karl Ludwig von

Bertalanffy, and by W. Ross Ashby, who was primarily concerned with the question of how systems deal with internal and external variety ("Law of requisite variety") (Rosnay 2000).

Building on these fundamental works and endowed with his own background in operations research, Stafford Beer applied cybernetic theories to managerial questions in organizations and is therefore said to be the founder of management cybernetics. Beer developed a comprehensive meta-model – the Viable System Model (Beer 1959) – that defines the structural conditions and managerial functions that need to be fulfilled in order to deal with the overwhelming amount of variety inside and outside of an organization, while still keeping the entire system "under control". The main characteristics of the VSM will be illustrated in the following section.

Basics of the Viable System Model

The origins and details of Stafford Beer's viable system model (VSM) have been described extensively in various publications (e.g. (Beer 1959), (Beer 1972), (Beer 1984) and (Espejo 1989)). Therefore, we can limit ourselves to introducing the main facets of the model, necessary for understanding the analysis executed further in this chapter.

The basic cybernetic model consists of operations, i.e. the primary activities, that constitute the purpose of an organization (also referred to as System 1) in a given environment. In order to provide guidance for those operations, a management function is needed. According to Ashby's law of requisite variety, complexity needs to be attenuated from left to right and amplified from right to left, as depicted in Figure 5-1. Elaborating on this, Beer came up with the first principle of organization: "Managerial, operational and environmental varieties, diffusing through an institutional system, tend to equate; they should be designed to do so with minimal damage to people and to cost." (Beer 1985).

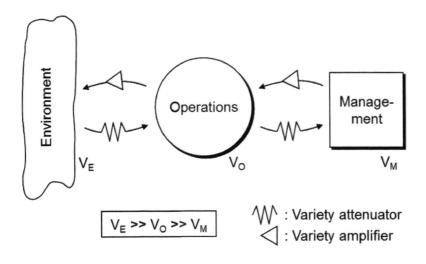

Figure 5-1: Balancing variety (Beer 1985)

In other words: As long as operations meet the needs of a particular environment on the one hand and follow the instructions of management on the other, the system in focus is able to maintain a separate existence as a recognizable entity. This is what Beer calls "viability".

In an attempt to further refine the management function, the VSM then comes up with five control systems that are highly specific in what they do. Figure 5-2 provides an overview of the interaction of these five systems with an arbitrary number of three embedded operational elements. Each System 1 contributes its specific share to the entire value chain and acts within its own environment. The wavy lines between the circles represent any type of relationship between operations. In a project environment, System 1 could be – at the lowest level – an individual project team member working diligently on their project task and, in doing so, is interacting with several peers (Britton 1993). In a manufacturing setting, the wavy lines represent the material flow between operations (Beer 1985).

System 2 then coordinates the primary units' activities, solely by mutual adjustment. Designed properly, this management function is a very powerful variety damper, as it does not require ongoing centralized, hierarchical intervention. System 3 is the so-called control or command function. It is concerned with reaching the highest possible level of efficiency, while orchestrating the activities of operational elements (i.e. Systems 1A through 1C). In a narrower sense, System 3 uses the allocation of tasks and resources, as well as target agreements and formal reporting, to fulfil its task. In a broader sense, System 2 contributes to the cybernetic function of System 3, which is to maintain internal stability of the primary units in focus. Another auxiliary function of System 3 is the so-called auditing channel 3*. If employed every now and then, and in an unpredictable (!) manner, it provides unbiased first-hand information on the various aspects of operations.

System 4, the strategic management function (also called the intelligence function), looks above and beyond the daily concerns of the lower systems. Therefore, it has a specific and vivid interest in the overall external environment and its future development. From left to right in Figure 5-2, information on changes in the marketplace, technological advancements, customer change requests etc., are communicated to the organization via filters (variety attenuators).

From right to left in Figure 5-2, the organization's identity, its products and service capabilities are advertised to relevant customers. In order to fulfil its cybernetic function, System 4 disposes of highly evolved models of both the internal and external environment.

Until now we have lacked an ultimate organizational mission or policy. This void is filled by System 5, the ultimate holder of identity. One of the main tasks of System 5 is to conciliate the views of System 3 (efficiency and stability) and 4 (effectiveness and change) with respect to the organization's direction.

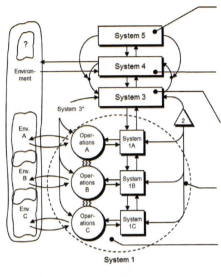

Normative management function defining fundamental goals of the systems in focus, its policy and **identity**; balancing of future activities (System 4) and current capabilities (System 3).

Strategic management function concerned with balancing current and future environment with the companies activities; concerned with effectiveness.

Command function striving for efficiency while balancing local autonomy and overall cohesion; provides resources and claims reports;
3*: auditing/monitoring activities

Coordination of System 1 operations; guarantees stability of the whole system without any hierarchy involved; anti-oszillatory function

Operational elements with own, local management (System 1) acting within their local **environment**; defining the purpose of the system; wavy lines: connections to other operative units

Figure 5-2: Simple representation of main elements of the VSM (Beer 1985)

So far, the description of the VSM has made implicit use of another key concept: recursiveness. On closer inspection, Figure 5-2 already shows two levels of recursion with each System 1, containing all the managerial functions and elements mentioned above. Just like a set of Russian dolls, this of course can work as well in the other direction, building up larger and even larger organizational entities.

Since our main objective is to explore and assess agile methodologies and frameworks from a cybernetic point of view, the introduction carried out so far will suffice for the upcoming sections. As previously mentioned, for delving deeper into VSM fundamentals and applications, we refer to the literature.

Matching Neuro-Logical Layers with Management Cybernetic Functions

Current enterprises are, to a great extent, pushed by a permanent demand for change and adaption. One of their main requirements therefore is their ability to react accurately and precisely to dynamic and quickly changing market demands. On top of this, it is becoming more and more apparent that organizations need to act in a much more proactive manner than previously. Addressing this challenge is hampered by the vast array of competitors in the market and shortened product life cycles, so that even small innovations and market advantages have to quickly realize the required profitability. All in all, the actual market environment can be characterized as a challenging combination of accelerating dynamics under growing competitive pressure.

One of the main topics of organizational structuring is to develop a safe and guarded setting, in which people are capable of mastering complex situations that originate from inside as well as outside. Under such circumstances, the still too often hierarchically and centralized company structures, prove to be too weak to successfully absorb the complexities at hand. Thus, the main defect of centralized structures is their tendency to focus managerial expertise on the shoulders of a small and distinguished group of people. As a consequence, such organizations lack collective empowerment and mind setting, which would otherwise enable them to quickly adjust to market changes and subsequently contribute to the survival of the whole company.

It is exactly this issue that is addressed by the management cybernetic approach. Management cybernetics provides a structural framework of managerial functions and the required interactions that will enable the long-term success of businesses. Based on the assumption that the Dilts' concept of neuro-logical layers (Dilts 2014) offers a theoretical framework applicable to both individuals and organizations, in Figure 5-3 we demonstrate the relationship of the latter two theories. For more details on Dilts' model please refer to the respective chapter 3.2.

Figure 5-3 shows that the strategic management function (S4) detects potential environmental parameter changes and transfers this information – amongst others – to normative management function (abbreviated to S5), which in turn may provoke a modification of the organization's actual mission and vision. According to Dilts' neuro-logical levels, this is equivalent to a re-evaluation of the "values and beliefs" layer, as well as the „identity" layer by top management.

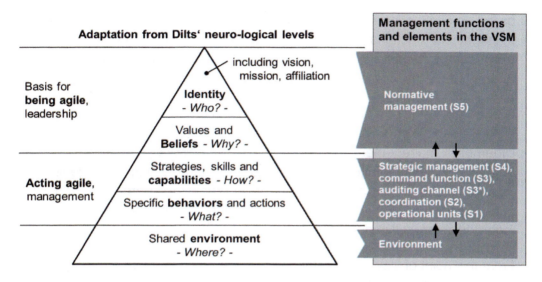

Figure 5-3: Dilts' neuro-logical levels relationship to management cybernetic functions

As a core conclusion of that relationship, we can say that every transformation on the operational level (S1) or even of management functions S2, S3, and S3*, needs to be preceded by a normative, cultural shift. The objective of such a normative transformation must be the development of a collective mindset that permits management to address the following principal criteria for successful collaboration:

- the values and beliefs of the acting persons
- their perceived identity during collaboration
- the knowledge of their common bond
- the determining driver of successful collaboration: the deeper sense, the superior mission and therefore the source and the inner value of work which will match the ethical foundation of work and profession (Patzelt 2010)

Obviously, changing the normative setting in an organization is crucial for reaching the desired synergy effects, i.e. initiating a process where "the whole is greater than the sum of its parts" (Aristotle). The main driver for a collective interconnection between people, is firstly the development of a collective vision or a shared corporate goal ("big picture"), and secondly a corporate culture based on confidence and mindful appreciation between the representatives of management functions and operational units. Hence, it is possible "to achieve extraordinary results with ordinary people" (a modification of the quote from Andrew Carnegie, indirectly cited by (DeMarco 1999)).

We see the vision of a collective mindset and a comprehensive agile corporate culture as the corner stone for linking the individual layers of Dilts' model to cybernetic management functions. This framework can serve as an organizational blueprint to handle complexity in a long-lasting, value generating way. Agile capabilities and behaviors of an organization are then, no longer pure reactions to market developments outside the organization, but can be regarded as proactive actions and measures.

From this point of view, it is pretty obvious that empowerment of organizations via agile transformation of their S1 operational units should not only trigger measures of structural reconfiguration, but involve all aspects of organizational adjustments and changes. This means that

1. it is not only a reassessment of the usefulness of individual operational units that needs to be considered, but also that the informal means of communication between S1, S2, and "higher" management functions (S3, S4, S5) also needs to be part of the corporate change;
2. it is not only the enlargement and enrichment of the mission of operational units that has to be a major goal, but also the way these entities interact with each other in order to address their market issues without greater friction;
3. it is not only the segmenting or reshaping of specific operational structures that has to be addressed in a process for an agile transformation, but also the basic principles of the corporate culture that have to be reshaped. This includes, such important issues as tolerance toward individual mistakes, non-hierarchical communication, appreciation and acceptance of diversity, risk managing, rather than a risk avoiding attitude, and many other aspects that will help enhance the corporate culture.

We cannot stress strongly enough how important it is from our point of view that any increase in S1's self-organizing capabilities should always be accompanied by an agile reshaping of the higher management functions S2 through S5 in the sense described above. Hence, it is dependent above all, on the leadership skills of management, to implement a vivid corporate culture, which embraces change as a steady companion of agile living. Once this fundamental system cohesion is destroyed, it is no longer possible to maintain the long-lasting existence of organizational unity as a whole. In addition, any interruption of connections within the management functions, i.e. a lack of communication, can easily cause the whole entity to perish. Therefore, knowledge of the connection between the management cybernetic model and Dilts' neuro-logical model can contribute to successfully leading a company towards increased agility.

In the next section, we will outline and investigate the widely available agile concepts Scrum, Kanban, and CCPM and evaluate their contribution in fulfilling the necessary cybernetic functions.

Evaluating Agile Methods and Techniques from a Management Cybernetic Perspective

The comparison of agile concepts with cybernetic management functions and their way of interacting adds a new aspect to the understanding of Agile Management. As far as we can see, (Figure 5-4), the literature covers the comparison of general and predominantly plan-based project management with agile techniques on the one hand (Schaden 2015) and on the other, the mapping between general project management and the control functions of the VSM ((Britton 1993), (Saynisch 2003), (Saynisch 2010), (Morales-Arroyo 2012), (Murad 2012)):

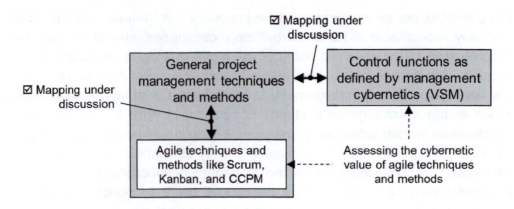

Figure 5-4: Area of investigation

Although Agile Management techniques and methods are discussed as a subset of general project management processes and practices (Wysocki 2014), a detailed examination with regard to their cybernetic value has not yet been carried out. Therefore, it would seem both reasonable and necessary for us to take a deeper look into this relationship in the following paragraphs.

Cybernetic Value of Selected Agile Concepts

The first agile concept we will evaluate is Scrum, because this is currently a widely applied framework. In order to better understand Scrum based on the cybernetic management model, we need to first look at its role concepts.

At the heart of the **Scrum role concept** there is a multidisciplinary team that builds up the required basis for the operative units. Schwaber and Sutherland (Schwaber 2013) recommend a team size of 3 to 9 members. Larger projects should be organized as clusters of autonomous teams, thus exploiting the complexity absorbing effect of various operative units each dealing with their own environment and objectives in a highly specialized way ('Scrum of Scrums').

In order to act in the most efficient manner, the cybernetic management model requires individual team members (operational System 1 units) to be managed via the System 2 coordination function, System 3 command function, and the System 3* audit channel. The Scrum Master supports these control functions methodically in various ways, thus supporting team members in their strive for self-organization, without the need for a formal leader. The cybernetic value of this role is therefore regarded as one of an enabler function – from supporting daily or weekly Scrum meeting routines, to promoting agile values deeply rooted in normative management (see Figure 5-5 and Figure 5-6). Through dealing with external impediments – stumbling stones and roadblocks, which are out of the team's sphere of influence, – the Scrum Master even fulfils a System 4 function to a certain extent.

Even though we have to take the high degree of autonomy of the team on the operational level into consideration, the leading role in Scrum lies in the hands of the Product Owners (PO). Their task is the careful investigation of all customer requests. The PO has then to turn these requests into so-called user stories, each endowed with a priority reflecting their importance for the customer. With Scrum, direct intervention in the team's autonomy is strictly forbidden, although task progress and resource consumption are monitored to satisfy the need for information of both team members and externals. For all these reasons, the primary cybernetic value of a PO boils down to strategic and normative functions in conjunction with a weak control task (see Figure 5-5).

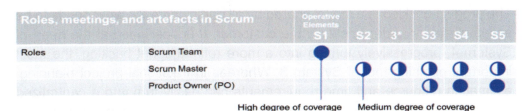

Figure 5-5: Cybernetic value of Scrum roles

Based on examination of the role models alone, it becomes obvious that some cybernetic control functions are not fully covered. Therefore, we have to take a closer look at what the role model holders are actually doing throughout the course of a project, as prescribed by the **Scrum process model** (see Figure 5-6).

Roles, meetings, and artefacts in Scrum		Operative Elements					
		S1	S2	3*	S3	S4	S5
Process Model	Vision					◐	●
	Product backlog, user stories, release plan					●	
	Estimation meeting, sprint planning, sprint backlog				●	◐	
	Daily, task board, time box		●				
	Sprint review					●	
	Sprint retrospective, impediment backlog with internal issues		◐	◐	◐		
	Sprint structure		●		◐		

Figure 5-6: Cybernetic value of Scrum meetings and artefacts

Every Scrum project clearly starts with a vision, i.e. the big picture of the product to be developed, which gives ultimate meaning to the initiative. The vision is represented by the PO and has to be rated as System 5, the most important element. Unlike more traditionally operated projects, Scrum requires each team member to be fully committed to this (product) vision, which, from a cybernetic point of view, is a highly effective way of managing a wide range of peoples' actions and attitudes.

The product backlog is a model shared by all participants, on what needs to be accomplished in order to satisfy the customer. It is positioned at the heart of System 4, progressively turning into a more refined sprint backlog, the most important planning tool of System 3. Whereas in traditional project planning, estimating resource and time requirements can easily turn into a centralized expert task, Scrum urges all team members to come up with a mutually agreed plan.

Each morning, there is a Scrum meeting (usually called "daily"), during which team members share information on their current work progress and coordinate upcoming tasks visualized on the task board. This is probably the most powerful non-hierarchical System 2 mechanism in Scrum (which is often missed in traditionally operated project teams).

At the end of each sprint, a sprint review takes place. As part of this, the team members get in touch with the customer and present the sprint results in the form of a "shippable product increment". Here, we are again dealing with a System 4 function, which might even change the direction of the project's next iteration. The second meeting at the end of each sprint is retrospective. Its goal is to ascertain improvement opportunities with respect to the team's operating mode (a focus on efficiency through cooperation). Although this is a highly institutionalized and predictable way of self-auditing, the execution of primary activities and retrospectives can still be interpreted as a System 3* function. The results of the retrospective meeting are written down in the impediment backlog and followed-up by the Scrum Master.

The fact that there is a process model defining steady and repetitive time slots for the sequence of meetings is a huge contribution to the coordination function. This is also true for more traditional process models where there are regular process checks at milestones.

In addition to Scrum, when looking at widely used agile concepts, we also need to take **Kanban and Critical Chain Project Management (CCPM)** into consideration. Kanban might not appear to be that different to Scrum, but it is more specific and powerful in the way that tasks are managed in a flow-oriented way, while at the same time excluding the organizational requirements of Scrum. It is also much more tolerant with regards to team members working in different places and coordinating their tasks by electronic means ("virtual Kanban board").

The essential idea behind Kanban ((Anderson 2010), (Hammarberg 2014)) is the use of tickets that represent project tasks, which are moved along a board from an input queue on the left, through a certain number of process steps, to the final output column on the very right. Each process column can be subdivided into an "in progress" step and a "done" step. Furthermore, it is recommended that swim lanes are added to the vertical column structure, with each lane representing a specific service class. The iron rule is that a Kanban ticket is only allowed to move further downstream if there is room in the respective column and work-in-progress (WIP) limits are not violated. For more details, especially on how to work with WIP limits in general, please refer to the respective chapters in this book and Anderson's book.

CCPM can be traced back to Eliyahu Goldratt's theory of constrains (TOC) that he applied to project management (Goldratt 1997). His major concern was the way in which time buffers are created and employed, especially in conjunction with network planning. He also demonstrated that it made no sense to schedule too many tasks to be worked on at the same time, which eventually leads to all tasks being completed much later, rather than being worked off in a strictly sequential fashion. In practice, and whenever applied in a team environment, CCPM looks a lot like Kanban. Even fundamental tracking and reporting techniques, like the cumulative flow diagram (CFD) are the same. However, if applied to larger projects that are spread out over several departments or even companies, Goldratt's approach of dealing with time buffers provides additional benefits for scheduling and project control.

That being said, we can look at the cybernetic value of the most important features of both Kanban and CCPM in Figure 5-7. The core concern of both methods is the efficiency and stability of the operative elements, i.e. the project team members, along with their self-organizing effects. Assigning tasks to individuals is carried out based on an agreed upon and often almost ritualized set of rules. System 2 functions are carried out mainly through the Kanban board and its compelling way of visualizing the entirety of all activities on hand, as well as through satisfying routines for filling the input queue, reporting work progress and such. All procedures dealing with project control in the technical sense – including metrics derived from the CFD – can be primarily considered System 3 functions.

Also, in Kanban, as with Scrum, it is highly recommended to continuously identify improvement opportunities regarding (a) the way in which a team employs the basic rules of the method and (b) the way of working together. As in many cases, the theory of constraints approach goes hand in hand with "lean thinking", no serious CCPM practitioner would exclude a search for improvements and the elimination of "waste" from their own way of working.

Selected properties and artefacts of Kanban and CCPM	Operative Elements S1	S2	3*	S3	S4	S5
Visualize workflow → Kanban board, Pull		●				
Limit work-in-progress (WIP), assign service classes		◐		●	◐	
Insertion of buffers				●		
Measure and manage flow → CFD, buffer control, …, metrics				●	◐	
Establish rhythms (for filling of input queue, delivery, …)		●		◐		
Identify waste and practice CIP			◐	●		

Figure 5-7: Cybernetic value of Kanban and CCPM elements

It seems that when assessing the cybernetic value of Kanban and CCPM (see Figure 5-7), there are a lack of higher system functions beyond system 3 – especially when compared to Scrum. This should not come as a great surprise, as we are able to demonstrate that Scrum includes a much higher degree of very concrete organizational concepts and role models. On the one hand, it is this absence of role models and organizational requirements that make Kanban and CCPM so flexible. On the other hand, there is a certain risk that these flow-focused methods are reduced to technical aspects, disregarding the need to ingrain the core values into the corporate culture.

First Insights from the Examination

The examination of Scrum, Kanban, and CCPM in the previous sections shows that all cybernetic management functions 1 through 5 are covered in one way or another. Not all agile concepts, however, are fully capable of filling out the strategic and the normative function. If we connect this insight with the need for a collective mindset, it becomes apparent that tools and techniques alone are not sufficient to serve the overall purpose of increasing the organization's level of agility.

The way in which Scrum resolves this issue is through the introduction of highly specific role models, the team concept in general, a call for a shared vision, and various meetings and artefacts. In particular, when it comes to serving the customer in a fast changing environment – undisputedly one of the most valuable features of an agile organization – the role of the Product Owner fulfils a crucial task that would otherwise be left unattended (or at least left to the more or less skillful implementation of customer management in an organization).

In addition to working with a set of five management functions to counterbalance a varied environment, the VSM works with the concept of recursiveness, in conjunction with the idea of breaking down a huge overall task into manageable chunks, which are then taken over by individual team members or teams respectively. In turn, those tasks then have to be coordinated and aligned, which falls under the jurisdiction of System 2 and 3. Scrum is familiar with this necessity, not only when dealing with individual team members, but also on a recursive level further up in the hierarchy, when coordinating several Scrum teams ("Scrum of Scrums"). So far, Kanban and CCPM do not seem to attest to much expertise in this matter.

A striking similarity of Scrum and Kanban is their strong emphasis on participative planning and control, as well as on striving continuously for process improvement. In practice, this requires a high level of transparency within a team and between teams, and high level communication skills of like-minded individuals. For that reason, it seems justified to remain skeptical as to whether every member of an organization will have the ability to live up to these expectations.

Conclusion for Successful Agile Management

Based on the cybernetic management background developed in this chapter, it can be demonstrated that it is imperative for agile transformation to always take all five management functions S1 through S5 into consideration. By using Dilts' neuro-logical model, it becomes obvious that there has to be specific emphasis on normative management function in order to really anchor an Agile Mindset in an organization. Furthermore, when "agilizing" an organization, the practitioner is challenged in addition, to consider several levels of recursion: tools, techniques, and practices from the agile movement have not only to be applied to individual team members, but also across teams and beyond.

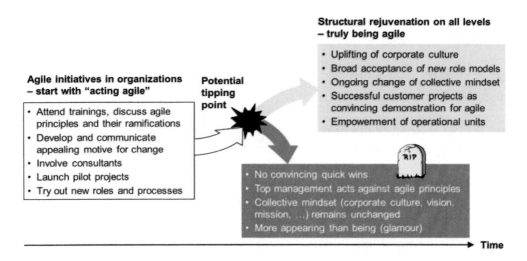

Figure 5-8: From acting agile to being agile

If these conclusions are not addressed by change initiatives within organizations, these efforts inevitably risk failing. In these unfortunate cases, the initial enthusiasm ("acting agile") will never result in an organization's deeply rooted rejuvenation ("being agile") (see Figure 5-8), but will remain superficially - and eventually disappear. This phenomenon is also described by Ken Schwaber: He stated in an interview that it would not be sufficient to demand a new type of employee who could incorporate a "bottom-up intelligence" in organizations and hope this could initiate a renunciation of the traditional model of "command and control" (Schwaber 2012).

Literature

Anderson D-J (2010) Kanban: Successful Evolutionary Change for Your Technology Business, Blue Hole Press, 2010

Beer S (1959) Cybernetics and Management. London: English Universities Press, 1959

Beer S (1972) Brain of the Firm: the Managerial Cybernetics of Organization. London: Pinguin Press, 1972.

Beer S (1984) The Viable System Model: Its Provenance, Development, Methodology and Pathology. In: The Journal of the Operational Research Society Vol. 35, No. 1 (Jan., 1984), pp. 7-25, URL: http://www.jstor.org/stable/2581927 (accessed 20.09.2016)

Beer S (1985) Diagnosing the System for Organizations. Chichester: Wiley, 1985

Beer S (1991) What is Cybernetics? Talk held by Stafford Beer to undergraduate students on October 3rd 1991 at Aquinas Building, Maryland Street, Liverpool, L1 9DE. Video property of John Moores University's Stafford Beer Collection, Liverpool, URL: https://www.youtube.com/watch?v=JJ6orMfmorg (accessed 20.09.2016)

Britton G. A. and Parker J (1993) An Explication of the Viable System Model for Project Management. In: Systems Practice, Vol. 6, No. 1, 1993, URL: http://link.springer.com/article/10.1007/BF01059678 (accessed 20.09.2016)

de Marco T and Lister T (1999) Wien wartet auf Dich, 2. German edition of "Peopleware" with 8 new chapters, Munich, Vienna; Hanser Verlag, 1999

Dilts R.B. (2014) A Brief History of Logical Levels, 2014, URL: http://www.nlpu.com/Articles/LevelsSummary.htm (accessed 20.09.2016)

Espejo R and Harnden R (ed.) (1989) The viable system model:

interpretations and applications of Stafford Beer's VSM. Chichester u.a.: Wiley, 1989

Goldratt E M (1997) Critical Chain. North River Press, Great Barrington, 1997

Hammarberg M and Sundén J (2014) Kanban in Action, Manning, 2014

Morales-Arroyo M A, Chang Y, Barragán-Ocaña A, Jiménez J and Sánchez-Guerrero G (2012) Coordination Mechanisms Illustrated with Project Management Using the Viable System Model (VSM) as Organizational Framework. In: Jindal Journal of Business Research 2012 1: 163, DOI: 10.1177/2278682113476161, URL: http://brj.sagepub.com/content/1/2/163 (accessed 20.09.2016)

Murad R S A and Cavana R Y (2012) Applying the viable system model to ICT project management. In: Int. J. Applied Systemic Studies, Vol. 4, No. 3, pp.186–205

Patzelt M (2010) Die Unternehmenspyramide als Vermittlerin zwischen Marketing-, Strategie- und Personalbereich. In: Brinkmann M (Hrsg.): Besser mit Business NLP, DVNLP e.V., Berlin 2010

de Rosnay J (2000) History of Cybernetics and Systems Science. In: Heylighen F, Joslyn C and Turchin V(ed.): Principia Cybernetica Web (Principia Cybernetica, Brussels), URL: http://pespmc1.vub.ac.be/cybshist.html (accessed 20.09.2016)

Saynisch M (2013) Neue Wege im Projektmanagement. In: „InterPM 2003" – Konferenz zur Zukunft im Projektmanagement durch interdisziplinäre Ansätze, d-punkt-Verlag, Heidelberg 2003

Saynisch M (2010) Mastering Complexity and Changes in Projects, Economy, and Society via Project Management Second Order (PM-2). In: Project Management Institute (ed.): Project Management Journal, Vol. 41, No. 5, 4–20, DOI: 10.1002/pmj.20167

Schaden B (2015) Projektmanagement und agiles Vorgehen. In: Deutsche Gesellschaft für Projektmanagement e. V. (ed.): Projektmanagement aktuell, 2.2015, pp. 28 - 30

Schwaber K (2012) in an interview in Objekt-Spektrum Nr. 5/2012

Sutherland J and Schwaber K (2013) The Scrum Guide (July 2013). URL: http://www.scrumguides.org/docs/scrumguide/v1/Scrum-Guide-US.pdf#zoom=100 (accessed 20.09.2016)

Wiener N (1948) Cybernetics or control and communication in the animal and the machine. New York: Wiley, 1948

Wysocki R K (2014) Effective Project Management: Traditional, Agile, Extreme. 7th Edition, Indianapolis: Wiley, 2014

5.2 Agile and Fluid Organization

Author: Norbert Schaffitzel

Summary: To become effective, agile thinking based on Agile Mindsets has to be established in organizations, or more generally in modern enterprises. We are therefore convinced that organizations of the future will be forced to build up agile units as temporary agents to handle their market needs. Once this development has been established, it could even be expanded by creating a more flexible structure that signifies a so-called fluid organization. Although fluid organizations may become very popular, it has been shown that ultimately, to remain successful, the objective of agile transformation in the direction of maximal fluidity is limited. The reason for that conclusion is simply the necessity to maintain a minimum of social and organizational coherence. This implies that much emphasis must be placed on a sophisticated normative management policy.

Key Terms: Agile Transformation, Agile Organization, Fluidity, Fluid Organization, Hybrid Organization, Normative Management, Order Parameter, Control Parameter

In the preceding chapter, it was shown that from a cybernetic management perspective there is a tight alignment and coupling between collective, Agile Mindsets and the identity and value-based principles of an organization. This connection is required to expand a company's agile practices and behavior in our defined sense. We know that the neurological layers of Dilts' Pyramid describe the individual inner elements of people's consciousness and their mental structure, to which people gravitate. The cybernetic model, on the other hand, provides an organizational layer structure that is regarded as essential for organizations to survive. We assume that both the individual and the organizational layer structure can be aligned in such a way that the individual mindset layer refers to an organizational counterpart and its equivalent cybernetic management function in agile transformation processes (see also the preceding chapter). This means that on every layer of the Dilts pyramid there is a corresponding system function. Furthermore, the vision and mission in Dilts layer structure coincides with the normative S5 and the strategic S4 system function in the VSM model. (see Figure 5-9).

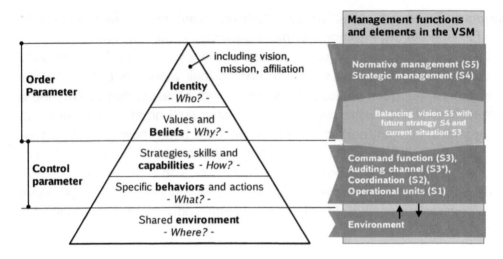

Figure 5-9: Relationship of Dilts neurological layers and the system-functions of the VSM-Model

As already stated in Chapter 3.4 of this handbook and in Oswald (2016), "self-organized systems are regulated by three types of parameters": setting, control and order parameters. From this perspective, the normative management function serves as an order parameter for the whole organizational system. But, we have to keep in mind that for the transformation of large corporations, the normative functions serve as external settings from top-management with which to organize the process of agile conversion. On the other hand, an internal correlate of corresponding normative settings for the upcoming self-organized teams and system units must also exist. From that point of view, the normative order parameters of the S5 and S4-system functions serve as facilitators for the whole organization, whereas the normative values and beliefs of the self-organized units need to be regarded as enablers for the performance of these structures. If these normative management functions correlate, we presume that the process of agile transformation can be orchestrated successfully. The best picture to illustrate this process is the recursive structure of Russian dolls, where Agile Mindsets and their inner normative values are shared on every existing layer (see Figure 5-9).

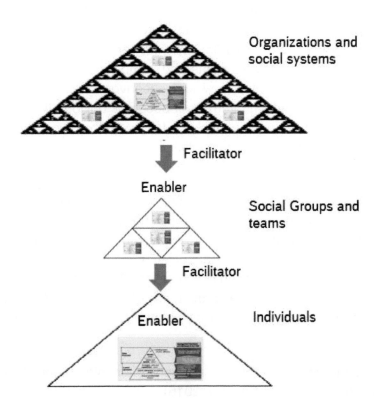

Figure 5-10: Normative system functions and their impact as facilitators and enablers

In addition to the normative fundamentals, a well-defined set of control parameters must also exist to manage the capabilities and behavior of the organizational actors and self-organized units. For example, the presence of multitasking is one of the main performance indicators that needs to be managed, and should be reduced to a minimum in organizations. We are aware that the absence of multitasking is governed by a well-defined control parameter, in this case, the work in progress factor (WIP), that should obey the equation WIP=1. It characterizes an optimal throughput and flow of work in organizations (for further details see the Wire Swiss example in chapter 11 of this handbook).

In addition to a measurable control parameter, we evaluate agility in organizations according their ability to cultivate individual and organizational behavior that allows enterprises to react flexibly, with versatility and with high speed, to adapt to new market environments and complexities. According to this point of view, this will also entail new and unconventional actions and activities that will need to be implemented. So it becomes obvious that within these activities, the ability of the people involved, to handle their work through self-organizing and self-enabling methodologies, has a high level of importance and significance.

But, agile organizational patterns do not evolve on their own. On the one hand, they are triggered by **external** market processes and developments. In this case, agile transformation processes are an expression of market induced pressure for action, the upcoming of unexpected new competitors or the emergence of innovative disruptors for an organization. But on the other hand, very often in organizations, there is a large body of **internal** defects and disadvantages, which should be regarded as pathfinders and promoters for agile reorganization efforts.

Serious warning signals in organizations are very often attributable to the following issues (cited according to Saaman 2015):

- Sluggishness in decision-making and slowness of implementation, provoked by complex planning procedures and long information exchanges
- Competence conflicts and undefined responsibilities
- A lack of readiness to take over entrepreneurial initiative
- Frustrated employees, underload, overload and burn-out
- Lack of creativity, innovation and change
- Tumbling market shares or market influence.

The process for transforming entire organizations in the direction of new Agile Management, needs to start on an individual level, by creating a big picture of the future mindset. Both the organizations and the social systems can grow by creating a new collective mindset (see Figure 5-11):

Figure 5-11: Level of influence within corporate changing processes

An organization's transformation path in this direction will become an experimental research field in which to train in a new form of mastering complexity from the outside. We believe that agile hybrid organizations will evolve. However, this process can only develop in large companies if agile transformation does not remain restricted to isolated islands within their entire organization. Furthermore, expansion cannot occur as long as a value- and identity- based mindset does not reach the normative management layer. Only the expansion of agile practices guarantees the survival and emergence of fluid forms of organization. Otherwise, the agile structures are under permanent pressure for legitimation against traditional enterprise departments and are in danger of, or become obliged to, reconvert into a traditional organizational structure. This could mean the return to normal, process-based and organizationally aligned departments and enterprises. This would indicate the opposite of an agile transformation.

But normally there is the need to be aware that "one of the main issues of productive social systems is the avoidance of exceeding stability as well as an excessive flexibility" (Weber 1996). Hence, fluid organizations are characterized by networks of temporary agile entities that adapt dynamically to their environment and "float along" quick changing environmental variables.

Depending on the environmental situation, organizational responses will need to be configured so that they adjust to requirements. The spectrum of organizational configurations needs to cover the whole range of possible structures: from traditional/traditional permanent organizations to temporary and therefore fluid organizational patterns. In between, a wide range of agile hybrid organization patterns will evolve (see Figure 5-12).

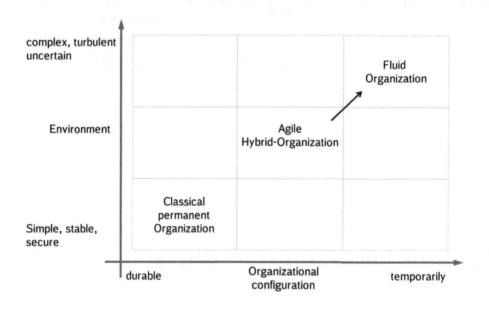

Figure 5-12: Relation between environmental complexity and organizational response (derived and adapted from Weber (Weber 1996))

Hence, we talk of an agile organization if a change process has started and isolated departments, or specific peer groups have started to use and adapt agile principles and methodologies within their work. Such agile (sub-) organizations or agile elements in enterprises are normally of a temporary nature.

In Figure 5-13 we show that at the beginning of agile transformation processes, agile hybrid organizations will evolve. In these organizations, different organizational structures must coexist. Beginning with specialized units in a business working with agile principles and self-organized teams, the development of an agile organization can become a reality.

Agile special units in organizations may evolve and attempt to absorb the environmental complexity quicker and more flexibly than before.

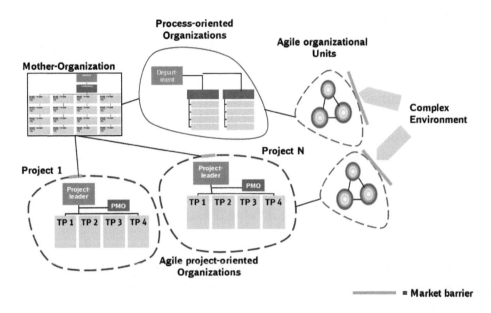

Figure 5-13: Transformation towards agile hybrid organizations as a response to complex market environments

If an agile structure is to be built, a certain range of required roles and responsibility patterns must be introduced to establish a functioning self-organized social system within these structures. According to the cybernetic management model, this structure can even be organized recursively. This means that every agile organizational unit also includes the complete structure of system functions from the top (S5) to the bottom (S1). Hence the goal must be the organizational formation of functions **beyond** traditional hierarchical relationships. The dominant principles needed to attain this are "networking, openness, agility and participation". In detail, this means:

- Networking addresses all activities which realize respectful dialogue at different stages and within different contact groups;
- Openness means providing all required information actively and in a completely transparent way, as well as not being dependent on a certain level in the organizational hierarchy (which can be seen in typical silo thinking organizations);
- Agility means a quick and sometimes unconventional or flexible reaction to new trends or unforeseen circumstances and
- Lastly, participation means to take part in self-initiative, in a voluntary way where the takeover of responsibility is self-organized – "even if it doesn't result in a direct personal benefit" (Lederer 2015)

Hence entrepreneurial success means the establishment of self-organizing behaviors and a new Agile Mindset in businesses. In the end, even fluid organizational structures may be achieved. They allow a more accurate response, with a higher level of effectiveness towards changes in the markets. Speed and flexibility become decisive features of differentiation. In an attempt to handle market requirements, the future organizations that emerge will be network based organizations to deal with the disruptive market environment in a better way.

As long as organizations (systems) and their environment (context) represent a mutual relationship (Oswald 2016), we assume that in future, organizations will react to these challenges with a heterogeneous structure of organizational answers. This means that the organizations will still belong to a legal entity where the mother organization has its origin. But within these same organizations, temporary task oriented units will grow that handle certain innovation issues within a project based organizational framework. On the other hand, temporary fluid organizations will also evolve and respond to disruptive market needs by operating on the basis of cross-linked, interconnected network organizational structures (see Figure 5-14):

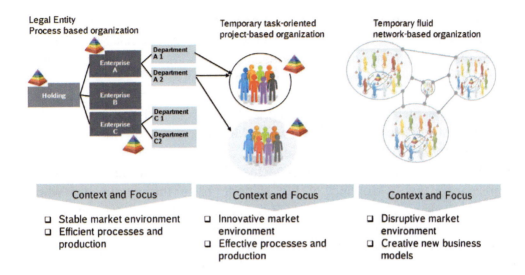

Figure 5-14: Fluid organizations are reactions to new market challenges

Based on variable interconnections between different organizations, such network-operating entities lead to an empowerment of organizations to manage market complexity in the direction of higher flexibility and greater speed. Furthermore, in such a network based organization, there is also the option to cooperate with external partners, in order to address market issues more accurately. But even when the cooperation structure of a network-based organization is expanded beyond the borders of the mother organization, there is a vital issue that needs to be considered:

To build up fluid organizations, the correlated organizational structures must share the same Agile Mindsets in order to handle environmental complexity. Furthermore, they need to be aligned along the agile control- and order parameter:
first an agile vision that signifies the order parameter, and second the enterprise strategy that is derived from this vision and defines the control parameter for each enterprise unit. Flexibility and speed serve as leading indicators for agile transformation. Based on a cybernetic point of view, S5 and S4 management functions can be regarded as a coherent fundament over all agile sub-entities

of an enterprise. The basis for flexibility and agility in an organization is in fitting company-wide compatible mindsets with the relevant skill profiles of individual employees. In fluid organizations, these mindsets must be interconnected across all management functions and departments.

But the range of these interconnections remains limited if the S5 central management function, in conjunction with S4 and S3, is not correlated and does not accommodate to that process. Hence, in addition to the basic regulation of individual values and beliefs, a collective mindset must be managed in organizations, by a clearing of the generic base throughout the whole enterprise. This means fundamentally that the management philosophy in fluid enterprises is based on a vision- and mission-oriented leadership, but that it needs to be accompanied by collectively shared values and beliefs as shown in Figure 5-15.

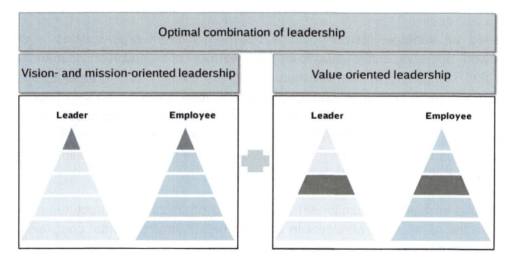

Figure 5-15: Combination of leadership

Only in this case an optimal order parameter hierarchy is established in organizations (for further details on this point see Oswald 2016).

However, what must also be taken into account is that the fluidity of such organizations from a cybernetic point of view is also limited: These limits are described by processes that lead to a dysfunction of S5 and correlated S4 and S3 management functions, and by developments where the order- and control structures of these enterprises are behaving in a completely divergent manner. In the worst-case scenario, this implies that such structures are no longer viable and the ability to flexibly adapt to market changes cannot be triggered any more in these organizations (as the disappearance of several large companies in recent years has proven).

As a result of these conditions, the opportunities to organize companies toward fluid structures are limited by the effectiveness of the overall management and value structure. This means that the agile transformation of entire enterprises towards fluid structures must avoid the disruption of organizational coherence.

In the context of the installation of effective self-organizing structures in fluid organizations, this relationship can be described as a function of the normative empowerment of Agile Mindsets and the agile maturity of the organization as follows (see Figure 5-16):

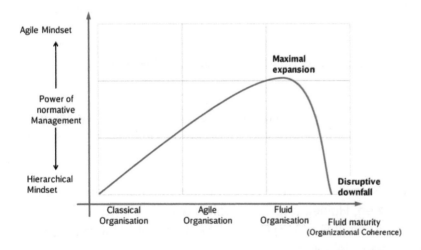

Figure 5-16: Relationship between the agile maturity of an organization and the normative power of the Agile Mindset

Summing up the previously described findings, we must concede that the progress of organizational maturity to fluid structures needs a minimum of common sense and common mindsets throughout the networks of organizations, and a setting of clear order and control parameters. A loose coupling of organizational units is insufficient to establish fluid organizations and can lead to disruptive downfall, as described. From our point of view, fluid maturity in organizations is limited by the individual ability to maintain organizational coherence.

Literature

Lederer A (2015) Digitalisierung: Leistungskultur und Fluide Organisation als Lösungsansatz der Zukunft. URL: http://www.it-finanzmagazin.de/digitalisierung-leistungskultur-und-fluide-organisation-als-loesungsansatz-der-zukunft-14280/

Saaman A G (2015) Organisation im Fluss – Ein radikal neuer Ansatz für die Zukunft

Saaman W (2012) Leistung aus Kultur – Wie aus „Arbeit-Nehmer" Bestleister werden

Weber B (1996) Die fluide Organisation - Konzeptionelle Überlegungen für die Gestaltung und das Management von Unternehmen in hochdynamischen Umfeldern

Oswald A, Köhler J, Schmitt R (2016) Projektmanagement am Rande des Chaos, Springer Vieweg, Heidelberg. This book is avalaible in English: Oswald A, Köhler J, Schmitt R (2018) Project Management at the Edge of Chaos, Springer Verlag, Heidelberg

6 Reference Model Agile Organizations

Author: Wolfram Müller

Summary: The agile community was and is very busy generating new methods and frameworks for agile organizations. Even for experts it is difficult to maintain a complete overview to be able to discuss advantages and disadvantages of these various approaches. The reference model we describe here attempts to integrate several concepts in order to define a generic structure along with consistent terms and definitions to enable fruitful discussions for continuing development.

Key terms: Reference Model, Agile Organization, Agile Mindset, Self-Organization, Viable System Model (VSM), Critical Chain Project Management (CCPM), Theory of Constraints (TOC)

Need and Use of a Reference Model

A Reference model is a minimalistic description that defines the core elements of a class of systems.

It can then be used to derive specific and more concrete models for special situations an organisation may encounter. Furthermore, it helps users compare any model from the class of models, to check whether they are complete, functional and valid.

The scope of this reference model is an "Agile Organization". With an organization defined as "an entity comprising multiple people, such as an institution or an association, that has a collective goal and is linked to an external environment." (Wikipedia Organization 2018)

This can be a team, a division or even a company – our reference model aims more at complete (company-wide) agile organizations with differentiated substructures, such as production, projects, marketing/sales, and even purchasing and distribution.

This implies this reference model must be applicable to the full spectrum of companies and company sizes.

Building Blocks

To describe an agile organization, it is not necessary to describe structures, processes, roles, artefacts, nor associated procedures. Instead, it is sufficient to define a common mindset, to understand self-organization and awareness of the systemic layers in a living organization. Finally, we must have knowledge of different types of work flow management techniques.

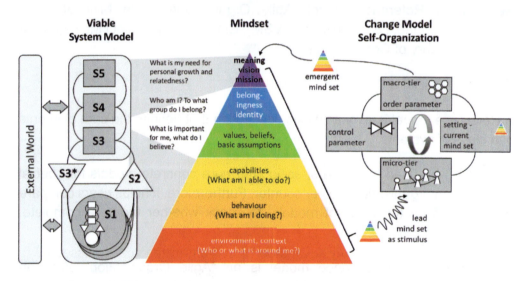

Figure 6-1: Building Blocks to Describe the Reference Model

To describe mindset, we use the Dilts-Pyramid, a commonly used model from the realm of psychology (Dilts 2014). For self-organization we rely heavily on Haken and Schiepek's "Synergetic" model (Haken 2010). For an organization's system layers, we propose using the Viable System Model (VSM) (Wikipedia Viable System Model 2018). For workflow management techniques, we propose the concepts described by the Theory of Constraints (TOC) (Wikipedia Theory of Constraints 2018), (Cox 2010), (Techt 2006). Since the beginning of industrialization there has been a clear development toward flow-oriented low level work-in-process control techniques. Practically all known workflow management techniques (e.g. Scrum, Kanban, Drum-Buffer-Rope) can be derived from the principles of the TOC (Goldratt 2006), (Müller 2012).

Agile Mindset in a Nutshell

As mentioned, a mindset can be described as neurological layers referred to as the Dilts Pyramid (for details see chapter 3.2 "Mindset of Agile Management 4.0"). The Dilts Pyramid represents an extension of the Maslow Needs Pyramid and is used in "Neuro Linguistic Programming" (NLP) as a key model for individual and organizational change work.

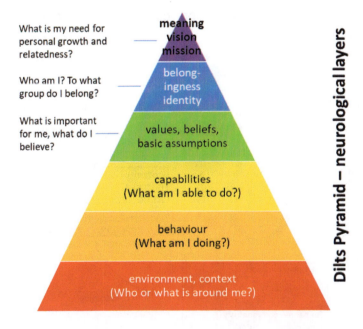

Figure 6-2: Mindset Described as Layers in the Dilts Pyramid

In Figure 6-2, we see the six elements of the Dilts pyramid: environment/context, behavior, capabilities, values/beliefs/basic assumptions, belongingness/identity, meaning/vision/mission, and how these elements are arranged in a hierarchical order. This order is referred to as the hierarchy of neurological levels.

The new (agile) mindset is then the key stimulus for self-organization and is the guiding goal for work flow management.

Self-Organization in a Nutshell

The next building block of the reference model of an agile organization is the concept of self-organization. We use the Haken and Schiepek self-organization model (for details see chapter 3.4 "Self-organization"). We assume an organization is a system of autonomous subsystems that communicate easily with one another and have a common goal (see Agile Mindset).

The model below contains several closed loop controls to explain the mechanisms of how self-organization works.

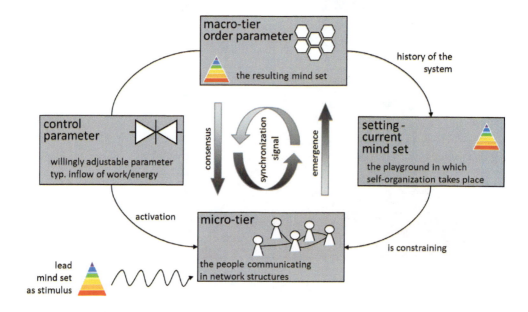

Figure 6-3: Model of Self-Organization according to Haken and Schiepeck (Haken 2010)

At the bottom of the Figure 6-3 is a system of autonomous subsystems (people, teams) that communicate within a complex network structure. We refer to this as the micro structure.

At the top is the macro structure, or state of the system – caused by the order parameter. This is the self-emerging resultant mindset.

The micro structure and macro state are connected by signals generated in the micro structure – typically based on objects processed by the autonomous subsystems (e.g. projects, stories, tasks or orders). These signals are used by the subsystems to organize, so that the system goal is achieved in the best and most effective way. It is the key to generate an emergent new macro state. This signal or order parameter is fed back down to the autonomous systems in order to synchronize them. This closed loop is the main corrective control mechanism.

On the right side, the diagram shows the context. This can be explained as the current mindset – the base line of the self-organization process. It is here that all current resources, processes and roles are defined.

On the left side, is the control parameter. It is necessary to provide the correct inflow of energy or work. It enables the system to change from one order parameter to another. If we assume the feedback loop between micro and macro layers is in place, then it is only a matter of adjusting the control parameter to provide the system with the ability to instantly shift between order parameters.

Finally, a stimulus is essential for the system to start its process. In our case, this is the new desired lead or primary mindset. It triggers the process and enables the system to reach an emergent self-organized order parameter (mindset). This emergent order parameter should preferably be very close to the lead mindset.

Viable System Model in a Nutshell

The Viable System Model (for details see chapter 5.1 "Agile Enterprise Structures from a Cybernetic Perspective") describes the necessary layers of control loops. Loops that are inherent (and necessary) in all living systems.

VSM Layer (Systems)	Synonyms
System 5: Top-Management Decisions (constitutional goal, final escalation level)	Top-management responsibility
System 4: Analysis and forecasting for future development (provide for resources)	Strategic Forecasting
System 3: Optimizing resource usage (load control, audits and continuous improvement)	Portfolio Management and the Continual Improvement Process
System 2: Operational management (location of self-organization)	Project Management
System 1: Operational value generation (team level)	Flow Control

Table 6-1: Viable System Model Layers and Naming

All layers must deal with control and order parameters stemming from the self-organization domain.

Disclaimer: Stafford Beer defined VSM in about 1959. Self-organization concepts appeared later – beginning around 1970. Momentum for self-organization grew increasingly around the millennium. The description of Systems 4 and 5 can be understood as "defined by management" or, in the world of self-organization, as an "emerging mindset from the underlying system". We apply the second definition.

Theory of Constraints Workflow Management in a Nutshell

As mentioned previously, we propose using workflow management techniques from the Theory of Constraints (TOC). The TOC principles are useful for describing systems focused on flow. All current agile workflow management techniques can be derived from the principles of the TOC.

The core concept of the TOC is the assumption, that *"All open systems (with an in and out flow) show exactly one constraint at a time"*. To reach optimum output, an organization must subordinate every decision on how to exploit the constraint.

In this core concept, the control and order-parameters are already visible. In typical working environments the work-in-process (in the constraint) functions as control-parameter and the signal that help every autonomous system to subordinate correctly to the exploitation decisionis is the order-parameter. The two parameters enable an organization to reach the optimum.

The TOC makes a second assumption: *"The more complex a system is – the more dominant this constraint must be, in order for the system to be viable and robust"*. In TOC terms this is called "inherent simplicity". This means nothing other than, the more complex a stable system becomes – the easier it should be to control it. This is true even if these complex systems consist of many nonlinear subsystems connected within a network.

The Theory of Constraints assumes two different classes of systems and therefore of work flow control techniques – each specific to the type of work.

To clarify the scope of this reference model, we have added a third class, which is not part of the TOC scope. All three control techniques provide concepts for both control and order parameters.

Type of Work	System Characteristics	Control Parameter	Order Parameter
Production (Goldratt 2006)	Many relatively small, more or less equally sized and independent work orders	Work in Process at the real or virtual constraint	Vast majority of the orders/projects have appropriate buffer left
Projects (Goldratt 2006)	Big new risky initiatives with a due date and defined scope. Work packages with high deviation and strong couplings	Longest critical chain of work packages	Buffer consumption compared to the progress on the critical chain
Disruptive Innovation	Undefined goal, resources and time fixed, alternating between creativity and selection	Resources (money, time)	Convergence of the results from the iterations

Table 6-2: Classes of Work and their Control and Order Parameters

The Reference Model for an Agile Organization

(1) The reference for an Agile Mindset:

There is no one and only standard Dilts pyramid/mindset for agile organizations. Every individual, team and organization has its own mindset. These mindsets have developed over the years by individual and team experience and are greatly context sensitive. The goal is not that everyone in an organization should have exactly the same mindset – but to be as well-aligned as possible. The following reference of an Agile Mindset is, potentially, a minimal list of concepts and requirements for agile:

Layer	Agile Mindset
meaning, vision, mission	- Generate the greatest possible value for customer and be good to the people in the agile team - Find a solution and create an effect
belongingness, identity	- Be part of a vanguard, be a changer or leader, be a problem solver
values, beliefs, basic assumptions	- People are valued and have positive intentions, - Generate useful value for the customer, - Learning from customers is key, - Embrace change → Focus on Flow There are more values that typically go hand in hand with agile: - Transparency - Courage - Openness - Commitment - Respect
capabilities	- Highly professional, educated people - Precise, concrete and clear communication - Cooperation - Reflect often - Able to build (integrate/deliver) a product in very short cycles (e.g. daily)
behavior	- Fast iteration - Joint planning - Daily stand-ups - Retrospectives, reflection most important see table below: - Management of Control & Order-Parameters to optimally apply self-organization
environment, context	- Product development

Table 6-3: The Agile Mindset Reference

To build an agile organization your mindset must be compliant with the mindset reference.

Your organization must avoid roles and processes that conflict with this mindset. The following concepts, methods or ideas are not compatible with an Agile Mindset:

- excessive cost controlling/accounting – cost cutting programs
- budgeting projects and teams – measuring hours spent per project
- local optimization – individual incentives at individual or team level
- excessive planning and controlling of adherence to the plan
- hire and fire mentality – excessive outsourcing to reduce cost
- ...

(2) The workflow management techniques reference to use with self-organization:

Control Parameter (CP) and Order Parameter (OP) for each VSM-Layer in the context of product development.

VSM-Layer	Type of Work	Para-meter	Agile CCPM (Hannan 2014)
System 3 Portfolio Level	Production	CP	staggering according to the virtual drum (integration phase)
		Short term OP	>90% of projects are yellow or green → buffer regain
		Long term OP	Process optimization to eliminate/reduce buffer consumption
System 2 Project Level	Projects	CP	critical chain
		OP	buffer consumption < progress on critical chain, resources distributed according to status = operational priority
System 1 Team Level	Production	CP	number of open subtasks on the task board
		OP	number of red/blue (blocked) subtasks

Table 6-4: Control and Order Parameters for the VSM Layers in the Reference Model

Reference Model for Implementation

It is possible to describe a reference implementation (transformation towards an Agile Organization) as a step-by-step reference process.

For the transformation, the constraining element is the span of attention management can spare. The control parameter is work-in-process (sometimes called change-in-process) and the order parameter is the predicted effects of each step.

Self-organization gives no hint as to in what order the steps of change must be carried out. Experience and logical thinking leads to a generic order of the change steps (Barnard 2010), (Techt 2015).

The following description is typically used for implementation of "agile Critical Chain Project Management" (Goldratt 1997), (Techt 2015), (Hannan 2014), for more details see chapter 10.2 "Scaling Agile by using Critical Chain Project Management").

This approach is principle valid for any other breakthrough transformation. Of course, this is not the only way to transform, but it is one that uses the principles and speed of self-organization and generates a huge impact.

There are five main phases/steps for a transformation:

(1) A radical initial adjustment of the control-parameter (Work-in-Process) – typically known as "freeze" or "stop multitasking". This step is a big enough reduction of work-in-process to obtain a significant effect, without endangering the system. The desired mindset is introduced by this stimulus into the organization or team.
(2) Establish full-kit – project work is typically not well prepared. It is important to complete preparations for active work in process and for those frozen projects waiting on their re-release.
(3) To apply the order parameter. Typically, there is no appropriate signaling system or data at hand – so the order parameter must be developed. CCPM uses "fever curves" that help a team to adjust their use of resources accordingly.
(4) At this point the signals that connect the micro-tier with the macro-tier are activated – the self-organization process starts and becomes operational. The new mindset emerges. Focus is to stabilize the new system. In this phase, leadership's full attention is essential.
(5) After the order parameter is stabilized – the system focuses exactly on the hot spot where the long-term improvement will be most effective. Only the useful improvement measures will be worked on. This starts the continuous improvement process.

The example below is an agile Critical Chain transformation. Each of these steps has typical subset work packages:

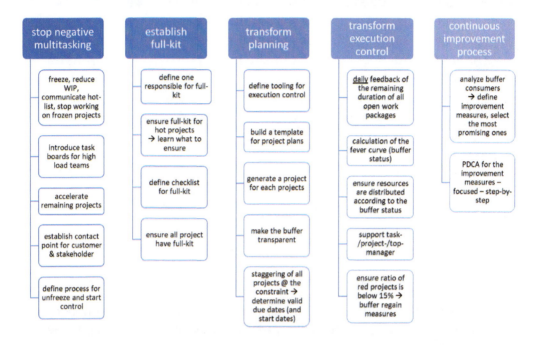

Figure 6-4: Example Work Packages to Follow the Five Change Steps in the Reference Model

For each of these steps there is also a known predicted effect – which can be seen as the order parameters of the change steps:

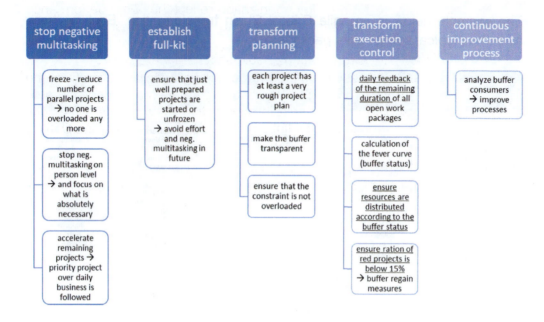

Figure 6-5: Example Order Parameters for each Change Step in the Reference Change Process

This approach is consistent with the Agile Mindset – each step or work package is regarded as an experiment within a PDCA-Cycle. It is impossible to predict the behavior of all subsystems in a complex process with feedback loops.

This explains why the approach has only one work package in process (CIP – Change in Process) at a time. In this way it is possible to detect (sense) unwanted behavior and adjust tactics until desired results (predicted effects) are achieved – or the approach is modified to the new situation.

Literature

Barnard A (2010) https://harmonytoc.com/What-Is-TOC-Strategy-and-Tactic-Trees, S&T Library: "Projects Co S&T_Aug2010"

Cox J F and Schleier J (2010) Theory of Constraints Handbook, McGraw-Hill, 2010

Dilts R B (2014) A Brief History of Logical Levels, 2014, URL: http://www.nlpu.com/Articles/LevelsSummary.htm (accessed 20.09.2016)

Goldratt E (1997) Critical Chain, The North River Press, 1997

Goldratt E (2006) Standing on the shoulders of Giants - Production concepts versus production applications, The Hitachi Tool Engineering Example, 2006, www.goldrattconsulting.com/webfiles/fck/files/Standing-on-the-Shoulders-of-Giants.pdf, accessed 2018-01-27

Haken H and Schiepek G (2010) Synergetik in der Psychologie: Selbstorganisation verstehen und gestalten, Hogrefe, 2010

Hannan M, Müller W and Hilbert R (2014): The CIO'S Guide to Breakthrough Project Porfolio Performance: Applying the Best of Critical Chain, Agile, and Lean, booklocker.com, 2014

Müller W (2012) Drum-Buffer-Rope als bessere Alternative zu Scrum und Kanban, http://speed4projects.net/know-how/forschung/drum-buffer-rope-ultimate-scrum/ and http://speed4projects.net/fileadmin/downloads/Speed4Projects.Net_-_Drum-Buffer-Rope_in_der_Softwareentwicklung.pdf, 2012

Techt U (2006) Goldratt und die Theory of Constraints – Der Quantensprung im Management, ibidem, 2006

Techt U (2015) Projects That Flow - More Projects in Less Time (Quistainable Business Solution), ibidem press, 2015 also available in German

Wikipedia Organization (2018) https://en.wikipedia.org/wiki/Organization, accessed 2018-01-27

Wikipedia Theory of Constraints (2018) https://en.wikipedia.org/wiki/Theory_of_constraints, accessed 2018-01-27

Wikipedia Viable System Model (2018) https://en.wikipedia.org/wiki/Viable_system_model, accessed 2018-01-27

PART II – BECOME AGILE AND STAY AGILE

7 The Impact of Working Agile on Human Resources

Author: Frank Edelkraut

Summary: Agile methods have a significant effect on several areas, typically in the field of Human resources. Organizational design, compensation & benefits, performance management, labor relations, and career systems are just a few examples. To make an agile transformation effective and sustainable it is critical to involve HR in the process. In the majority of companies facing agile transformation, the initial analyses and decisions will have to be in collaboration with HR and will also define the future role of HR.

Key Terms: Organizational Design, Human Resources, Agile Transformation

Although the use of agile methods is widespread, they still are mostly seen as an IT and software development related matter. But as soon the "IT bubble" has burst, agile becomes a major challenge for HR management. Looking at it from an HR point of view, agile is much more than just a method like SCRUM, or an experiment on future ways of working. Nearly all key systems in HR are affected by agile and it will have a serious impact on the way HR management is carried out in the future.

If you are an HR representative, it makes the most sense to have a look at the big picture and the major trends affecting the business world, in a holistic way. Then it will become obvious that agile is just one out of several topics following similar patterns and logic, all resulting in the need for organizational adaptions. Looking only at agile methods would be short-sighted. The modern business world is characterized by the digitalized Internet of Things (IoT), agile methods and other trends, all leading to a context we currently describe by the acronym VUCA. VUCA stands for volatile, uncertain, complex and ambiguous. In business this means, companies face fast changes, which are increasingly less predictable, leading to a more complex environment, and making management decisions much harder. For example, the increasing speed of business increases pressure on managers to decide and act faster. At the same time, the increasing amount of relevant information and contradictions leads to more options and lower levels of predictability with respect to the outcome of decisions.

All these effects are driven by technological innovation, new business models, networking models and individualization. One of the goals of modern industries is one piece flow, which means every product is unique. This corresponds well to the way in which HR views employees who are unique in themselves, with Digitization and globalization too having increasing importance. But, this new ideal of individual treatment for each employee is met with reality in a world where standardized HR systems in a command & control logic are still widespread. A move into an agile world will have a significant impact on HR systems and create a need for major changes.

Looking at the discussion around agile methods it becomes clear that it has an effect on other topics, such as team management or leadership. This is also true for this handbook, where you will find corresponding chapters. Fewer discussions relate to the impact of working agile on a company's organizational structure and processes. In this chapter we will discuss in more depth, how agile methods may effect Human resources management.

A first agility check of any existing organization may be based on the DGfP reference model. (Figure 7-1). For each of the topics in there it may be asked which impact agile working may have. This rough analyses may reveal certain aspects, which are related to agile method use and HR systems:
1. Culture and values
2. Organizational structure and process organization
3. Role of managers and administrative departments
4. Learning & Development, career models
5. Working hours and locations
6. Performance management

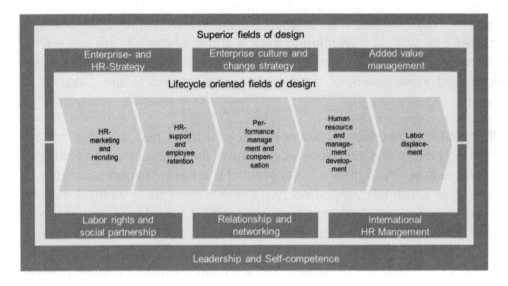

Figure 7-1: Reference Model of HR Management (DGfP 2010)

As a next step, it has to be analysed, what the concrete situation within the identified clusters is, how other companies have handled similar questions. This is a sufficient information base to define possible next steps.

In many companies we will find a potential conflict of interest that could occur during a transition to a more agile future. The Agile Mindset and methods needs a certain level of experience and expertise, and it is quite tempting to stick to common approaches.

Overall most areas of HR management are affected by using agile methods. This ranges from easy to design and decide aspects, to legal conditions, which can not be influenced, yet will cause severe problems. Since many topics are interconnected (e.g. performance management is related to compensation&benefits and career models and HR information systems and others) it is quite difficult to find a good starting point for an agile transformation. The lack of well documented experience in the form of benchmarks, blueprints etc. does not make it any easier for HR. So where to start and how to proceed?

First of all, a HR managers may decide to find some kind of structure to help to define a more systematic approach. One of these may be the Dilts pyramid, which was originally created as a coaching tool by Robert Dilts. The decision is based on the insight, that personal change and agile transformation of a whole company have different complexities, but follow more or less the same patterns. Additionally, the levels in the pyramid can be used to structure the different aspects in agile methods.

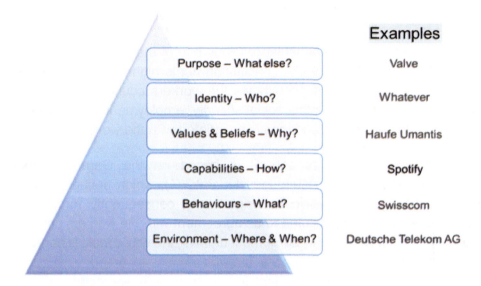

Figure 7-2: Dilts Pyramid and the levels of an agile transformation

Interviews with HR managers in 37 companies (Edelkraut 2016) who are already using agile methods revealed that only a minority of HR managers had started to find ways in which to handle consequences. Those who had already dealt with the topic reported two major insights:

1. There is a high level of complexity in an agile transformation, as they mostly had to find ways to run agile and "traditional" systems in parallel. Different views, expectations and competencies of employees also resulted in many conflicts of interests.

2. The best way to solve the problems was to use agile methods from the start and quickly learn where agile has advantages and where other approaches are preferred. Customer orientation, iterations, simulations, prototypes etc. all helped move from the "old world" into an agile setting.

Agile Methods and works constitution act (Betriebsverfassungsgesetz in Germany)

From an HR point of view, national labor law is one of the key factors to look at. Located in Germany, the works constitution act is highly relevant since it affects HR on a daily basis, especially via the workers council. Additionally, legal regulations for working times, social security, employment of freelancers etc. all have to be considered and mostly negotiated with the workers council.

Cooperation with the workers council is based on the German works constitution act (Betriebsverfassungsgesetz; BetrVG), which defines a wide range of consulting and participation rights and consequently forces the company to co-determine and come to an agreement with the workers council. The standard result is a company agreement defining the way a topic is handled in daily operations.

If agile methods become standard, the following paragraphs will have to be considered:

§ 111 BetrVG will look at new standards and procedures which lead to a change in operations

§ 96 BetrVG defines the rights of a workers council in relation to personnel development measures

§ 87 BetrVG is highly relevant for the standard interaction of HR and workers council, since it defines powerful employee rights with respect to any measures that effect the individual employee. This may be relating to compensation&benefits, recruitment, performance measurement, working hours and shift systems, technical installations and so on.

From a workers councils point of view, the most relevant aspects of working agile will probably be:

- new ways of organizing work, including changes in roles and consequences for individual employees
- defining objectives and measuring progress
- compensation&benefit schemes and performance measurements
- equal treatment within the workforce

All of these topics will change in those units that are working agile, and for HR this will mean hard and long negotiations.

One exemplary company, which already started the communication and negotiation process with its workers council is Deutsche Telekom AG. Both parties agreed on a company agreement defining the general outlines for working agile. The aspects integrated in the agreement are:

- Assignment to agile teams
- Management
- Working times
- Holidays and representations
- Retrospective
- Measuring performance and behavior
- Qualification

The agreement was discussed in 2011 and is based on little operational experience. Therefore, the individual paragraphs are rather vague. On the other hand, an early start followed by later refinements may be an excellent blueprint for other companies. It fits well into the Agile Mindset and allows both negotiation partners to gain relevant experience.

Develop individuals and organizations – Create spheres for learning and experience

On the next level on the Dilts pyramid, "Behavior – What", Swisscom may be an example showing how agile working methods can be introduced into an organization. Swisscom has already started to prepare itself for changes and conditions in the telecommunication market. The whole industry is in the midst of a fast moving process of change, fueled by competitive pressure. The ability to act flexibly and agile is critical for success. One of the many consequences is a more intense use of Design Thinking, supporting the strategic principle to become an Experience Driven company (Haas 2015). The intention is to create more innovations and foster the development of the whole company.

At the head office in Berne, a Design Thinking Lab has been installed to develop new products and services following the principle of User Centric Design. At the same time, the Lab is being used as a development center for employees and managers. They can learn to use agile methods in a "Safe Harbor" here, using agile principles and gaining experience in agile operations. This approach catalyzes the use of agile methods in day to day operations and the probability for success increases significantly. Participants trained in the lab showed a higher level of motivation and willingness to transfer new experiences, than is usual in standard development settings.

Organizational design for agile Organizations – Rules and Behavior

Within the Dilts pyramid the level "Capabilities – How" is very much related to skills and capabilities. On an individual level, this is mainly a matter of competencies (see previous section), on a company level, it is related more to the procedural structure. Due to the strong relation between organizational and procedural structure, HR would need to combine both in an organizational design process.

The objective for an organizational design process is to build an organization that:
- supports the company´s strategy
- allows efficient cooperation of all business units
- ensures all necessary information is available where needed

Most companies are organized by functional units, following the logic of dividing work into units that process work sequentially by respective experts. In an agile world, cross-functional teams have proved to be more effective and often more efficient. Customer orientation and continuous delivery are easier, if all relevant functions cooperate directly and organize themselves.

An example of an organization following this logic is Spotify. Their organizational design has been published and discussed several times and is well documented (e.g. Kniberg 2012). The principle of Spotify´s organization is enablement of Scrum teams, and it uses social group structures as an orientation. In the end, again it is a kind of matrix organization, but the needs of the employees and teams are said to be served better. Cooperation, learning and (individual) development are key objectives for the organization, which has proved to be highly innovative and motivational.

Squad: The central org-unit and backbone of the organization is a team (Squad) which acts as a kind of mini start-up. Teams get all competencies they need and are co-located. Squads work on exactly one task until it is ready. All teams are asked to use 10% of their working time for active learning. The topics and methods covered in this learning time are decided by the teams.

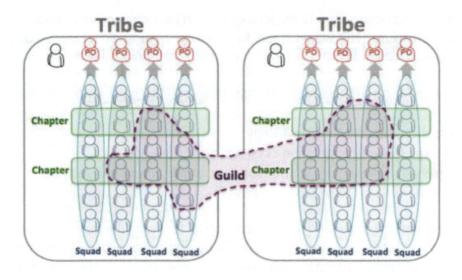

Figure 7-3: Organizational structure at Spotify (Kniberg 2012)

Tribe: A tribe is a group of Squads working on the same or interconnected tasks. The tribe is seen as an incubator for the "start-ups" (Squads). A tribe is managed by a tribe leader whose main responsibility is the creation of a supportive framework.

Chapters and guilds: Chapters and guilds are Spotify's answer to the main disadvantage of self-organized teams. The decrease in central control may lead to doubling of work, and loss of strategic focus and knowledge exchange. Chapters are meant to bundle those team members into tribes with similar expertise, to share knowledge and work on related topics. Whereas chapters are communities within a tribe, guilds are a kind of community of interest for the whole company. Every guild has a guild coordinator to facilitate topics and processes.

As a whole, the organization of Spotify is focused on delivery of projects and cooperation of the project teams. Functional units are secondary and mainly for development and strategic coordination.

Values and Beliefs – A foundation for cooperation

An example for level „Values & beliefs – Why" in the Dilts Pyramid may be Haufe Umantis. The company became famous in 2013, when the CEO at the time, Herrmann Arnold, stepped down and asked employees to elect his successor. Since that time, all managers in the company are elected democratically. The logic behind this step is described by the current CEO Marc Stoffel, who said: "The employees anyway elect the managers every day. If I as a manger act in a way the colleagues do not understand or agree on, they will not follow instructions and in extreme cases leave the company." (Haufe Umantis 2015).

At Haufe Umantis they use the so-called Haufe-Quadrant (see Figure 7-4). It is meant to show the link between organizational design and the self-conception of employees. It is formed by a two axis Organizational design denoted as "controlled" or "self-driven", and the role of employees denoted as "Executer" or "Creator".

The resulting four boxes represent four different ways of interaction:

Command & Control: Executers act within a structured design, which is still a common way of working in companies. Employees expect and need clear instructions, which are executed within a defined framework of processes.

Agile Network: In some ways this is exactly the opposite. In a flexible organization, design employees work in self-organized and self-responsible teams. Agile networks are based on trust and quick action in flexible markets. Agile networks are used to handle complex topics and react quickly to changing demands.

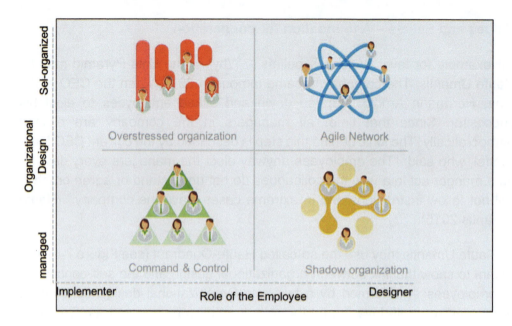

Figure 7-4: Haufe-Quadrant (Haufe 2015)

Shadow organization: Here employees want to act pro-actively and self-responsibly, but a rigid organizational design does not allow any non-conformist action. Consequently, breaking rules and creating work-arounds are standard behavior, as they seem to be the only chance to achieve better solutions.

Overloaded Organization: If executers find themselves in an open organizational design they tend to feel lost and insecure. They are unable to act in a self-directed and self-organized way to reach objectives.

The Haufe-Quadrant is a good tool for initial analyzes of teams or larger units in an organization to find out how employee expectations and competencies fit into the current and any future organizational design.

Vision and Guiding Principles in an agile economy – Purpose and Alignment in an organization

Most companies have a vision describing the fundamental alignment and basic principles to follow. In an economy, that will become more and more VUCA oriented, alignment and certainty will progressively be lost or be only short-term. Many of the existing vision statements are no longer able to fullfill their purpose.

During a conference the Chief HR manager of Whatever mobile Ltd. (Cortinovis 2015) talked on her experience. At Whatever mobile Ltd. the trigger for change was the IT department, because software had to be programmed more efficiently. Introduction of agile methods rapidly influenced all other departments. That resulted in, among other things, teams no longer being organized according to function, but according to value chain (marketing, sales, project management, development, operations). As a consequence, managers (in terms of position) were replaced by leadership. Subsequently, an apparently simple methodical topic (agile programming) had far-reaching implications that influenced even the company's self-understanding. It revealed that processes, structure and culture cannot be separated from each other.

According to this perception, work at Whatever mobile (WM) is currently based on a corporate understanding of how work is understood (WM 3.0 Principles) and a common behavior codex (WM Style: Respect, Fun at Work, Speak up and speak out, Openness, Excellence).

At Whatever mobile, the principles of work consist of:

- in team we trust
- fever to deliver
- freedom to act, duty to correct
- thinking value
- sharing lead to caring

A quick consideration of these principles reveals high expectations for all players. Employees must act self-reliantly and self-critically, managers must trust employees, and there is an overall need for strong team spirit and corporate goal-orientation. During the transition period, not all participants at Whatever mobile wanted or were able to join the change towards a new culture and basic principles.

The change towards an agile organization also had consequences for HR. Today the focus and therefore basic attitude is on the transformational and strategic design of processes. Administrative duties have significantly declined. Work in HR is guided by agile principles and agile instruments and follows the above described principles.

The HR manager stated the following as her learning experience from agile transformation at Whatever mobile:

- The need for communication rises enormously
- Topics get more complex
- HR automatically focusses on organizational development and cultural topics
- A "Safe Harbour" has to be created, which means adhering to the basic principle that mistakes can/should happen and things need to be tried out.

Valve is a game producer in Washington which completely dispenses with managers/leaders. The financially independent company was founded in 1996 and aims to represent "greatness". Therefore, the employees have all over freedom. Small scale, this means anyone can place their desk anywhere, everyone can decide what they are working on and in which team. On a larger scale it relates to the handling of mistakes, which plays a large role as learning potential, or decisions concerning product rollouts.

The logic of this way of working at Valve is formally described in a manual every new employee receives. Everything they need to know is described within it. At Valve there is neither a boss/superior, nor HR. Everything necessary is carried out by the employees themselves.

Figure 7-5: Valve Handbook on the question, how to work without a manager. Source: http://www.valvesoftware.com/company/Valve_Handbook_LowRes.pdf

Modern HR Management for Agile Organizations

One benefit from the current discussion on agile methods is the opportunity for organizations to critically revise their current HR systems. Comp.& Ben., Objective Agreements, budgeting, and other systems are common to many companies, but will not necessarily work in a more agile setting. Often, these systems have existed for many years and have been developed in an almost "evolutionary" way, but have seldomly undergone critical revision. They may even have a tendency to limit the organization, therefore getting rid of these limitations may be a good trigger for a new organizational design.

Example 1: In a Taylorisitc working system all resources should be close to a 100% work load. Experience from project management (even the "old" waterfall systems) showed, that this is not an ideal way to view resources. Any kind of unexpected or changing matter will cause problems if resources do not have the capacity to react.

Example 2: In agile methods like Scrum, sprint is a core logic. This can only work, if resources are able to focus on one task and take the next one from the backlog when ready to do so.

Looking at HR systems the two HR managers ask themselves, which instruments have to be addressed within HR. They create a list showing all topics already discussed with the different departments and even at this stage, the initial version contains a many topics:

Agreement of objective: Agreeing objectives with all employees in a yearly process does not appear to be meaningful in an agile environment. Additionally, it will become increasingly difficult for the line manager to see and influence the process to reach the agreed objectives.

Individual bonus payments: The logic of an individual bonus, i.e. to value individual performance, does not fit into an agile world, where team performance is key and individual contributions are not even possible to measure. Individual bonuses violate the mindset of peer support.

Personal development has to be organized on an individual level and instruments and formats have to be more flexible to address short-term or very specific learning needs.

Knowledge Management (KM): The basic question of KM "How do we learn in this organization?" becomes more relevant in an agile organization. Agile working teams create a lot of new knowledge and experience and this new knowledge has to be documented, and analysed for its value to other teams, and if meaningful then taught to others. Here again individual teams are the basis for the new system.

Organizational Structure: An analysis has to be made as to whether the existing org chart and the therein defined roles and responsibilities still make sense in an agile organization. It may be necessary to create new structures more oriented to the work flow as shown in the Spotify example.

Liquid Workforce: In a more agile and faster moving world, competencies and manpower are more difficult to plan. Therefore all companies will increase the number and type of freelancers, Interim Managers and other flexible workforce. Due to a number of regulations, partly in direct conflict with the company´s interests ("Scheinselbständigkeit", social insurance etc.) plus the increasing need to involve freelancers more heavily in all learning and knowledge processes, a more structured approach needs to be defined.

IT for HR: The actual IT system at Meier is designed to support managers in their role as department heads. In an agile future, the self-organization of teams has to be covered too.

Performance Management: To work in an agile environment performance management has to be redesigned from a manager-to-employee-related system into a 360° system. Feedback from peers and customers (internal as external) becomes more relevant and part of all performance matters.

Career models: The current career model focuses on managerial and project related careers. In an agile system, career has to be redefined and a modified career system established.

These topics alone will create a lot of work for HR and have significant potential for conflicts. They therefore look at two topics in further detail.

Summary and Outlook

All discussions on agile methods and the consequences of their use, have shown a massive need for clarification and for redesigning the organization. Clarification starts with a definition of agile. There are different concepts of agile in different departments and at different managerial levels, and the reasons for becoming more agile may be vary. The already agile working departments see agile more as a method for organizing work, whereas HR and the management team see agile more as an organizations capability to adapt to change. Step number one in any agile transition or transformation therefore, must be to define the purpose, definitions and scope of any activities.

The logic of agile work affects three levels: Individuals, Team and Organization. HR is an excellent example of how these three levels and the effects of agile are interwoven. Any change in one little aspect will cause several side-effects, which then have to be dealt with. An individual bonus for example, is part of an organization wide salary scheme, which is agreed on with the workers council and so on. For HR, this is a big challenge, since this complexity means every change will take time to be defined, negotiated and implemented. Long processes on the other hand, are in direct conflict with a key benefit of agile work: Speed. Only time will tell how this conflict of interest can be managed properly.

Success in agile transformation depends on several factors:

- Ability to analyse context and options to act

- Let go: Processes, power, ... skip what is not working anymore and change what needs to be changed
- Tolerance: different approaches may lead to the best results and may be tried, even in parallel
- Endurance: There will be a lot of problems, mishaps and "failure". Stand up and move on!
- Experiment: There will be no plan and no one and only way. Experiments are the best way to find proper solutions and save energy.
- Learn, learn, learn

For HR this will mean redefining its future role. Depending on the company´s strategy and the respective context, there is ample room to define what to be. An administrative specialist can be as helpful as a business driver and enabler of agile teams and the whole organization. The future will tell. Agile!

Literature

Cortinovis S (2015) Veränderung als Normalzustand – Agile Praxis aus Personalmanagement-Sicht, Vortrag auf der Zukunft Personal 2015

DGfP - Deutsche Gesellschaft für Personalführung (2010) DGfP Langzeitstudie Professionelles Personalmanagement, http://static.dgfp.de/assets/publikationen/2011/03/dgfp-langzeitstudie-professionelles-personalmanagement-pix-2010-1342/dgfplangzeitstudiepix2010.pdf

Edelkraut F (2014) Der letzte räumt die Erde auf! Wie sich „agil" auf die Personalabteilung auswirkt. Vortrag auf der Manage Agile 2014, http://de.slideshare.net/fredel00/hr-in-agilen-umgebungen

Edelkraut F, Eickmann M (2015) Agiles Management – jetzt wird es ernst! Wirtschaftsinformatik & Management

Edelkraut F (2016) Personalmanagement in der agilen Organisation; Management Innovation Camp 2016, http://managementinnovation.camp/

Haas A (2015) Führung in einer Experience Driven Company, Beitrag auf dem DGfP-Lab 2015. Interview und Hintergründe: Wilkat B., Haas A.: Human Centred Design bei der Swisscom, http://www.the-new-worker.com/human-centred-design-swisscom/

Haufe (2015) Whitepaper: Agile Unternehmen – Das Betriebssystem für die Arbeitswelt der Zukunft, http://www.haufe.de/personal/download-agile-unternehmen-whitepaper_48_319054.html

Haufe Umantis (2015) http://presse.haufe.de/pressemitteilungen/detail/article/ceo-marc-stoffel-erneut-demokratisch-gewaehlt/

Komus et. al. (2014) Status Quo Agile - Zweite Studie zu Verbreitung und Nutzen agiler Methoden, http://www.status-quo-agile.de/

Klumpp B, Guillium L (2012) Betriebsverfassungsgesetz und Scrum – Wie passt das zusammen? Vortrag auf der Deutsche Scrum 2012, http://deutschescrum.de/sites/deutschescrum.de/files/article/Deutsche%20Scrum%202012_Betriebsverfassungsgesetz%20und%20Scrum.pdf

Kniberg I, Ivarsson A (2012) Scaling Agile @ Spotify with Tribes, Squads, Chapters & Guilds, http://de.slideshare.net/xiaofengshuwu/scalingagilespotify

PMI (2015) Capturing the value of project management through organizational agility http://www.pmi.org/~/media/PDF/learning/translations/2015/capture-value-organizational-agility.ashx

Quartz (2016) http://qz.com/428813/ge-performance-review-strategy-shift/

Stoffel M, Grabmeier S (2015) Mitarbeiterzentriertes Betriebssystem, Keynote auf dem Talent Management Gipfel, https://www.haufe.com/vision/mitarbeiterzentriertes-betriebssystem/

8   Reliable and Ultimate Scrum

Author: Wolfram Müller

Summary: Agile methods are product focused and team oriented approaches and therefore by definition do not follow dictionary definitions of projects with firm deadlines and many dependencies. Nor do agile methods concern themselves with the fact that most project organizations are multi-project. To use the best of both worlds it is necessary to modify traditional project management to make it a little more agile, and the agile world to make it faster and more reliable to be compatible for the multi-project world. There are two possible approaches, based on ideas from Critical Chain Project Management and the Theory of Constraint, to enable agile methods to be much faster and reliable in the multi-project World.

Key Terms: Critical Chain, Fever Curve, Buffer Management, Task Board, Drum Buffer Rope, WIP Limits

Differences between Projects and Production (Agile!)

To begin to understand how agile methods can be made faster and more reliable, we need to review the underlying production and project system characteristics, especially what makes them different.

Definition of Production: There are many definitions of production – we will use just one. The Theory of Constraints perspective (Goldratt 1992) tells us production is characterized by:

- An overall touch time to produce an article of "something", which is far shorter than the overall lead time – typically <10% and often considerably less.
- A production batch, which is usually made up of many items of the same article. For example, when a batch of 100 items is produced, only 1 item can be processed at a time, so the item waits 99% of the processing time.

- Every part taking more or less the same amount of production time.
- The production sequence of these items being immaterial and able to be changed with wide ranges.

Compare this system with agile projects and you will see lot of commonality. Agile works with many small tasks or jobs, referred to as stories. Stories are held in a batch called a backlog and the production sequence can easily be changed by the product owner. Even sprints are types of batches. From the perspective of a story – it waits a long time in the backlog or within a sprint to be processed. Modern agile methods are often even referred to as production systems e.g. Kanban systems.

Production sounds negative somehow, but it has nothing to do with Taylorism at all. Production can be very creative. If you look at modern creativity methods, such as "Design Thinking" or IDEO, you will see that they are very much a strict process of generating as many ideas as possible. So, high creativity processes are even more like production.

Modern production steering methods are flow and pull oriented and are easy to apply. Due to the low touch time to lead time ratio, there is a buffer of plenty of time. This can be used to change the order of work whenever urgent demand makes it necessary. Because of the huge number of work items that are more or less equal in size – it is also easy to predict the release due date.

Modern production management and control methods all use the same concepts. They seek to increase Flow, or in other words reduce production times. They all use a mechanism to signal when NOT to produce. They all seek to eliminate the drive for efficiency everywhere, in order to focus on where a significant reduction of lead time can be realized. They all have a mechanism to continually improve flow.

There are three known production control concepts. One of the first was by Henry Ford, who invented Flow Lines that limit space in production to permit only just enough work in process to run at the optimal throughput and to prevent over production. This concept is very inflexible. It requires a very restricted product line. Henry Ford stated this with his famous line, "You can have any color as long as it's black." Scrum has many similarities to Ford's production system and his way of limiting space on the assembly line.

Tachii Ohno developed the Toyota Production System (including Kanban) from which Lean was born. Lean, containing Kaizen as method, focuses on continuous improvement and Kanban (the pull principle) to prevent over-production by limiting stock. Kaizen, was never very focused on the critical hot spots (which is waste!) and Kanban requires many buffers at each stage and is therefore relatively slow or inflexible to demand changes. Toyota also needed to take measures to limit product variability.

The third generation of production management and WIP control was developed by Eliyahu M. Goldratt. He called his process "Drum-Buffer-Rope (Goldratt 1992), (Goldratt 2008). It focuses solely on constraint in the value chain. A buffer is placed in front of the constraint (the limiting factor) to protect it from running out of work. The buffer is managed to minimize its size, to prioritize work and to determine where work should focus on improvement. New work is released as the Drum (the constraint) completes tasks. The rope is the signal to start a new order. The process maintains just enough work in the production system to prevent the constraint running out of work. This enables much more flexibility and brings WIP towards the minimum (without jeopardizing Throughput). This methodology has evolved over the years. "Simplified Drum-Buffer-Rope" (Schragenheim 2009) is the (evolving) latest version. It is very easy to implement even with just a backlog of work.

At their core, all agile methods e.g. Scrum, Kanban and SAFe are versions that and are (could have been) derived from the above three methods.

To use these simple methods, you have to pay the price – projects must be cut down into small portions and lead time should be expected to be much longer than touch time.

Simply because of the missing steering elements of dependency and buffer management, it is not possible for agile methods to really both commit to due dates and deal with all the internal and external dependencies. In these cases, project management is needed.

Definition of project management: While production produces an item many times, projects are large and, usually one of a kind, initiatives with a critical chain made up of many physical (critical path defines only physical dependencies) and many resource dependencies. Commonly, projects also show huge deviations in the work packages they contain. The goal with projects is to manage them with a touch time close to the lead time. Or, it is all about finding the shortest possible lead time. A project is defined by the network of work items or tasks modelled with the dependencies.

In typical organizations, it is rare that only one active project exists. Usually there are several to many projects with resource dependencies between or among them. These dependencies across several projects require resource management within a single large project and across all the projects in the organization.

Current project and portfolio management methods are inadequate to make good strategic decisions. The dynamics involved require greater flexibility, speed and agility. The key is to prevent vital resources from multi-tasking.

One option is to use the methodologies around "Critical Chain Project Management" (CCPM) to make traditional project organizations more agile.

The following section gives a short and rough description of Critical Chain and its ideas – to attain more in-depth information, "Critical Chain" by Eliyahu Goldratt (Goldratt 1997) or "Projects that Flow" by Uwe Techt (Techt 2014) provide most of the insights you will need.

Critical Chain starts by reducing the number of projects active in the organization. Typically more than 50% of projects are frozen until projects are in the final stages of completion. At that point, the load in the organization is maintained by (re-)releasing (frozen) projects as projects are completed. With this simplified portfolio, it is much easier to manage resources so that they do not multi-task and are therefore much more effective. Instead of fully loading all teams, the organization accepts that the system has constraints that in any case, limit its output capacity. Because management tends to overload the organization, constraint seems to move/jump/dance from resource to resource. If you look closely, you will usually see that the constraint of a project organization is not an individual person or a skill – it is the integration phase, the point at which projects are finally assembled. In this integration phase, you usually need the best of the best, employees with many years of experience and (top) management representatives. With this kind of load, you know for sure that you can only integrate very few projects at a time.

Critical Chain portfolio management (Harmony 2010), (Techt 2014) sets the virtual drum (the constraint) capacity, so that the constraint is not overloaded and multitasking is eliminated (largely). By managing constraint (virtual drum), all other resources are also not overloaded and therefore do not multi-task. By staggering at the virtual drum (limiting the number in integration) resource management is simpler; prioritization decisions and due date estimates become much easier (Müller 2006).

Critical Chain also simplifies project controlling and operational prioritization. Critical Chain assumes that resources, because they have to be reliable, include buffers for their work package estimates. Resources do this because in today's environments they know that they will suffer disturbances and multi-tasking. Critical Chain reallocates part of these buffers from work packages to place an aggregated buffer at project end. This buffer can be reduced, because due to the aggregation of risks, the complete original buffer time is not required (it works just like any insurance that aggregates many risks).

Project management and controlling is now reduced to the monitoring of progress on the critical chain, relative to buffer consumption.

The buffer has a key role in managing projects. Management focus is to protect the critical chain, the longest chain of dependent work packages. When your % progress on the critical chain is greater than your % buffer consumption, the fever chart (Figure 8-1) indicates everything is fine (the project is in the green zone). If the buffer is consumed more quickly than project progress, the fever chart will show the project moving more and more into the red zone. The red zone indicates action to repair the situation is required. Without action, the project is at risk of being late! Management looks at projects in the red zone and expects the relevant project managers to tell them what corrective actions will be taken and whether or not they need management support.

The diagram below provides a good overview of the status of one project. A project's traffic light status is derived from this diagram:

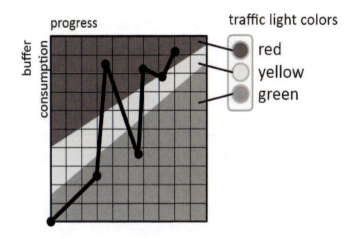

Figure 8-1: Typical Fever Curve used in Critical Chain

The x-axis shows project progress while the y-axis shows buffer consumption – both in %. All projects start at the lower left corner and are expected to move to the left and upwards, finishing near the top right hand corner. Projects are expected to end at 90% buffer consumption to have a final buffer should something go wrong in the final few days.

Critical Chain does not control just a single project. The traffic light status of each project is fed (reported) back to the organization's management, so that everybody is aware of the criticality of all projects. This overall picture allows management to reallocate resources from projects in the green to those (deep) in the red. The overall objective is to complete all projects on time. Overall reliability can be exceptional.

Project managers' objectives cause them to have an intrinsic interest in completing their projects as quickly as possible. Hence they are always interested in and pushing for more (than enough) resources. Plans with shorter lead times ensure a greater focus, because these tend to go quickly into yellow, sometimes touching the red. This mechanism leads to a reduction in estimations until the buffer has the right size.

The information received on which teams consume more buffer than others, is a good starting point for finding those problems - although that team is seldom causing delays. A simple Pareto analysis focuses the organization on those problems that when solved, have the greatest effect.

Work in Process is significantly reduced when Critical Chain Project Management is applied, so that lead-times are shorter and Throughput (rate of project completion) is increased. Proper Critical Chain Project Management maintains work in process at the correct level and consequently maintains the benefits. The organization is much faster and more agile.

Buffer management with fever curves as signals for the organization is a tool for self-organization. The flexibility on operational team level increases. Through Critical Chain reporting everyone knows which tasks are most urgent and can think about how to help according to clear priorities. Tasks or work packages have no fixed time plan, only the project due date counts. Measuring only progress and buffer consumption, is a very agile approach.

Critical Chain can be regarded as an agile method at the project and portfolio level.

What are still missing, are reliable and fast agile methods at the team level and how to use these in a CCPM Environment. Therefore, CCPM und TOC/Lean ideas are integrated into Agile.

Within larger work packages (releases) or sub projects, situations as described in the definition of production can often be seen. That provides the option of using agile methods within these work packages. To do this in a project compatible way, reliability has to be ensured – this can be achieved by adding CCPM buffer management to agile approaches.

Reliable Scrum

For Scrum or Kanban to be more reliable, the same concepts that Critical Chain uses should be applied. Regardless of Agile Management method, two elements from Critical Chain should be added:

1. Limit work in progress to prevent multi-tasking and accelerate work and to reach the goal at or near the due date – allocate the right number of resources to maximize speed.
2. Enable buffer management and use fever curves to manage priorities.

The goal of Reliable Scrum is to provide teams with a realistic scope and due date that the team can achieve and to keep the backlog (WIP) under control.

For a detailed description see "Tame the Flow" (Müller 2013/1), (Tendon 2015, Chapter 23) and (http://reliable-scrum.info). Below is a rough overview of the process.

1. The first Step is to carry out a quick clean-up of your backlog. Start by defining the release goal with the product owner. Check the backlog to make sure that based on current knowledge, all known stories (small development packages) are included with their estimated size. All stories, that are just nice to have or wished for, are postponed to a later release date – just those stories absolutely necessary for a minimal viable release will survive. Add a buffer for surprises (any additionally needed stories identified during implementation) with the product owner and other stakeholders. Make sure you have a significant buffer – around 30% is usually good enough.
2. Your second step is to get a feeling about future velocity. Use current velocity – but also consider expected/probable deviations in productivity

or resource availability until the release date.

Divide the backlog (including buffers) by the velocity to get your realistic due-date. If this does not fit into the expectations of the stakeholder, this is a good time to negotiate this.

This is a simple way of ascertaining a realistic due date. If stakeholders are not that cooperative, you can use a more sophisticated mathematical calculation. With three-point-estimations of backlog times and velocity it is possible to calculate a curve of the absolute probability of success. This is normally not necessary, but can be useful. More details and useful excel files and descriptions are available on the website (http://www.reliable-scrum.info). No matter how you estimate, be aware that people will estimate based on their experience, expectations and their level of need for security. Very often these estimations are far too conservative.

Once you have a realistic due date, including an approx. 30% buffer, you have burn down monitoring, as shown in the diagram below. Your current estimated completion date is today plus the current backlog divided by the expected velocity until the due date. The estimated finish date should be somewhere within the buffer period.

enhanced release burn down

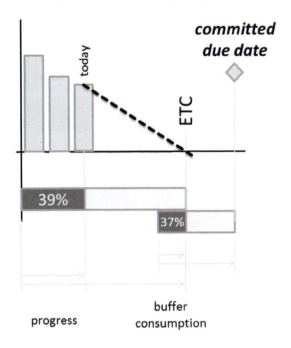

Figure 8-2: Burn Down Chart to Calculate Progress and Buffer Consumption

With the estimated time to completion, it is very easy to calculate progress and buffer consumption in %. These numbers can be used to draw a fever curve as with Critical Chain.

The fever curve is an excellent tool for the product owner. If the release is in the green zone – new stories can be added – if in red, trade-offs will have to be made.

It is also a very good tool for the team to get a feeling of whether they are on track or whether they need to speed up or focus on efficiency. All the time, the fever chart shows the available buffer at the end of the release. While some buffer remains, the team has always got a realistic chance to achieve the release. If the buffer consumption is too high, the fever chart will move into yellow. But, this is visible at a very early stage, so counter measures to get back into yellow can be reasonably carried out without urgency. The team is always in the driving seat and the release is under control.

If more than one release or team run concurrently, fever curve status can be aggregated into one scatter plot to show the status of all releases relative to each other.

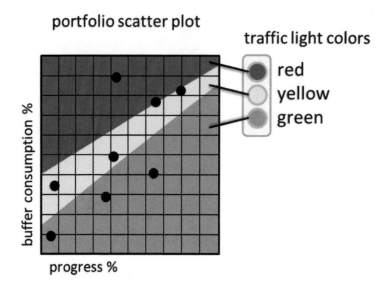

Figure 8-3: Fever status of a portfolio of releases shown as a scatter plot

The scatter plot enables control of more than one team – if releases are in yellow or green everything is fine. And even team overspinning dependencies should be able to be managed easily.

Applying Buffer management to Scrum or Kanban improves reliability significantly. Explicit buffers reduce the need for local buffering in every story/sprint, or at each stage – velocity and quality usually increase almost immediately.

Ultimate Scrum

What remains is to avoid any damaging multitasking at team or personal level. It is all about absolute focus on flow. This leads to optimal throughput, lowest possible WIP, shortest possible lead times and even greater agility.

The concept behind this is known as "Drum-Buffer-Rope" (Goldratt 1997), (Schragenheim 2009) – and it is a type of production methodology. It has some similarities to Lean's one-piece-flow.

It is always the same – you start by reducing WIP. To achieve (and maintain) flow, you simply have to ensure that the constraint is not (never) overloaded. But who (or what) is the constraint?

With several skills in your team, then it could be anyone. If there are several stages a task has to perform to be completed, then the constraint could be any stage.

But to solve the problem, there is no real need to know exactly, except for the application of some logical thinking (as suggested by the Theory of Constraints).

Here we refer to knowledge workers – they are the ones that add value. Just imagine a team with some members, then all of them are a constraint, since all of them have the capacity to address just one problem at a time.

Forget about the 'Multi-tasking is good' story, because it is not. There are many evaluations (e.g. Komus 2016) that show humans are not good at multi-tasking. Yes, we can multi-task, for example talking while driving a car, but if something becomes interesting, then we (need to) focus and sometimes we even forget to eat! Therefore, the first rule is: The number of open tasks is always less or equal than the number of people in your team.

Sometimes this limit is too high. Your team may well have (valuable) jobs they must carry out that are not part of the release. Such jobs consume your capacity. If you have other non-release jobs to accomplish, it is vital to reduce the number of active tasks appropriately. If you do not reduce the number of tasks, your team will likely multi-task and suffer the consequences of that.

Sometimes even this limit is too high. If you want to produce high quality, then you need to carry out peer reviews for all concepts or work you do. While reviewing, two or sometimes more than two people work on the same subtask. This reduces the number of open tasks to a number that is always below the team size.

Quite often, the optimal number of open tasks is half, or slightly more, than the number of people in your team. Since you are unaware of who the constraint is, or even which phase it is in, we refer to this constraint as a 'virtual constraint'.

In order to reach optimal flow, reduce the number of open subtasks to a value significantly lower than the number of team members; this is the same tactic as applied in multi-project management.

You need to monitor the number of tasks that are ready to start. Normally just a few ready to start tasks are enough. Below a certain number, the team risks (work) starvation. If the ready to start number is too low - there is enough time available to generate new tasks from your backlog. This is described in Müller (Müller 2013/1), (Müller 2013/2) and in Hyper-Productive Knowledge Work Performance (Tendon 2016, Chapter 24).

Typically, this work is managed with the help of a task board (Müller 2015).

Your next key step is to detect and correct all barriers to flow. Therefore reduce the duration of the subtasks. Subtasks should have durations smaller than one day (or something like 4-6 hours). Sometimes this will be difficult – but if you are not sure of what to do the next day, it is a good idea to take some time to prepare a concept or plan.

If you are able to reduce subtask size, you will almost immediately be faced with hurdles or barriers to finish them within the allotted time. These problems and the chance to solve them immediately becomes a valuable process that needs accelerating. If a problem can be solved by the team, the blocked subtask is marked (e.g. with a blue dot). A new subtask to solve this blockage is generated and processed with highest priority. If blockages occur that cannot be solved in the team, they are marked (e.g. with a red dot) and are escalated immediately to the appropriate manager who takes responsibility for resolution.

Ultimate Scrum is effective at team member level, eliminates multitasking completely and removes all barriers that prevent work from optimal flow. Team members will be very grateful and will repay you with innovation and quality.

Agile Project Management

These three concepts …

- portfolio management based on the virtual constraint (integration phase),
- project management based on the management of the project buffer and fever cure,
- task management within the team, based on backlogs, buffer and task board

… integrate into what can be considered as true agile and scalable project management.

Critical Chain ensures the right number of active projects and that no resource is overloaded.

Reliable Scrum helps agile teams deliver negotiated releases (work packages) on time, based on a scope and set of resources that fit the time frame.

Ultimate Scrum is used to eliminate negative multitasking at team or person level and to eliminate all barriers to optimal flow.

These concepts can be combined with all known agile and lean methods. All roles will still be applicable; artefacts and meetings can still be applied.

Sprints alone are no longer necessary, since it is all about creating a continuous flow with the goal of the shortest possible lead time. Applied well, these processes free capacity to focus on people development and to reach the highest levels of empowerment.

Literature

Goldratt M E (1992) The Goal: A Process of Ongoing Improvement, North River Press

Goldratt M E (1997) Critical Chain, North River Press

Goldratt M E (2008) Standing on the Shoulders of Giants - Production concepts versus production applications. The Hitachi Tool Engineering example, Goldratt Consulting

Harmony (2010) Strategy & Tactic Tree Library - Projects Co S&T_Aug2010, available at https://harmonytoc.com

Prof. Dr. Komus A (2016) in Kooperation mit VISTEM GmbH & Co. KG., Studie Multitasking im Projektmanagement –Status Quo und Potentiale 2016, http://multitasking-projektmanagement.de/

Müller W (2006) Erfahrungsbericht der 1&1 Internet AG - Projekt-Priorisierung in einem dynamischen und inhomogenen Projektumfeld, Projektmagazin.de, 17.10.2006

Müller W (2012) Das Beste aus zwei Welten kombinieren: Scrum + Critical Chain = Reliable Scrum, Projektmagazin.de, 19.09.2012

Müller W (2013/1) Agiles Projektmanagement: Schneller geht's nicht – Ultimate Scrum, Projektmagazin.de, 06.03.2013

Müller W (2013/2) Agile Project Management: Critical Chain and

Reliable/Ultimate Scrum equals to an Agile Enterprise, TOCICO 2013 Bad Nauheim, available on YouTube:
https://www.youtube.com/watch?v=9SQbhAKq5_M

Müller W (2015) TameFlow-Scrum-Board in Practice, available on youtube: https://www.youtube.com/watch?v=rk4hfjutZAk

Schragenheim E (2009) Using SDBR in Rapid Response Projects

Techt U (2014) Project that Flow – more Projects in Less Time (Quistainable Business Solution), ibidem-Verlag, Stuttgart - available in German, French and Spanish

Tendon S, Müller W (2015) Hyper-Productive Knowledge Work Performance – The TameFlow Approach and Its Application to Scrum and Kanban, J. Ross Publishing – Chapter 22 to 25

9 Agile PMO 4.0

Author: Norbert Schaffitzel, Marcel Schwarzenberger

Summary: We regard Agile PMO 4.0 as an organizational result and reaction for businesses to reach an appropriate level of readiness for the VUCA environment.
Therefore, we are convinced that in its new role, Agile PMO 4.0 must define itself as a servant leader for developing self-organization in modern enterprises. Based on this role, PMO 4.0 supports senior management in enabling the change towards self-organization and agile thinking. To be equipped for this future organizational setup, agile PMO 4.0 itself must be organized according to agile thinking and principles.

Key terms: Agile PMO 4.0, Agility, Management Techniques, Organizational Development, Agile Project Management, Agile Techniques, Project Management Offices, Volatility, Uncertainty, Ambiguity, Complexity, Future Organization.

Why Agile PMO 4.0?

In previous chapters we have outlined a multitude of ways that the management approach of the future will rely more and more on agile principles. Moreover, the development of management approaches that allow organizations to introduce and support self-organization in daily work will become very important. From this point of view, it becomes clear that on the one hand the PMO of the future must promote self-organization. On the other hand the PMO of the future can only convince in that new role, if it works and organizes itself according the principles and methodlogies of self-organization. To differentiate it from the actual PMO we call it PMO 4.0, because it follows our Management 4.0 approach. We therefore understand Agile PMO 4.0 to be the fundamental unit in organizations for establishing self-organization and enabling management, as well as project teams, in agile methodlogies.

PMO – Actual starting point

Today, companies are increasingly working in project organizations. For this reason, the creation of a center of competence for project management receives his right to exist. Projects management offices were designed to give management committees the opportunity to manage, structure and lead organizational projects in a specific and individual way. Project management offices (PMOs) are responsible for defining company-specific project management processes and standards, adapting them to the actual process conditions and implementing them within the organization.

PMOs can be implemented in a company-specific way in various forms. Differences are made according to their organizational embedding and their entrepreneurial orientation. A PMO is mostly integrated in a hierarchical, reportable manner or attached to a management area as a service department. A PMO has different tasks within an organization and the variety of tasks can be summarized in the following way:

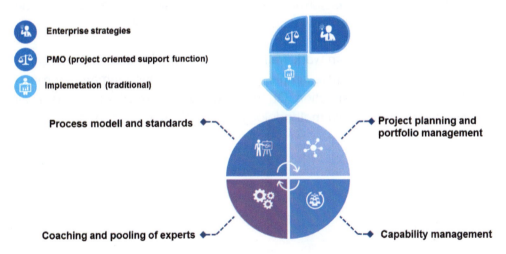

Figure 9-1: Organizational incorporation and responsibilities

The PMO of today mostly occupies itself with the standardization of projects, the planning and controlling of projects, and project portfolios, and the coaching and pooling of project management professionals, as well as their formation to support the project professionals maintining their knowledges and capabilities on an actual level.

PMO – Driver of the change

Based on the traditional relevance of the PMO we are convinced that the PMO of the future must become a relevant part of organizational transformation in the direction of agility. To differentiate it from the actual PMO, we refer to it as PMO 4.0. We see our PMO 4.0 concept as the driver of agile transformation and as an agile competence center for facilitating the operational implementation of agile, self-organized processes.

The reason why a move towards agility will emerge as a necessity can be deduced from the Stacey matrix. As Figure 9-2 shows, for every project, there exists a different grade of innovation and novelty. Every project type in the Stacey matrix requires different skills to manage these projects adequately. Agile project management is normally required for missionary projects that lead to new techniques and even new disruptive business models.

Hence, an Agile Mindset can work well in harmony with traditional techniques, if the project complexity is quite simple, and the project management approach should be adapted to this situation. On the other hand, a traditional mindset will be unable to implement agile methodology if it is not used to agile thinking.

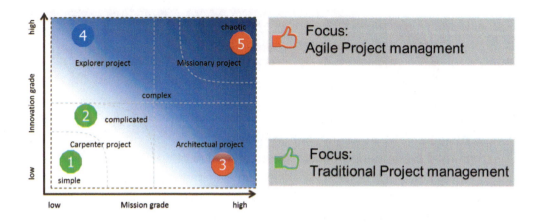

Figure 9-2: Project management perspectives of an agile working PMO (Oswald 2016)

Future requirements of PMO 4.0

Without question, we can say that in many ways, we are going to face disruptive changes in the world.

These changes will be triggered by huge fundamental challenges. Regardless in which area these changes occur, they will impact our future life in many ways. And all of this will subsequently generate market conditions that can be described in terms of high **v**olatility, massive **u**ncertainty, rising **c**omplexity and huge **a**mbiguity - in one word: the VUCA world.

This new "VUCA-world" demands different and fundamentally new requirements for businesses and their relevant markets. To master these conditions, from our point of view, it is essential that we accompany these changes by adjusted, new and different working methodologies. We favor therefore our Management 4.0 approach for organizing the future world of work. In this context, Management 4.0 means nothing more than the following (see Figure 9-3):

199

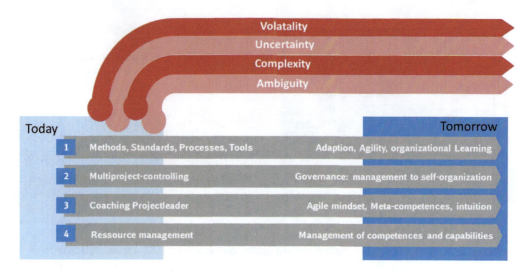

Figure 9-3: The world goes VUCA! And what should the PMO do?

1. The focus of standard procedures and processes is changing in the direction towards competencies that support adapting quickly and accurately to changing environmental conditions. Agile thinking and acting, as well as readiness for permanent organizational learning, will become important working requirements. Learning and formation must also grow in the same direction based on such fundamental basic principles as fault tolerance, mindful cooperation and short, but efficient incremental cycles of work in progress.

2. Multi-project control in the traditional sense, will be reshaped by the introduction of self-organizing principles. This means that, based on our management approach, every organization must develop its own specific setting, order and control-parameter structure, to achieve a self-organization culture in their company. For our new PMO 4.0, this signifies new governance for the project culture.

3. Beyond this, a new style of governance will also emerge. It will signify a shift of project management knowledge and project management capabilities. In the future, such knowledge must be widened by the fundamentals of an Agile Mindset, meta-competence of basic structures of self-organizing behaviour, and by knowledge of their systematic interrelationship. Furthermore, the importance of intuition and its mental and neuronal foundation will play a more important role in project proceedings.

At a minimum, we would assume that a successful management 4.0 approach will no longer regard employees as working resources, but guide their potential to develop. On that basis, it is essential for management to help every employee evolve their outstanding capabilities.

All these factors will influence the PMO of today and will change the actions of tomorrow's PMO. To summarize, the main objective of our PMO 4.0, is to facilitate and enable self-organization, to achieve value-creating complexity.

What is agile PMO 4.0?

It is obvious therefore, that agile PMO 4.0 is both on the one hand, an organizational unit that follows agile principles, and on the other hand, a governance unit for establishing agile transformation in project organizations and supporting change in direction of self-organization.

In brief, PMO 4.0 must be designed by the following components (see Figure 9-4):

Self-organization
Supporting and demanding
Self-responsibility of acting

Agile and 'raditional' techniques
Techniques and framework for acting
with respect to agility,
capability to adapt and learning

Mindset
Establishing an agile mindset and
meta-competences as a reaction to the
environment
Coaching and developing competences

Leadership
PMO as mediator of the guidelines of the
enterprise and of the organizational vision
Governance to facilitate self-organization

Figure 9-4: New tasks of an Agile PMO 4.0

1. An Agile Mindset:
   As already mentioned in this book (see chapter 3.1) an Agile Mindset is a cornerstone of our Management 4.0 approach. Therefore, the coaching and learning of agile principles is one of the main objectives a PMO 4.0 must support.
2. Self-organization:
   Self-organization becomes an important prerequisite for mastering complexity. PMO 4.0 must support and coach self-organization in companies.
3. Leadership:
   Self-organization cannot evolve without leadership. Therefore, PMO 4.0 must manage that leadership function in a way that defines the rules for leaders in self-organizes processes. The governance of that ruling is the leadership function of PMO 4.0
4. Agile and traditional techniques:
   In project-management, the PMO serves as the owner of the preferred project management techniques. This function will not disappear. In contrast, it will be enlarged by the range of agile techniques the PMO 4.0 must master.

Competitive advantage of self-organization

In chapter 3.4 of this book we have already described our understanding of self-organization. Therefore, in this chapter we will focus on emphasizing the fact that in our opinion, in today's large organizations, self-organization is a basic principle for achieving a competitive advantage. Along with actual observation of multiple moves toward agile techniques and practice, we regard it as an expression of mastering new, highly competitive, and sometimes also disruptive, market environments.

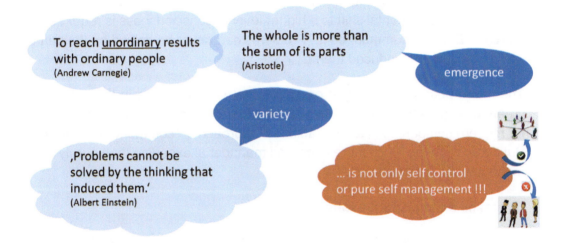

Figure 9-5: Competitive advantage with self-organization

To evaluate the competitive advantage of self-organization, it is essential to understand that a successful change to self-organization supports emergent behavior and a higher capability to regulate higher complexity. Therefore it provides an organization with a more varied range of capabilities to respond to environmental requirements.

Emergent behavior in an organizational context is best described by Aristotle's one-liner that "the whole is more than the sum of its parts".

Andrew Carnegie expresses the existence of such an emergent phenomenon when he states how "unordinary results" are reached by "ordinary people".

But in an organizational environment, at every given moment, with self-organization, there is the danger of provoking negative value-destroying complexity. This means that self-organization does not naturally lead to higher level performance. Self-organization can only lead to higher organizational variety if the organization learns to manage the power of self-organizational diversity. It is fundamentally clear that only the networking of thinking, and the orchestration of different varieties, will lead to a greater capability for resolving complex problems. But at times, it may also be necessary for completely new and innovative solutions with disruptive effects to be created. In such cases, we assume that a mental shift to a higher level of consciousness is required, or as Albert Einstein summarized it: "Problems can never be solved by the same way of thinking that induced them".

The future potential of modern organizational structures lies in their ability to create emergent behaviour. If they succeed it offers many more opportunities for modern companies than the traditional approach of "command and control". But it also requires much more effort and managerial expertise than purely self-management or self-control.

Scrum as an important example

To illustrate our point of view about a future PMO 4.0 and its main objective of regulating and fostering self-organization in modern organizations, it makes sense to compare it with a widely used framework like Scrum. The basic question is whether and how Scrum could be sufficient for establishing and maintaining conditions that facilitate self-organized processes in large organizations. As an answer to this question with respect to our Management 4.0 approach and its theoretical premise that self-organization requires an Agile Mindset and a proper introduction of setting, control and order parameters in an organization, we have derived the following:

1. The Scrum framework can be regarded as a technique that theoretically defines a range of basic requirements to shift teams in the direction of self-organization. By defining specific roles, like the PO, and the requirement of a product backlog, Scrum theoretically achieves the setting parameter of a project. But the vision parameter, as well as the order parameter of a project is normally not very well defined and elaborated. This reduces Scrum's self-organizing capabilities.
The main elements of Scrum supporting the requirements of the control parameters. Here Scrum involves using a well-defined set of tools, such as a backlog of work-items, daily stand-up meeting, the meeting sessions every week, sprints to carry out backlog tasks, reviews to improve team performance, and retrospectives to inspect and adapt team organization. All of these artefacts of Scrum support in a certain way self-organizational behaviour. But we regard their deeper impact on self-organization as limited simply because applying Scrum stresses the mere technical aspects of organizing work in a team but it is not going further. From our perspective, Agile Management first addresses the Agile Mindset and its governance. Although the technical aspects are relevant, they should not serve as the primary aspect for transforming organizations in the direction of agile proceedings (see also chapter 4.0: Agile leadership 4.0)

2. Furthermore, we must concede that the Scrum framework is restricted to regulating self-organization for single teams, scaling up this methodology for larger organizational units will inevitably entail great difficulties. Therefore, upscaling self-organizational regulation and governance to cover different teams and larger organizational units, requires a newly defined set of parameters and further shaping of the relevant order, control and setting parameter.

According to such insights, using a detailed analysis of the Scrum regulation parameter, it can be seen that the theoretical framework and implemented practice also differ (see Figure 9-6):

Parameter	Theory	Practice
Setting parameter	As far as the PO is able to protect the Scrum-team from massive interventions from the external world it is theoretically fulfilled.	Rarely achieved because of scarce availability of team members and/or of multitasking requirements for specific team experts
Control parameter	Value orientation supports the fulfilment of this requirement. But it often lacks of models or concrete instructions for the team members in the daily business (see for example the issue of mindful communication)	Rarely fulfilled because unexperienced POs and SMs could not support this requirement
Order parameter	Vision is a central element of our Management 4.0 approach as well as in Scrum. But in Scrum it is normally a exogenous factor defined by the PO	The vision is very often not in the focus. The accomplishment of backlog tasks is the main driver. The capabilities of the PO to communicate the vision determine to a great extent whether the vision governs the team members

Figure 9-6: Setting, order and control parameter in Scrum

For an implementation and regulation of self-organization throughout an entire company, overall governance in the direction of self-organization is required that must be actively designed by the company as a whole and which must be accompanied by coaching and mediation measures. This task will be the main area of work for our PMO 4.0.

Governance is the basis for self-organizing enterprises

Therefore, looking at the management practice of self-organized enterprises in more detail, each organization should be regarded as a conglomerate of a variable and differently organized number of organizational units. In their underlying structure, they will have a multitude of exchanges with their neighboring departments, as well as with their essential external market environment.

The primary goal of every organization is to survive in their relevant market, according their specific environmental requirements. To successfully achieve this objective, every business is forced to individually specify its own structure. The main question for businesses is how to survive in their markets and how they should organize themselves to overcome different market challenges.

From a self-organizational perspective, this implies a relatively poor set of management parameters for a simple reason: As long as we rely on our governance of self-organization, it is necessary to define and carry out the practice of having an order, control and setting parameter. In our case, the definition of central organizational governance is the task of top level management. The implementation and coaching of this governance lies in the hands of the future PMO 4.0. It becomes the servant leader for mediating agility and the self-organizing capacities of an organization.

In detail this means:

1. The business model with which the enterprise wants to succeed in the market competition defines the fundamental setting parameter.

2. The vision and mission of the business, as the big picture for all employees, coupled with the organization's underlying fundamental values and beliefs, signifies the compulsory order parameter of that business.

3. The decisive control parameters of the business, which regulate the activities of the different organizational units.
   In this area, management of the competencies for evolving Agile Mindsets and strategies to prioritize organizational efforts, become the most important mission.

For further details, please see chapter 3.4 of this book and the description of the leadership parameters of self-organization for a multi-project organization.

From our point of view, these parameters must be defined on every layer of a multi-project organization. In practice that means a specific set of leadership requirements must be developed for portfolio management, as well as for program and project management.

In fact, when examining the different parameter structures of self-organization (order, control and setting parameter) along the different layers of an organization, the most interesting point – in our opinion – is that the same parameter structure exists on every layer of the organization. This implies that to achieve the best fit for the relevant portfolio, program and project level, the order, control and setting parameter must be organized and shaped accordingly.

In the overview of Figure 9-7 the relevant parameters of the respective organization layer are listed:

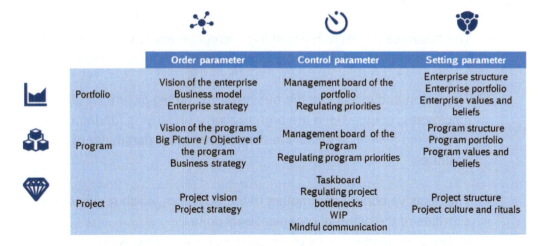

	Order parameter	Control parameter	Setting parameter
Portfolio	Vision of the enterprise Business model Enterprise strategy	Management board of the portfolio Regulating priorities	Enterprise structure Enterprise portfolio Enterprise values and beliefs
Program	Vision of the programs Big Picture / Objective of the program Business strategy	Management board of the Program Regulating program priorities	Program structure Program portfolio Program values and beliefs
Project	Project vision Project strategy	Taskboard Regulating project bottlenecks WIP Mindful communication	Project structure Project culture and rituals

Figure 9-7: Examples of Framework, order and control parameter in a multi-project organization

As we can see, the essential order parameter on the portfolio layer must be regarded the vision, the business model and the strategy of the enterprise. The management board of the different portfolio-projects manages operational practices. The required and relevant portfolio measures pay attention to possible bottleneck factors that limit the throughput in the project portfolio. For further details on the possibilities for visualizing work in progress, please refer to chapter 9.1 of this book: Reliable and Ultimate Scrum.

Both the business structure and the business portfolio, act as the setting parameter. But in addition to this, the values and beliefs of the enterprise as a whole, are setting parameter that impact on the Agile Mindset.

Therefore, the primary task of a PMO 4.0 will be the coaching and directing of the individuals, to enable and empower them to carry out self-organized processes and principles. This entails a wide range of requirements, from establishing a certain Agile Mindset, to the acceptance of certain agile techniques.

Conclusions

We have summarized our findings in Figure 9-8:

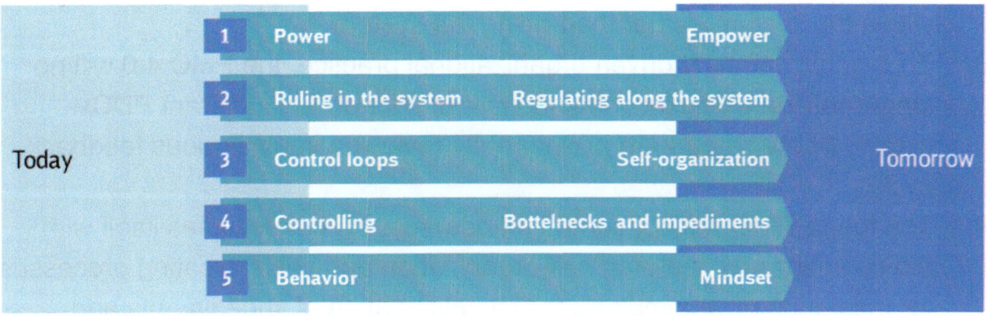

Today			Tomorrow
	1	Power	Empower
	2	Ruling in the system	Regulating along the system
	3	Control loops	Self-organization
	4	Controlling	Bottelnecks and impediments
	5	Behavior	Mindset

Figure 9-8: Conclusions

Our Management 4.0 approach is characterized by new requirements for management and leadership, and a reduced intervention structure in the system. Coaching and supporting businesses in establishing improved organizational capacity for handling their range, defines the role of the future PMO.

The new PMO 4.0 is necessary, because self-organization will not grow on its own. Moreover, businesses must be trained and educated.

In contrast to the actual scope of work of a PMO, we assume that the fundamental content and basic tasks of the future PMO will shift. Their new requirements are fueled by the essential drivers of organizational innovation, which we assume lie in self-organization and organizational agility. The detailed modifications for the future work of a PMO are described by the following features:

1. The PMO of tomorrow will act less as an authoritative owner and governor, and more as a facilitator of individual empowerment and as a coach to establish the actual governance in practice (from government to governance);
2. In contrast to current practice as controller of the rules, a future PMO 4.0 must establish an appropriate order and control parameter setting for the organization. The future PMO 4.0 empowers individuals to handle their situation adequately.
   In brief, the focus of the future PMO 4.0 will be organizational regulation within the system, rather than ruling the system.
3. To organize a result driven organizational practice, the PMO 4.0 will no longer rely on ex-post control loops, but support fault tolerant PDCA-cycles, where results are permanently reviewed in continuous feedback cycles.
4. The future PMO will not control ex-post results, but occupies itself with the conditions for realizing self-organization and value-creating processes for mastering new complexities. The elimination of impediments and obstacles will be one of the most important building blocks for the PMO of tomorrow. Others are: coaching, and mediating agile principles and self-organizing behavior throughout the whole organization (see also (Müller 2017)).

At the least, we must clearly emphasize that individual behavior is not the goal of the new PMO 4.0 governance. Its focus is to create a climate and a mindset where self-organized processes can develop and grow.

In this case, individual behavior is regulated by the new Agile Mindset.

Literature

Müller Ph-J, Hüsselmann C (2017) Agilität im Projektmanagement, S. 49 – 57, In: projektManagement aktuell, Ausgabe 2, 2017

Oswald A, Köhler J, Schmitt R (2016) Projektmanagement am Rande des Chaos, Springer Vieweg, Heidelberg. This book is avalaible in English: Oswald A, Köhler J, Schmitt R (2018) Project Management at the Edge of Chaos, Springer Verlag, Heidelberg

Komus A (2016) Studienbericht zur Studie „agiles PMO", BPM-Labor, S. 18-32, Hochschule Koblenz 2016.

Christian A, Braun L, Ribeiro M, Rietiker S, v. Schneyder, W, Scheurer S (2014), Das PMO in der Praxis, S. 28 – 38, ifmme – Institut für moderne Managemententwicklung an der Hochschule für Wirtschaft und Umwelt Nürtingen-Geislingen (HfWU) 2014.

IPMA Organizational Baseline Competence for Developing Competence in Managing by Projects (IPMA OCB®) Version 1.1 (2016)

10 Agile Scaling

10.1 Scaled Agile Management 4.0 - new

Authors: Alfred Oswald, Wolfram Müller

Summary: The scaling of an Organization, especially an Agile Organization, is characterized by first principles. Three scaling principles and the principle of self-organization allow a better understanding of organizational scaling and the characterisation of "off-the-shelf" scaling frameworks. Scaled Agile Management 4.0 integrates these insights into a meta-framework of agile scaling.

Key terms: Scaling, Sublinear Scaling, Linear Scaling, Superlinear Scaling, Team of Team, Agile Organization, Conventional Organization, Scaling Principles, Fractal, Invariant Ends, Impedance Match, Collective Mind Team Effect, Self-organization, Hierarchy Representation, Circle Representation, SAFe, LeSS, Holacracy, CCPM

Introduction

The scaling properties of an organization refers to the characteristic functions of an organization (e.g. sales, net income, number of patents or number of defects), which vary according to independent variables, such as the number of employees. The main question for Agile Scaling is: "How does performance (e.g. throughput) of an Agile Organization relate to the number of employees using self-organization as a characteristic governance guideline?"

In his remarkable book "Scale", Geoffrey West collected the "Universal Laws of Growth, Innovation, Sustainability, and the Pace of Life in Organisms, Cities, Economies, and Companies". Using a log-log-plot, Figure 10-1 outlines one of the many results: The net income of American companies displayed alongside number of employees.

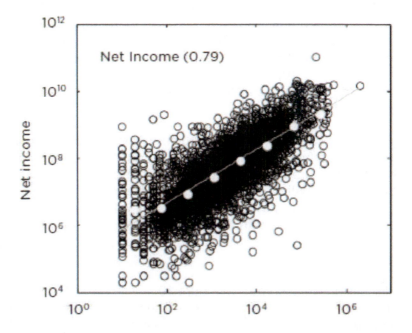

Figure 10-1: Scaling of Net Income for American organizations (West 2017)

Using NI for net income and NE for number of employees, NI scales with NE with the following function:

$NI = a*NE^n$, where "a" and "n" are characteristic constants.

By using Log NI = Log $(a*NE^n)$, a log-log diagram can be plotted with the following relations: $y = a' + n*x$; y = Log NI, a' = log a, x = Log NE. The exponent of n = 0.79 is in the log-log plot slope of the line. Figure 10-1 shows this plot.

We refer to sublinear scaling if the exponent "n" is lower than 1, linear scaling if the exponent is equal to 1, and superlinear scaling if the exponent is larger than 1. Functions like the one above, $f(x) = ax^n$ demonstrate a so-called "scale invariance" (Wikipedia 2018, Feldmann 2018): If x is scaled by factor b, then $f(x)$ is scaled by b^n: $f(bx) = ab^n x^n = b^n * f(x)$. The net income of an organization is scaled by a factor of $b^{0.79}$. – It is also worth mentioning that scaling has a great affinity to the concept of elasticity in the field of ecomomy.

In other words, according to this sublinear scaling, an organization loses performance. If there is an increase e.g. from 10^2 to 10^3 employees, then the performance scale with a factor $(10)^{0.79} = 6.2$. Compared to linear scaling, organizations lose about 38% of their performance. And this is true for each scaling, going from 1 to 10, from 10 to 100, from 100 to 1000 and so on, resulting in a performance of 23.44 % compared to 1000 independent persons – a frightening result!

West has shown that characteristic infrastructure functions of organisms (e.g. metabolism power as a function of mass) scale sublinearly with an "n" near 0.8. Similarly, the infrastructure of cities (e.g. the number of gas stations) scale at 0.8. But other characteristics of cities (e.g. the number of patents created, related to the number of citizens) scale superlinearly with an "n" near 1.15. With respect to scaling, it would seem that organizations behave like organisms: As far as their performance is concerned, they are bound by their infrastructure scaling!

For further discussion we assume that Figure 10-1, with n = 0.8, represents the scaling for "conventional" organizations. This assumption is based on the belief that the data used reflects "conventional" organizations and that Agile Organizations or IT-Tech giants do not have a substantial role to play in these data. This performance function is our reference function for the evaluation of the performance of Agile Organizations.

En route to Agile Scaling Principles

Based on this insight, the following questions can be posed:

- How does an Agile Organization scale? Linearly, sublinearly or superlinearly? Is the scaling better than for a conventional organization?
- The offset "a'" of the function $f(x) = nx + a'$ roughly represents the performance of a small number of people. A team of about 10 team members seems to be a reasonable starting point for scaling. Does the

scaling function of an Agile Organization reflect the better performance of a self-organized team compared to a "conventional" team? This means that the performance function (e.g. the straight line in Figure 10-1) of an Agile Organization should shift to higher values.
- What are the characteristic patterns of an Agile Organization from the point of view of scaling? Which design patterns support a self-organization performance shift in conjunction with scaling? Can Agile Organizations retain a potential self-organization performance shift by scaling?

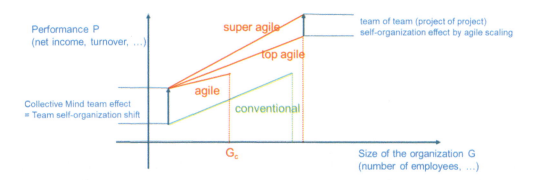

Figure 10-2: Scenarios of Agile Scaling

Figure 10-2 illustrates these questions: Using a log-log plot, it outlines the performance P of an organization, related to the size of the organization G. We assume that the scaling law starts with a team, for example of 10 team members. Additionally, we assume that the scaling does not continue ad infinitum, but that the scaling ceases at a critical size G_c, which will differ for different organizations. If the performance of a self-organized team of 10 team members is higher than the performace of a conventional team, then there should be a shift for the function off-set "a'". We call this the Collective Mind team effect. Figure 10-2 shows three scenarios for the performance of an Agile Organization, assuming that a Collective Mind team effect is (always) observable:

"n" is lower than 0.8: The scaling factor of an Agile Organization is lower than that of a conventional organization. Because of the Collective Mind team effect we call this scenario "agile", but there may be a company of a specific size where an Agile Organization has a lower level of performance than a conventional organization.

"n" is equal to 0.8: Scaling of an Agile Organization is not better than that of a conventional organization, but at least the Collective Mind team effect is retained. We refer to this as top agile scaling, because the Agile Organization always performs better than a conventional organization.

"n" is higher than 0.8: The scaling of an Agile Organization is better than that of a conventional organization. We call this the super agile scenario. If we compare this scaling scenario with the scaling of cities, we can interpret the infrastructure of an Agile Organization as supporting a scaling with at least n = 0.8 and that the Agile Organization supports further "social synergies" resulting in n > 0.8.

Agile Scaling Structure Principles

Figure 10-3 and Figure 10-4 outline the team of team (ToT) structure, the basis of Agile Scaling. Figure 10-3 shows the ToT structure as a hierarchy representation and Figure 10-4 shows a circle representation. The representations are different, but the pattern is identical.

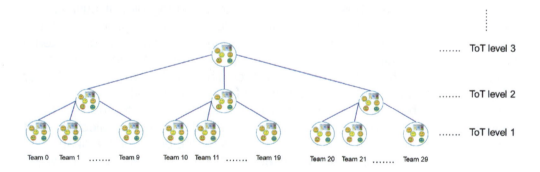

Figure 10-3: Agile Scaling: team of team (ToT) structure, hierarchy representation

For the sake of simplicity, we have assumed as the basis, self-organized teams of 10 team members. We call this team of team level 1 (ToT level 1). 10 teams are grouped together and are led by a self-organized team of again 10 team-members. We call this team of team level 2 (ToT level 2). And so on...

Conventional organizations have a very similar structure. The difference is that self-organization does not play a prominent role, neither at ToT level 1, nor at the higher levels. ToT level 2 and higher, in particular, are not represented by self-organized teams, but are usually led by one person. Conventional organizations lose about 38% of performance from level to level.

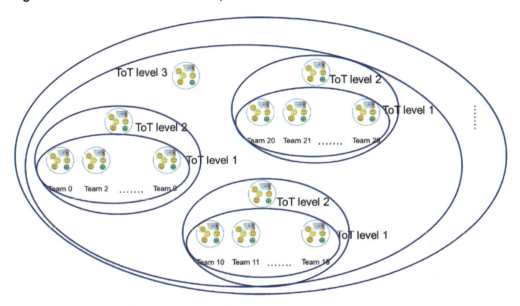

Figure 10-4: Agile Scaling: team of team (ToT) structure, circle representation

The circle representation is the preferred representation of the Holacracy framework (Robertson 2015, Holacracy 2018), which is based on the Sociocracy framework (Rüther 2017). Both frameworks include design elements of self-organization.

So-called Scaled Agile Frameworks SAFe (SAFe 2018) and LeSS (LeSS 2018) are also based on these agile structure principles.

The circle representation in Figure 10-4 shows the same structure pattern as the structure representation of a self-organized multi-project organization: See Figure 3-4 and replace "team" by "project".

Scaling Principles for Agile Organizations

According to the theory suggested by West et al. (West 2017) with respect to natural and urban infrastructure systems, three principles apply:

1. These networks are self-similar (fractal) and space-filling (fractal space-filling).

2. The ends of the networks are "the same everywhere" (invariant ends).

3. These network designs are such that the flow of energy (and information) through the network does not experience "impedance" barriers. We speak of an impedance match if the flow is not disturbed.

We have added a fourth principle:

4. Self-organization is fostered on all levels. For all levels, the setting, control and order parmeters are defined and continuously adapted.

With West's first three principles, we assume that we can achieve at least a sublinear organizational scaling of "n = 0.8". As Figure 10-1 shows, the data reflects a great variance, which also reflects the fact that it is not easy to get at least a scaling of "n = 0.8".

With the fourth principle we also assume that offset "a'", the Collective Mind team effect and a superlinear scaling effect "n > 1" will be achieved by using the self-organization principles for scaled organizations. Both assumptions are hypotheses which should be tested by scientific methods. Unfortunately, we are not aware of any scientific validations of these hypotheses.

The first principle, the principle of self-similarity, is based on fractals, which form, shape or structure an object on all levels, from the micro-level to the macro-level. In nature, many objects, such as trees, shrubs or ice crystals, are built on similar shapes. With respect to organizations, we can assume that groups are such fractals. Looking at Figure 10-3 and Figure 10-4, it is instantly clear how Agile Organizations are based on fractal, "self-organized" teams. And this structure is space-filling: The team structure imbues the whole organizational space, with no other shapes mixed in the organization. An example of an additional shape, for example, could be a (conventionally organized) department.

Therefore, the second principle is directly linked to the first principle: The ends of the network, the ends of an Agile Organization, should be "the same everywhere". If the organization is based on self-organized teams, then it could be said that the whole network is based on invariant ends. If one department is conventionally organized via groups, which are not self-organized, then it must be stated that the second principle has probably been damaged. Here we can see first-hand that a mixure of different shapes (i.e. self-organized team and conventional team) are able to induce impedance barriers. Although we actually have no way of measuring if "the ends are the same everywhere". Space-filling and invariant ends are the only conditions necessary to enable the flow of energy to suffuse the whole system (i.e. body, city or organization).

From our point of view, the third principle is the pivotal principle of (infrastructure) scaling: Energy and information need to flow throughout the whole network from the highest ToT level to the lowest ToT level and vice versa without obstacles.

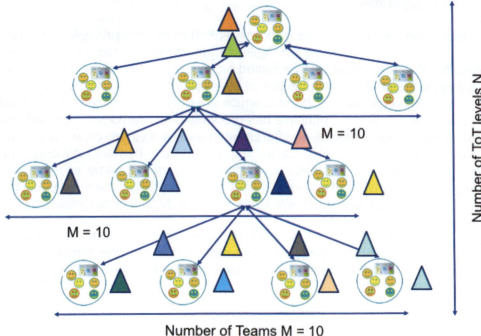

Figure 10-5: Impedance matching of Agile Scaling

Figure 10-5 shows an Agile Organization with N ToT levels, where there are always 10 teams grouped together: The fractals are "self-organized teams", which space-fill the organization, and all ends are invariant. In addition, impedance is modeled by the Dilts Pyramid. Each self-organized team is represented by one Dilts Pyramid. If the teams are not self-organized, the team has to be represented by 10 Dilts Pyramids (one Dilts Pyramid for each team member) and the second principle is broken: The ends are no longer the same. Each team is represented on the next ToT level by representatives, indicated here by another Dilts Pyramid (each link line is associated with a Dilts Pyramid). To fulfill the third principle of "impedance matching", all Dilts Pyramids on all levels must be aligned. Alignment of the Dilts Pyramids means that the higher levels of the Dilts Pyramids must be similar: The vision and the mission must be the same, and there must be the same feeling of belongingness resulting in one identity, the organizational Collective Mind. Last but not least, the values, belief systems and principles should be such that the energy and information flow (from top to bottom and vice versa) are not blocked. In other words, this means that the control and setting parameters on the different ToT levels need to be adjusted.

The order parameter of self-organization of the fourth principle is directly connected to the third principle "impedance matching". If the "impedance matching" requirement is not fulfilled as a necessary condition, the order parameter can not be scaled. Scaling of the order parameter means that the organization has a "living" target hierarchy.

In summary, to scale an organization, we require an interwoven scaling of infrastructure (mainly principles 1 and 2, and setting parameters), of action (mainly principle 3 and control parameters), and of information (mainly principle 3 and order parameters).

Practical Implications

The goal of Scaled Agile Management 4.0 (SAM 4.0) is to design and lead an Agile Organization 4.0. The principles outlined in this handbook are used to design and lead such an organization. In particular, we have used the above-mentioned four main scaling principles. This may include "off-the-shelf" Agile Frameworks, or parts of these frameworks being utilized. SAM 4.0 applies the principles as guidelines to assess Agile Frameworks, to recognize potential handycaps, and to find ways of combining parts and beneficial aspects of Agile Frameworks. A listing of current "off-the-shelf" Agile Frameworks based on Scrum can be found in an overview given by Komus and Bell (Komus 2018).

None of the frameworks have been scientifically validated. There is no scalability data. As we have seen, such data on conventional organizations has only recently become available (see Figure 10-1). Based on the qualitative experience of the authors, an improvement factor (Collective Mind team offset) of a' ~3 is feasible, provided the team or the organization practices team self-organization. Other publications would also appear to support this assumption (Olbert 2017).

There is also a lack of data and qualitative experience for the scaling factor "n" for Agile Organizations. We assume that the average scaling of Agile Organizations is no worse than the scaling of convential organizations, i.e. n ~ 0.8. But, we also believe that organizations which practice scaled self-organization at all levels of the organization will demonstrate superlinear scaling n > 1. But this is only if all four principles, i.e. fractal space-filling, invariant ends, impedance match and self-organization are fulfilled.

In Table 10-1 we list some "off-the-shelf" Agile Frameworks with comments relating to principle fulfillment. We have done this to support learning from these frameworks. Our motivation for doing this is not to assess these as good or bad frameworks. All frameworks are based on valuable ideas or concepts.

Holacracy (Robertson 2015, Holacracy 2018)

- A "line organization" framework

Principle 1: Fractal space-filling	Fulfilled by circles (teams)
Priniciple 2: Invariant ends	Invariant ends = Holacracy teams (circles)
Principle 3: Impedance match	Impedance match of two special roles (lead link and rep link), the design and documentation of Governance guidelines by the circles. With the introduction of two roles, impedance matching can be enhanced, provided the two individuals do not have a Mindset mismatch!
Principle 4: Self-organization	Setting parameter: Holacracy Constitution (Holacracy 2018) Control parameter: Tension concept, special roles, such as facilitator, secretary, and cross link; organization specific Governance design and documentation on all levels Order parameter: Purpose ("Holacracy… its governance of the organization, through individuals, for the purpose." (Robertson 2015))
Scaling impact (our hypothesis)	$a' \sim 3 \cdot a'_{conv}$, $n > 1$ (a'_{conv} is the offset of a conventional team) We believe that these parameters are possible, but the danger exists that with the strict role and process concept of the Holacracy Constitution, Holacracy transforms complexity into complicatedness. If this occurs, any potential performance benefit is lost. In addition, the purpose of Holacracy has no finer structure; we recommend that the purpose is implemented as a target hierarchy. Furthermore, for Agile Organization implementation we recommend using the basic implementation ideas of self-organization, but not all the rule details of the Holacracy constitution.

Agile Critical Chain Project Management (see chapter 10.2 and Full Scale Project and Agile Framework (2013))

- a multi-project management framework
- with agile practices included

Principle 1: Fractal space-filling	The goal of the network is to exchange all necessary control information with the invariant end points (projects). The fractal structure of an agile CCPM system includes an oscillating combination of production and project system controls. Four layers are recognized (roughly similar to the VSM see chapter 5.1): Layer 1A – a portfolio – looks like the production of projects – few dependencies – coupled via a constraint – production control used (VSM System 3/4) Layer 1B – a project – looks like a network of work packages - tight dependencies/strong coupling and high touch time – project controls used (VSM System 2) Layer 2A – a work package = release backlog – looks like production – loosely coupled tasks or stories – production control is used in the form of checklists, backlog oriented burn down controls (VSM System 1) Layer 2B – a task or story – looks like a small project (very simple network = a chain) of tightly coupled subtasks – taskboard with process dependent steps is used (VSM System 1) Cross Layer X – continuous improvement process (CIP) – root cause analysis on how to reduce lead - generates structural improvement projects
Priniciple 2: Invariant ends	Invariant ends = Projects (because projects are the ends which determine the CCPM macro-structure)

Principle 3: Impedance match	Only very simple, objective and operational signals (progress versus buffer consumption – fever curve or estimated time to complete) are used. Minimal room for personal bias due to separated responsibility and real data for generating the signal. Layer 1A/B – the percentage of red projects should be ~10% and projects should be in the "green" or yellow" zone Layer 1X - all events that touch the "red" zone are analyzed and patterns need to be detected, which lead to evasive measures (CIP projects) Interaction between Layer 1B and 2A – this is a closed loop corrective signal, the fever curve status goes to the lower layer (i.e. the operational priority) (2A) → what leads to an estimated completion time (ETTC) (1B) → what leads to progress and buffer consumption per project (2A) the fever curve Layer 2A/B - a systematic backlog and velocity management to determine the estimated completion time daily Layer 2X – explicit deblocking management The impedance match is established by using the identical signal between the A/B Layer and the cross layer X CIP
Principle 4: Self-organization	See Figure 3-4 and chapter 9: Agile PMO 4.0 Setting parameter: (1) top management that is willing to reduce the WIP and does not interfere with the order parameter (2) a culture that allows open, fast and transparent feedback (3) lack of local optiminzation KPIs (like the utilization of teams or efficiency or cost per unit) Control parameter: organizational WIP on layer 1 and operational WIP on layer 2 Order parameter: Multi-project management visualization - fever curve and scatter plot diagram on layer 1 and systematic

	deblocking on layer 2
Scaling impact (our hypothesis)	Unfortunately there is no valid comparison of data for the scaling of companies applying and not applying agile CCPM. The only data available is with respect to gains in throughput that were achieved by applying agile CCPM to traditional R&D departments/companies: 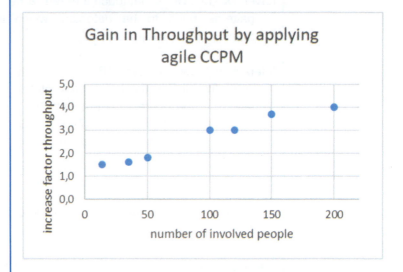 *Figure 10-6: Reached gains in project throughput increase versus number of involved people in the organization (Source: data out of consulting projects see partially made public on VISTEM 2018)* Obviously the gain is significant and it increases according to the number of people involved (part of the R&D system). Based on our experience (see Figure 10-6) we estimate $k \sim 1.5$ ($a' \sim k*a'_{conv}$) and $n \sim 1$ for systems up to 200 people. It would seem that the gain in throughput by applying agile CCPM, increases with the number of people involved. There is no valid data available for companies of > 200 people, because the gains here will be constrained by other factors, such as maximum market capacity. Agile CCPM must therefore have a significant effect on the

downside (sublinear) scaling of the underlying support (control) network of R&D systems.

Typically the gain achieved by applying agile CCPM is so huge that the constraint of the company jumps immediately upstream to sales/marketing, or in rare cases, downstream to production. In such cases, further optimizations need to be achieved to ensure super linear scaling of the whole company.

Important Detail: a gatekeeper and organizational WIP control (Layer 1 and 2) are necessary prerequisites for introducing self-organization, even more so for agile CCPM. But this is not sufficient for achieving scalability. CCPM must be accompanied by self-organization at team level (Layer 2) and long term optimization (CIP Layer X).

The best results with agile CCPM can be achieved in multi project organizations with more than 10, and up to a hundred projects connected via a constraint phase or resource. Here, the major effect of agile CCPM is the dynamic reallocation of ressources to achieve optimal load distribution and reduction of residual underload.

LeSS – Large Scaled Scrum (LeSS 2018)

- A product development framework

Principle 1: Fractal space-filling	Fulfilled, the fractals are Scrum teams
Priniciple 2: Invariant ends	Invariant ends = Scrum team
Principle 3: Impedance match	LeSS uses Scrum as its basic framework and in the small version, with only one Product Owner for eight teams, cascaded Sprint Planning (product level Planing followed by team planning) and one Product Backlog are used. In the huge version requirement areas are build following the ToT concept. There are no special tools, processes or structures to illuminate impedance barriers (i.e. different mindsets (Dilts Pyramids)).
Principle 4: Self-organization	As stated in the chapters above, especially in chapter 9: Agile PMO 4.0, Scrum isn't a self-organized system. And LeSS offers no scaled self-organization structures (e.g. no target hierarchy).
Scaling impact (our hypotheses)	$a' \sim k*a'_{conv}$, $k \sim 1\text{-}2$ (because Scrum is not a self-organized system), $n < 1$ (because LeSS has no scaled self-organization)

SAFe – Scaled Agile Framework (SAFe 2018)

- A software product development framework

Principle 1: Fractal space-filling	Different fractals are used, so the space-filling is not perfect.
Priniciple 2: Invariant ends	Different team settings are used: Scrum team, Kanban teams and different other teams.
Principle 3: Impedance match	SAFe implements a structure hierarchy from portfolio, release and program to team level accompanied by a target hierarchy via a story map (Epics, Features, User Stories). Lean concepts can play a substantial role in detecting impedance mismatchs. But no mindset oriented impedance matching measures are used.
Principle 4: Self-organization	As stated in the above chapters, especially in chapter 9 Agile PMO 4.0: Scrum is not a self-organized system. SAFe offers certain scaled self-organization structures Setting parameter: Different roles and structures on the 3-4 SAFe levels Control parameter: Cadenced release and architecture planning, monitoring and coordination. Order parameter: Target hierarchy via story mapping.
Scaling impact (our hypotheses)	$a' \sim k \cdot a'_{conv}$, $k \sim 1\text{-}2$ (because Scrum is not a self-organized system), $n > 1$ (because SAFe has measures to support scaling). The danger is that the setting is so complicated that complexity is transformed to complicatedness. If this happens, the benefits of scaling measures are lost.

SAM 4.0 - Scaled Agile Management 4.0

- A general-purpose Agile Organization framework

Principle 1: Fractal space-filling	Fulfilled by circles (self-organized teams)
Priniciple 2: Invariant ends	Invariant ends = self-organized teams (circles)
Principle 3: Impedance match	Impedance match by mindset alignment (alignment of the top Dilts Pyramid levels)
Principle 4: Self-organization	The design and implementation of setting, control and order parameters is one of the key tasks of Management 4.0.
Scaling impact (our hypothesis)	$a' \sim 3 \cdot a'_{conv}, n > 1$ SAM 4.0 uses different parts of the "off-the-shelf" frameworks, especially the Collective Mind framework for team self-organization, combined with the CCPM framework for multi-project management organizations and the nested ToT circle structure with a transparent and documented Governance process.

Table 10-1: Agile Frameworks and their scaling principles

Literature

Feldman D (2018) Scaling and Fractals, https://www.complexityexplorer.org/courses/85-fractals-and-scaling, accessed on 26/07/2018

Full Scale Project and Agile Framework (2013) https://speed4projects.net/know-how/forschung/project-agile-framework/ accessed on 23/12/2018

Holacracy (2018) https://www.holacracy.org/ accessed on 26/07/2018, constitution v4.1

Komus A and Bell L(2018) Skalierung als Herausforderung – agile Skalierungsansätze und Frameworks nutzen, projektManagement aktuell 4.2018 GPM Deutsche Gesellschaft für Projektmanagement, Nürnberg

Olbert S, Prodoehl Hand G, Worley C G (2017) Organizational Agility AS A Competitive Factor – The "Agile Performer Index", NEOMA business school and goetzpartners

Robertson B J (2015) Holacracy: The New Management System for a Rapidly Changing World, Kindle Edition

Rüther C (2017) Soziokratie, Holakratie, Lalouxs "Reinventing Organization" und ...: Ein Überblick über die gängigsten Ansätze zur Selbstorganisation und Partizipation, 3rd edition BoD, Kindle Edition

LeSS (2018) Large-Scale Scrum: https://less.works/ , More with LeSS, accessed on 26/07/2018

SAFe (2018) Scaled Agile Framework http://www.scaledagileframework.com/, accessed on 26/07/2018

VISTEM (2018) consultancy specialized on implementing agile CCPM https://vistem.eu/referenzen/

West G (2017) Scale: The Universal Laws of Growth, Innovation, Sustainability, and the Pace of Life in Organisms, Cities, Economies, and Companies, Penguin Press, Kindle Edition

Wikipedia (2018) Scale invariance, https://en.wikipedia.org/wiki/Scale_invariance, accessed on 26/07/2018

10.2 Scaling Agile by using Critical Chain Project Management

Author: Wolfram Müller

Summary: Many agile concepts develop their power at team level and by concentrating on one single product. Larger projects or organizations have more than one team or one product – they have many projects. This chapter shows how to use the Critical Chain Project Management (CCPM) to make your portfolio and project management more agile by combining CCPM with the power of agile methods at team level.

Key Terms: Full Scale Agile Enterprise, Scaling Agile, Critical Chain Project Management, CCPM

Up until now we have talked solely about working in small teams. Sometimes this is not enough. If you want to achieve something great or on a large scale, then it will be necessary to work with many internal teams and external partners. You are in the project world, or even in the multi-project world. In this environment, totally different rules apply. You will need to deal with dependencies and deviations - not just in one project, but across many. This is much more complex than working with "just" one team.

But there is still hope. It is possible to still use some of the agile ideas. You must however, do a little bit more: you must manage several or many projects in an agile way.

Critical Chain Project Management

Projects are more complex compared to a single team's agile initiative. Real projects have lots of dependencies internally and externally. Furthermore, in projects, you want to make sure that the touch time (effective working time) is very near to the lead time (project duration) – so that there is as little waiting time as possible. Thus, duration deviations are far more critical. You must actively manage deviations by using buffers at appropriate places, before the integration point, at the end of feeding chains and at project end. These buffers do not prolong the project – they are taken from the work package time estimates and merely reallocated. Critical Chain Project Management (Goldratt 1997), (Techt 2014) has proven to be a very powerful approach for dealing with project management deviations in an agile way.

Critical Chain is not only management of single projects. It is mainly for portfolio or multi-project management. From this perspective, from the portfolio, project management looks like "production" – it is all about producing as many projects as possible, on time, and of good quality. Here, the focus is changing. In such an environment, the goal of increasing overall productivity means you must use your company constraint in as good a way as possible.

The Critical Chain approach at portfolio level is roughly like this:

1. First, the constraint needs to be identified. In project environment, this is not at all easy – the availability of resources fluctuates and estimates are unstable, so that it is impossible to fix the constraint at resource level. But, there is a phase in all projects that is extremely critical and where you need your best people handling it – this is the integration phase, where the feeding chains come together and the product is integrated and tested for the first time. In project environments, this phase is usually used as the constraint, because there will never be enough experienced people to eliminate this constraint. This constraint is not a real resource, so we refer to it as "Virtual Constraint" or "Virtual Drum".
2. Staggering projects according to the (virtual) constraint and accepting these due dates, is like threading pearls on a string – one after another. The time that a project is in the integration phase is the pearl. Some Companies are able to integrate more than one project in parallel – they have more strings. The load on the constraint (the number of strings) is adjusted in such a way that neither the constraint, nor any other resource or team is overloaded (Harmony 2010), (Techt 2014).

This ensures that the whole development system is optimally loaded, but not overloaded, which means that the work-in-progress is absolutely under control.

At its very core, this is Drum-Buffer-Rope scheduling (Goldratt 1992) – similar to the Ultimate Scrum (Tendon 2015, Chapter 24) concept. "Staggering at the constraint" builds the top layer of managing a project organization – the portfolio management layer.

One layer below, at the projects level, the core element of Critical Chain is the fever chart. It is calculated equal to Reliable Scrum (Müller 2014), (Tendon 2015, Chapter 23). The fever chart visualizes progress through time on the critical chain (the longest chain of dependent work packages with respect to resource availability) and consumption of the project buffer. To get this data estimate, every day the remaining duration of each open work package is reported and based on that the position in the fever chart is calculated. The chart gives you the traffic light status.

If you combine agile and CCPM work, packages are the connecting element. Work packages are equal to a (minimum marketable) release and its release backlog. From the perspective of a project, a release looks like a work package. Other stakeholders and work packages depend on this (your team's) release.

What makes Critical Chain so powerful is that resources are prioritized according to the traffic light status. The project with the least progress on the Critical Chain and the most buffer consumption gets all the focus and all necessary resources, to get it back into the yellow zone.

This has a huge advantage for agile teams. In organizations of a certain size, it is impossible to set up completely self-contained teams. The overall constraint of the organization is the final integration phase (not to be mistaken for continuous pre-integrations). In this phase the team needs the most experienced enterprise architects (always plural) and system/business engineers or very experienced employees. Sometimes the team needs decisions from top management or any other cross functional team. So, the traffic light (if red) could help the teams to get access to these rarely available resources. The visibility that is achieved by the traffic light ensures the success of the whole team.

Additionally, in Critical Chain, an overall closed loop corrective action process is established to keep the number of red projects below 10%. If this is the case, the work-in-progress control is working correctly and allocation of resources based on the traffic lights is also working. If less than 10% of projects are red, you can be sure that the due dates will be met with high levels of reliability.

And there are additional advantages. Because the system is controlled by focusing on the red projects, there is always a driver towards shortening the lead time. To get resources, the project manager is interested in having projects in the yellow, or sometimes in the red zone. Therefore, he has an intrinsic interest in reducing the lead times of his project. On the other hand, top management aims to reduce the number of red projects and will offer all possible support. This is the engine to avoid over buffering and over load at the same time – it is a closed loop corrective action system.

An additional benefit: you will get information as to which teams use a disproportional amount of buffer. These teams are not necessarily the root cause of delays, but a very good starting point to look at for the core problem and to start your continuous improvement process.

Agile Enterprise

Together with the concept of Reliable and Ultimate Scrum at the lowest team or release layer, you will get a blueprint of a very lean, agile, flow oriented, but also reliable, product development organization (Hannan 2014).

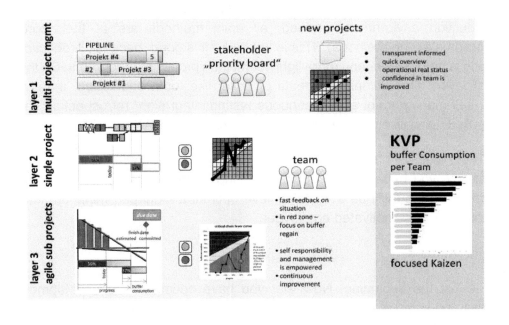

Figure 10-7: Layout of a Full Scale Agile Product Development Organization (Hannan 2014)

At the top level, you have Critical Chain as the multi-project management process, to ensure due dates are reliable and work-in-progress is under control. Taking a deeper look, you will see that the product development organization resembles production and is steered like a factory. Staggering at the constraint is no different than the production planning system of the third generation – Drum-Buffer-Rope or Simplified Drum Buffer Rope production management.

On the level below, single projects are the entities of concern. Single projects are much more complex - dependencies need to be taken care of and deviations handled. Here, Critical Chain buffer management (fever curves) can be used, to increase stability and reliability. This is real project management.

And if you look at a level lower, you will perhaps see sub projects (or even some smaller projects), work packages or releases that have very few external dependencies. These can be broken down into very small tasks. For these low-level work packages, releases or sub projects, fully-fledged project management would require far too many overheads. Again, it looks more like a production environment (indeed, all agile methods are at their core, production steering methods). This is not bad – it is good, because production steering is much easier and more lightweight than project management. On this lowest layer, all additional concepts of agile, like team orientation, iterative work, self-management and continuous testing/integration/ retrospection can be applied, to realize all the positive effects promised by Agile.

This is the blue print for an optimal development organization. At all levels and complexity, you have an appropriate steering method at your disposal, and consequently, you will be able to achieve optimal throughput, minimum lead time and the most motivated employees.

People Business

This is just the beginning. Now that you have optimized the development process and some of the supporting processes, you will have even more free capacity. But what will you do with this free capacity?

You can use this newly gained capacity and ability, to invest in people, in your vision and in all other relevant ideas, to finally achieve hyper-productivity.

Literature

Goldratt M E (1992) The Goal: A Process of Ongoing Improvement, North River Press

Goldratt M E (1997) Critical Chain, North River Press.

Techt U (2014) Project that Flow – more Projects in Less Time (Quistainable Business Solution), ibidem-Verlag, Stuttgart - available in German, French and Spanish

Hannan M, Müller W, Robinson H (2014) The CIO's Guide to Breakthrough Project Portfolio Performance – Applying the Best of Critical Chain, Agile and Lean, Fortezza Consulting

Tendon S, Müller W (2015) Hyper-Productive Knowledge Work Performance – The TameFlow Approach and Its Application to Scrum and Kanban, J. Ross Publishing – Chapters 22 to 25

Müller W (2013) Agile Project Management: Critical Chain and Reliable/Ultimate Scrum equals to an Agile Enterprise, TOCICO 2013, Bad Nauheim, available on YouTube:
https://www.youtube.com/watch?v=9SQbhAKq5_M

Harmony (2010) Strategy & Tactic Tree Library - Projects Co S&T_Aug2010, available at https://harmonytoc.com

11 Agile Transformation 4.0 - new

Author: Alfred Oswald

Summary: Agile Transformation 4.0 is based on a four-phase cognitive PDCA Transformation. In contrast to changes and transitions, transformations accept fuzziness in all aspects. We outline the relationship to methods like Design Thinking or Theory U. The Theory of Transformation and its related interventions are based on recent scientific insights. We summarize the key characteristics of Agile Transformation 4.0 using a transformation example.

Key Terms: Change, Transition, Transformation, Collective Mind, Learning Organization, Design Thinking, Theory U, Neuro Linguistic Programming (NLP), Dilts Pyramid, PDCA Cycle, Cognitive Bias, Tipping Point, Social Network, Social Contagion, True and False News, Theory of Change, Business Model Canvas, Governance

Introduction

As we have already stated at the beginning of this book, we live in a complex world and many believe that with the realm of digitization, connectivity inside the social and the technical domain will grow, as well as that between the social, technical and natural domain. This will result in previously unknown emergent phenomena with turbulent and sometimes chaotic dynamics. On the other side is complexity directly linked to our existence (Oswald 2018) and to innovation and welfare (Hausmann 2012).

The challenge for individuals, organizations and societies is to cope with complexity and the resulting dynamic phenomena. Individuals, organizations and societies need to learn how to cope with complexity, based on their different starting points. We speak of a transformation process of an individual, an organization or a society, because awareness of the characteristics of the starting point, of the future, and of the route from the starting point to the future, are fuzzy to differing degrees. The literature rarely differentiates between change, transition and transformation (Doppler 2008, Bridges 2003, Kotter 2012). In Figure 11-1, we emphasize the difference between change, transition and transformation management (Oswald 2018).

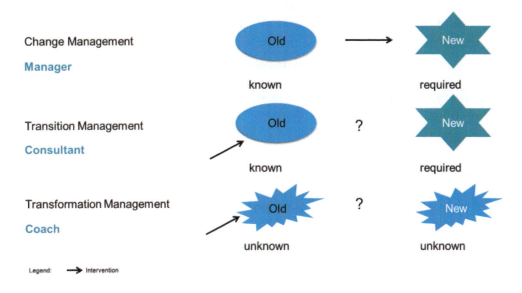

Figure 11-1: The characteristics of change, transition and transformation management (Oswald 2018)

We speak of Agile Transformation 4.0, if

- an individual, organization, or society enhances their meta-competence to regulate complexity, or in other words, to become more agile. The degree of agility required depends on the specific context of an individual, organization or society.
- the starting point of the transformation is fuzzy. We do however, try to fix the starting point using theories or models, whilst being aware that we can never be sure how close to reality we are.
- the end point of the transformation is fuzzy and is a preliminary end point. The end point is probably the starting point for a new transformation process.

- the route from the starting point to the end point is also fuzzy. In our role as transformation coach or as part of a team, we make interventions, checking the interventions and their effectiveness by comparing the actual intervention results and the planned route to the current fuzzy goal. In chapter 4.1 we have already outlined some of the aspects of transformation to agility. Success of the transformation is measured by assessing agility within the relevant, specific context.

In summary, it is the goal of Agile Transformation to enhance the agility of an individual, an organization or society, and to use theories, models and intervention techniques to lead that transformation.

Transformation Model

We use the transformation model proposed by Oswald et al. (Oswald 2018), which is outlined in Figure 11-2:

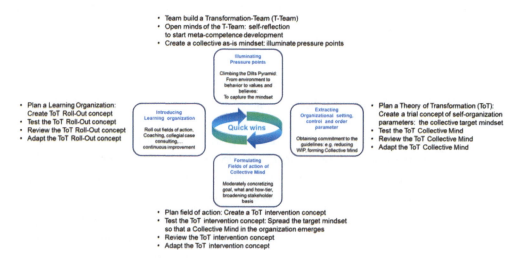

Figure 11-2: Transformation Model

The central ideas of the transformation model, which follows a nested Plan Do Check/Inspect Act/Adapt cycle, are the following:

Illuminating pressure points: A transformation team (T-Team) with open minds is required, capable of self-reflection and meta-competence. The T-Team includes personality diversity, which allows the team to think out-of-the-box and to transport a Theory of Transformation (ToT) later on to the whole organization. T-Team members know their own mindset and the interaction of different mindset and potential conflicts. The illumination of pressure points is carried out by analysing the different organizational mindsets in an organization using Dilts Pyramids. Analysing the Dilts Pyramids means analysing the specific levels of the pyramid from bottom to top, from specific context and behaviour, to mission and vision. Pressure points are pain points where processes, structure, roles or behavior are deemed to be inadequate.

What is essential in this phase of the transformation is that the T-Team develop a Collective Mind with respect to the As-is situation.

We refer also to the close link to other methodologies: Design Thinking methodologie (Hasso Plattner Institute 2017), especially the process steps 'understand', 'observe' and 'define point of view (as-is part)'; Theory U process steps 'downloading past patterns', 'seeing with fresh eyes' and 'sensing from the field' ((Scharmer 2018), see also (Veit 2018) for the link between Theory U and the integral model Spiral Dynamics); or the core transformation of NLP using the Dilts Pyramid (Mohl 2010).

Extracting organizational setting, control and order parameters: The T-Team plans a Theory of Transformation using open mindsets. For the main sub-organizations and the organization as a whole, an estimate (e.g. hypotheses) of self-organization parameters and the To-be Dilts Pyramid are created. The As-is Dilts Pyramids and the To-be Dilts Pyramids are linked by intermediate Dilts Pyramids. This reflects potential steps and interventions that are en route from the As-is to the To-be situation. Figure 4-6 in chapter 4.1 outlines an organization with different sub-structure levels and their related self-organization levels, emphasizing an iterative process (PDCA-cycles) and different interwoven self-organization parameters for different organization levels.

It is essential in this phase of the transformation that the T-Team creates a Collective Mind of the Theory of Transformation and that the team tests, reviews and adapts the load-bearing capacity of the Theory of Transformation. This can be carried out using gedanken experiments, testing quick wins or by dedicated feedback from a selected few people.

In addition, links to known methods can help an understanding of the essentials of this process step: Design Thinking with the process steps 'define point of view (to-be part)' and 'ideate', Theory U with 'prescensing' and NLP Core Transformation with 'core states'. In particular, the design of the target hierarchy (the order parameter) may also benefit from experiences of the Theory of Change (Wikipedia 2018).

Formulating fields of action of the Collective Mind: Based on the Theory of Transformation (As-is Dilts Pyramids, intermediate Dilts Pyramids, To-be Dilts Pyramids and related self-organization parameters), fields of action are defined and prioritized. In a larger organization it is likely that different As-is Dilts Pyramids will be found, which should be analysed and assessed with respect to their necessity and potential to enhance the agility of the whole organisation. Interventions are expected to bring an intermediate organizational mindset (e.g. the culture modelled by a Dilts Pyramid) to the next intermediate organizational mindset en route to the To-be Dilts Pyramid(s). It may not be necessary to reach only one To-be Dilts Pyramid, but the difference in the organizational mindsets of the sub-organizations should not be too great. The test (we refer to it as a test, because it is possible that the implementation of the Theory of Transformation transforms the transformation itself) of the To-be Dilts Pyramid and any related intermediate interventions are reviewed and adapted based on implementation insights. The T-Team creates a self-organized learning environment to support the emergence of the transformation.

During this phase of the transformation, it is essential that the T-Team is open to accepting a transformation of the Theory of Transformation resulting from implementation insights.

We would like to point out the similarities with other methodologies: Design Thinking steps 'prototype' and 'test'; Theory U steps 'crystalizing (vision and intention)' and prototyping (creating the new by linking head, heart, hand)'; or NLP core transformation step 'transform the experience by the core state'.

Introducing Learning Organizations: During the previous phase, the organization has already started to become a Learning Organization. The implementation of the Theory of Transformation is based on practices which support learning by self-organization. The organization lives by the Management 4.0 thumb rule of continuous improvement (PDCA-Cycle): Management 4.0 = Mindset*Governance*Techniques.

The similarities with other methodogies are: Design Thinking does not include an explicit Roll-Out delivery process step, Theory U involves 'performing (by operating from the whole)', and NLP core transformation 'integrates the revealed core states' in all past, present and future experiences to perform with a more holistic and agile perspective in the future.

Scientific Insights

As stated above, we believe in evidence-based management based on scientific models and theories. We believe that the above transformation process can benefit substantially from the following scientific insights. We are aware that these scientific insights are achieved using different contexts or settings than those found in a transformation process, but nevertheless, based on our own qualitative experiences, we are convinced that these insights provide strong guidelines for the design of the setting and control parameters of a transformation:

Insight 1: The spread of true and false news have different characteristics (Vosoughi 2018). Vosoughi et al. have shown, using a large scale data analysis of Twitter between 2006 to 2017 that true and false news reports online have different characteristics:

"Falsehood reached more people at every depth of a cascade (a rumor cascade begins on Twitter when users makes an assertion about a topic in a tweet) than the truth, meaning that many more people retweeted falsehood than they did the truth." "… we found that falsehood were 70% more likely to be retweeted than the truth.." "…user characteristics and network structure could not explain the differential diffusion of truth and falsity…" "We found that false rumors inspired replies expressing greater surprise…, corroborating the novelty hypothesis, and greater disgust …, whereas the truth inspired replies that inspired greater sadness …, anticipation…, and trust…"

Insight 2: Leveraging cognitive biases and social influence can make transformation efforts more effective (Cinner 2018). Cinner used the insights of cognitive biases to support efforts of sustainability. Based on Kahneman and Tversky's theory, Oswald et al. (Oswald 2018) discussed similar insights in the context of complexity regulation.

We have adopted Cinner's crucial insights with respect to transformation processes:

Cognitive biases	Social influences
The status quo bias: Most people prefer to maintain the status quo. This can be addressed by setting the default options so that people need to "opt out" rather than "opt in" to transformation options	People want to fit in with what "most people do" and what "should be done". Communication social norms about transformation can help to encourage transformation behaviors.
Anchoring: People tend to rely on initial information. This bias can be leveraged by setting cognitive anchors early, and at a distance from critical thresholds.	Observabilty: People behave more prosocially when they think others know what they are doing. Increasing observability can promote sustainable behaviors.

Cognitive biases	Social influences
Issue framing: People tend to have a strong aversion to losses. Highlighting what they stand to lose by keeping practices and policies without transformation, helps to catalyse action.	Block leaders: Those who we receive information from can be as powerful as what we receive. Trusted messengers and block leaders can amplify uptake.
Decoys: When people have trouble making decisions, the desirability of transformation options can be emphasized with the use of less diserable "decoy" options.	Public commitments: People want to maintain prestige and reputation, which can be leveraged through public commitments or pledges to change behaviour.

Table 11-1: Leveraging behavioral insights for transformation (Cinner 2018)

Insight 3: Behavior is spread by complex social contagions (Centola 2018a): "While simple contagions spread most effectively when bridges are long, complex contagions depend on bridges that are wide. (Annotation: Simple contagions are e.g. news; complex contagions require e.g. an individual behaviour change. In a social network a bridge links nodes via ties in the network. The length of a bridge is the distance that is spanned, the width is the number of ties it contains.) Wide bridges create redundancies that slow diffusion, thus for simple contagions, too much clustering means that there are too few long ties, which slows down the diffusion process; while for complex contagions, too little clustering means that there are too few wide bridges, which not only slows down diffusion but can prevent it entirely." "Relational factors aside, the results …show that placing people into clustered patterns of association - whether in an urban neighbourhood or in an online community – can significantly improve the spread of behaviour (Annotation: clusters are built by wide network bridges)."

Insight 4: Evidence for tipping points in social transformation (Centola 2018b): "Once the tipping point is reached, the actions of a minority group trigger a cascade of behaviour change that rapidly increases the acceptance of a minority view. …the power of small groups comes not from their authority or wealth but from from their commitment" to the transformation. The social systems cross a tipping point if the the critical group size, the "critical mass", is about 25%.

Example

Let us imagine an organization, for example a bank, an automotive supplier, a medical device manufacturer, or any other enterprise, which has been confronted by the effects of digitization. Figure 13-1 in chapter 13 outlines the key elements of digitization: This requires leaving the previous comfort zone, to become more agile, to create a new digital business model, and to transform the organization into a learning organization.

Let us furthermore assume that our organization has 1000 employees with 10 departments. Figure 11-3 outlines an As-is situation in a traditional, more or less hierarchical organization. The As-is situation is fuzzy, because we can not be 100% sure about the structure of the organizational mindset (i.e. the culture of the organization). In the figure we assumed that leaders' mindsets are different and that the related organizational mindset in their department corresponds to the leaders' mindset. But e.g. for Team 11 we assumed some uncertainty about the team mindset, indicated by a second Dilts Pyramid.

The first phase of the transformation process "Illuminating Pressure Points" starts with an initiation team of perhaps 2-3 people whose task it is, to start the whole process.

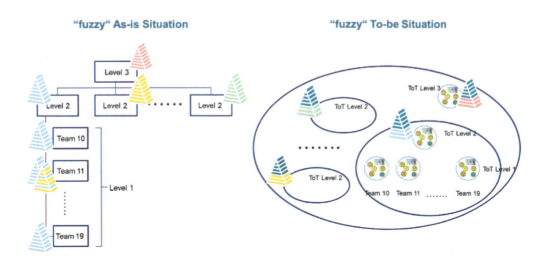

Figure 11-3: As-is and To-be situation of an example organization

They assess the As-is situation and make a potential first assumption about the organizational future (To-be situation). This small initiation team looks for appropriate members for the future T-Team in the organization. The T-Team should contain no more than seven people. On the assumption that the transformation project is a missionary project (Oswald 2009, Oswald 2018), they look for appropriate people (mainly with _NT_ or _NF_ temperament - a slightly more extroverts, a balance of Judging and Perceiving preferences, a v-meme mixture including green and yellow - maybe even turquoise value memes). In addition, they take into account Insights 3 and 4: It is better to choose the appropriate members, so that wide social network bridges can be built. This will probably result in T-Team members coming only from 2-3 departments containing ten employees. It is also a good idea to identify hubs in the social network. Hubs are influencers who have many more ties than other people in the organization. Hubs who are not convinced by the transformation may act as blockers. If these hubs cannot be included in the T-Team, because they do not have the right mindset, the T-Team will need to find a strategy later on to convince these hubs. Based on Insight 4, T-Team members should be selected who can contribute with their existing social network, so that the tipping point limit of 25% is exceeded as early as possible in the transformation process.

Once the T-Team has been selected, the first transformation phase can be started: To start with, T-Team members are trained to use the Dilts Pyramid with its related level models (MBTI, basic needs, motives and values, basic assumptions, Spiral Dynamics, target hierarchy, Collective Mind and self-organization (synergetics), as well as context evaluation by e.g project type evaluation). In this way, Management 4.0 principles and techniques are introduced. The T-Team will discover their own personal preferences and start to understand the current As-is situation. Enlightenment starts when potential contexts, related behaviors and capabilities are understood. Pressure points are identified in the organization and at the interfaces to the external environment (customers, market, external stakeholders). Based on this information, the higher levels of the Dilts Pyramides can be analyzed. It might be that the As-is situation reflects a more heterogenous organization mindset structure. Initial estimates of potential intervention areas for the transformation can be identified. Based on Insight 1, a communication strategy and activities for the whole organization can be started, whilst explaining the transformation process and using real news with a high surprise factor. These communication strategies may e.g. include news similar to the following:

- Agility does not mean that everyone has to use Scrum!
- Agility starts in the head!
- Practice is not correct or beneficial, because it is just practice!
- Mindset has a factor 1000 more essential than the usage of techniques.
- Agile Techniques are the least significant of all essential factors!
- Agility may mean that nothing changes!
- Leadership is essential in a self-organized team!
- Self-organization does not mean self-management!

In addition, organization-specific news with a high surprise factor on the organizational aspects of digitization can also be used. The T-Team can analyse rumors in the organization and also feed these back as actual news with a high surprise factor!

The second phase of the transformation "Extracting organizational setting, control and order parameters" is dedicated to finding a Collective Mind of transformation in the T-Team by developing a Theory of Transformation. The focus in this phase lies on the To-be situation. The T-Team develops To-be Dilts Pyramids, emphasizing that more than one Dilts Pyramide can exist, but taking care that the differences in the Dilts Pyramids (e.g. the overall organizational mindset, departmental mindset and individual mindsets) are not too heterogenous. In particular, there should be one target hierarchy, which should be adapted by the Learning Organization in the later transformation phases. Frameworks like Design Thinking (Hasso Plattner Institute 2017), Theory of Change (Wikipedia 2018), Theory U (Scharmer 2018) or Business Model Canvas (Osterwalder 2010) can be also used to find a Collective Mind target hierarchy. Using the target hierarchy, the first trial of the order parameter can be found. The first trials of the control parameters and the setting parameters are also defined. These three parameter types constitute the first trial of the Governance of the organization. On the behaviour and capabilities level (e.g. structures, process, roles), it may not be necessary for all departments to be organized in such a manner that self-organization is necessary to make the organization as a whole agile. But nevertheless, at a very minimum, the key persons in these organizations will need to develop an Agile Mindset during the transformation. This guarantees that the sub-organizations stay open to future transformations and that the interface to the whole organization is designed in an appropriate manner to allow agility of the whole.

A first draft of an organizational Transformation Charta has been published. The transformation Charta is a small document which contains only the essential guidelines of the organizational mindset and related Governance.

If a Collective Mind in a trial version of the future To-be situation is found in the T-Team, the T-Team needs to implement the Theory of Transformation and start one or more PDCA cycles in the third phase of the transformation.

For the third phase of transformation, "Formulating fields of action of Collective Mind", we recommend starting the trial implementation in the 2-3 departments from where the T-Team members have originated. This takes into account Insight 2, surmounting the 25% threshold as quickly as possible. The T-Team has to be very open minded and must not bring any mental bias into the departmental teams. Testing includes a collective understanding of the pressure points and approval of the predefined Governance parameters. The departmental teams start with a T-Team vision and develops their own target hierarchy and discusses and (optionally) approves predefined control and setting parameters. In all of the transformation phases, but especially here, transformation can be supported by systemic organization constellations or role play, to illuminate "real causes" (Klein 2010, Oswald 2018).

Subsequently, all results of the trial implementation (testing) will be checked, consolidated and fed back to the departmental teams. Departments not involved in these PDCA cycles, will be kept informed via workshops and trained by the T-Team and other members of the 2-3 departments. If necessary, Governance parameters will be adopted and detailed Governance parameters derived from these for the departments.

The organizational Transformation Charta is then updated.

Based on Insight 2, communication strategies use the following design principles:

- Novelties are not highlighted: The link to past roles, processes and structures are always emphasized.
- Self-organization parameters are defined as social norms and hinted that they are already well-accepted in the organization.
- The link to the true news in phase 1 of the transformation is emphasized.

- The retained processes, structures and roles, values and basic assumptions are highlighted.
- Hubs in the social network receive a lot of attention and are monitored.
- Those people with high values in the fields of appreciation, prestige, status, reputation and power, will receive a microtargeting strategy with the aim being that these values are minimized or substituted.
- All activities are monitored by a public commitment, e.g. sign up the Transformation Charta and related documents.

The fourth phase of transformation, "Introducing Learning Organization", is the final "test" of a successful transformation. A successful transformation can be recognized by the fulfilling of the following principles:

- The majority of the members of the organization have a certain level of meta-competence (a minimum of learning Level II, see chapter 3.2). Meta-competencies are practiced and trained. In all departments, agile techniques like time-box, visualisation, fast delivery and testing are practiced. In addition, if full agile frameworks are not practiced, this is because they are not appropriate.
- A sufficient number of organisational members (about 25%) are capable of designing new Governance guidelines if the context requires it.
- Social factors are accepted as the difference that makes the difference. Coaching and collegial case consulting are accepted as tools for supporting personal growth. A community of Agile Transformation Coaches will accompany the Learning Organization.
- Complexity is monitored and regulated. The principles of self-organization are understood and practiced to assess e.g. (Scaled) Agile Frameworks
- Setting parameters are monitored and adjusted: The design of space (e.g. rooms) and time (e.g. appointements) reflects an Agile Mindset.
- Control parameters are monitored and adjusted: E.g. In all departments WIP (Work-in-Progress) is monitored and regulated. Agreed organizational values are monitored and adjusted.

- Order parameters are monitored and adjusted: The target hierarchy is contionuously adjusted from top to buttom and vice versa. Each member of an organization shapes the target hierarchy with their contribution.
- Each department develops an Agile Mindset, also if (off-the-shelf) Agile Frameworks are not appropriate for their work.
- Each department chooses the Framework best suited for its work. Frameworks or tools are not agile or not agile per se. The tool repertoire is always hybrid.

In particular, we have observed the following resulting Agile Practices:

A multi project management organization implementing the principles of Critical Chain Project Management

A product development organization with a medium degree of innovation using an agile team structure.

A product development team with a high degree of innovation using frameworks like Collective Mind Method and Design Thinking.

Literature

Bridges W (2003) Managing Transitions. Making the most of change, Da Capo Press, Cambridge MA

Centola D (2018a) How Behavior Spreads: The Science of Complex Contagions (Princeton Analytical Sociology, Band 3), Princeton Univers. Press

Centola D, Becker J, Brackbill D and Baronchelli A (2018b) Experimental evidence for tipping points in social convention, Science 360, 1116-1119, 8 June 2018

Cinner J (2018) How behavioral science can help conservation, Science 362, Issue 6417, 889-890, 23 November 2018

Doppler K, Lauterburg C (2008) Change Management, 12. Aufl. Campus Verlag GmbH

Hasso Plattner Institute (2017) Documentation Design Thinking workshop

Hausmann R, Hidalgo C et al. (2012) The Atlas of Economic Complexity, Puritan Press, Cambridge MA.

Klein P, Linder-Hofmann B (2010) Buddha, Freud und Falco – Ein Dialog im 21. Jahrhundert, Szenische Aufstellungen im kollektiven Bewusstseinsfeld, Verlag arcus-lucis, Oberrohrbach, Österreich

Kotter J P (2012) Leading change, Harvard Business Review Press, Kindle edition

Mohl A (2010) Der große Zauberlehrling. Das NLP-Arbeitsbuch für Lernende und Anwender, Teil 1, Verlag Junfermann, Paderborn

Osterwalder A, Pigneur Y (2010) Business Model Generation, John Wiley & Sons, Inc., Hoboken NJ

Oswald A, Köhler J and Schmitt R (2018) Project Management at the Edge of Chaos, Springer Heidelberg

Scharmer O (2018) Essentials of Theory U, Berrett-Koehler Publishers, Kindle edition

Veit H (2018) Praxishandbuch Integrale Organisationsentwicklung – Grundlagen für zukunftsfähige Organisationen, Wiley-VCH Verlag, Weinheim

Vosoughi S, Roy D, Aral S (2018) The spread of true and false news online, Science 359, 1146-1151, 9 March 2018

Wikipedia (2018) Theory of Change
https://en.wikipedia.org/wiki/Theory_of_change, accessed on 17/10/2018

PART III Agile Management in Practice

12 Learnings and Guidance for the Implementation of Agility - new

Author: Norbert Schaffitzel, Steve Raue, Frank Edelkraut, Rüdiger Lang

Summary: This chapters discusses a selection of potential "fuckups" that may occur when implementing agility in an organization. The fuckups and the aim for the sweet spot of agility, will hopefully provide a practical guidance during the move to agility.

Key Terms: Agility, Fuckups, Social Romanticism, Agile Dogmatism, Agile Scaling, Agile Governance

Introduction

Any new way of organizing work and organizations includes a wide range of chances and risks. This is especially true for agile working. The aim is to deal with complex topics and context, but there is no one way, rather a wide range of possibilities and merging practices. Every organization that implements Agile will experience its own pitfalls, drawbacks, resistance etc. The nice part about the agile community is how failure is seen. Quite the opposite to many organizational cultures, the agile community celebrates failure as a chance to learn and improve. And it is!

One recently implemented "agile format" is the so called "Fuckup Night". Here people describe problems they faced and errors they have made. They are proud to share these experiences, to enable others to do better. In the following, we would like to address a few of the many fuckups, which may occur in your agile transformation process. We hope they will help you by fostering the essential factor of success: critical thinking!

Fuckup "Social romanticism in agile management"

Conspiracy of optimism

Description

Agile is a trend and a buzzword. The vision quickly emerged from a team of quality engineers in a large production company. They were asked to improve performance by leadership, and at the same time, they were also given permission to think of a new form of organization, and were given responsibility as a team. Individual KPIs were to be dropped in favour of overall project and team measurement.

The first thing they discovered on the Internet was the Agile Manifesto and it read well. "Individuals and interactions over processes and tools" sounded just what they were looking for. They pondered over the idea of more freedom and self-guided work. They thought of self-responsibility as a way of delivering what each individual feels capable of doing. But then the optimism ended right there, when the team and its lead had further talks with higher management about their expectations, interfaces and alignment with other parts of the organization.

Once the team had received training in agile principles it quickly understood that Agile means high performing teams, which follow an even more structured way of collaboration. Self-responsibility means setting your own to be able to function with the rest of the team, but even more importantly, with other departments. It implies a strong level of competence to be able to know what the team needs and how each individual contributes to improve the delivery of a product. It also implies continuous improvement of work processes and critical reflection of the team itself.

The romanticism around Agile needs to take into account an optimism which is grounded in reality. In reality it is to deliver better products, faster and with continuously improving performance. This is not an easy task. The question is whether your teams are ready to agree on this reality and be honest about what is working and what it is not.

Discussion

When teams decide to integrate Agile, it is important that they understand two dimensions first.

According to Noel Tichy, a leader has to perform two core functions: Define reality and mobilize resources. This means the leader needs to retain a fine balance between rallying the team to accept a new way of working and creating optimism about Agile in general, but at the same time ensuring that this optimism is grounded in reality. Most teams in rigid structures are aware of the benefits of their current way of working. Employees either hide mistakes or hope not to make them. Or they live in a competitive environment where being better than everyone else is essential for survival. Both have their limitations: either comfortable invisibility reduces performance in the company, because talent is lost, or individuals are in a constant survival mode for achieving success.

Creating optimism for agile working is crucial. Teams need a vision and a desire to embark on a journey where everyone has the freedom to realise their potential. Initially, the team will need to lose its fear of sharing and working together, of breaking with old habits and being more trustful. Yet, all these grand words can create two traps which need to be avoided.

The first is the conspiracy of optimism. Being overly optimistic often occurs when employees create unreasonably high expectations about their new freedom. For instance, when liberal work attitudes are interpreted to mean that anyone can do what they want. Or on the other hand, when it results in a laissez-faire attitude. This means that there is danger of losing sight of the fact that the company is still competing in the market for the best product and to attain clear targets for financial success. Such optimism is not grounded in reality and will lead to failure. In most companies this surfaces when team members are so optimistic that they fail to speak up about mistakes and failures when they should. Everyone is hyped up by the success of finally being agile, that they do not wish for any problems to cloud the view. It becomes imperative that everyone tries to keep the ship on course, even though there is a hole in the hull which needs urgent repair. Team members who speak up are branded as pessimists.

The second trap is more common, but also needs mentioning. It is the conspiracy of pessimism. It is easy to be overly negative at the beginning, highlighting all the pitfalls of changing to a somewhat successful status. The logic is, why change something that has worked so far. This kind of pessimism, grounded in fear of change, creates negative scenarios, which eventually also become a self-fulfilling prophecy.

Tipps & Tricks

While the trap of being overly pessimistic is the more common scenario, the conspiracy of optimism carries a very real potential of failure. In the end, no one in the organization will understand what really happened and Agile will be blamed as being dysfunctional, when it was the team itself. There are a few key aspects which are critical, and they all revolve around optimism grounded in strict and clear reality. The leadership and the team need to have a clear understanding of why Agile should be implemented in the first place and what it is that it can actually improve. This implies a very clear picture of the status quo, including an unconditional investigation into current problems and challenges. This is the baseline for choosing the right agile practices and building a business case around it.

Secondly, whilst integrating Agile, it is important to keep a clear overview of business targets, KPIs and the market. It is of no use integrating Agile just because it is cool. New ways of working actually need to align to these targets and KPIs.

Literature

Tichy N M (2007) Leadership Engine: Building Leaders at Every Level (Rapid-Read Handbook), Pritchett

Agile Manifesto (2001) Agilemanifesto.org, accessed on 17/10/2018

Fuckup "Agile methods dogmatism"

How dogmas influence behavior and complicate the path to agility

Description

The scene could be at any agile community meeting: People are standing together and discussing agility. Quite often a young "agile influencer" leads the discussion giving his version of truth. If believers do not follow the rules, downfall is certain. This may formulated as:

- Only if scrum is played by the rules, can it deliver any outcome.
- The Agile Manifesto says...
- If companies do not become 100% agile, they are doomed.
- The older generation do not really understand Agile as it has never been part of their world.
- Agility needs self-organised teams and managers are hell in this respect. So we should get rid of all managers. At least we should not have any contact with them.

All of the above statements have been actually heard at conferences or other gatherings. You may have heard something similar yourself.

Discussion

Unfortunately, such attitude are to be found frequently, but they represent just one side of the coin. The opposite, in the form of dogmatism can also be found, i.e. denial of any benefit agile methods may contribute to an organization, or with statements such as "this will never work here". One way or the other, such dogmas can not help in finding a proper approach for handling a complex business environment.

With respect to such opinions for and against agility, it would be pertinent to take a closer look at these statements, or more precisely, the context (person, situation, pre-experience etc.) in which these statements have been made. There is the chance that some "truth" may lie amongst these dogmatic views. Let us take an example. One such statement may be: "All our functions and roles have to be purely agile, otherwise Agile will not work at all." This statement has some truth at its core, i.e. agility requires end-to-end responsibility and appropiate organization design. On the other hand, this view ignores facts as for example legal or structural restrictions, the inability of some employees to show the required self-responsibility, and so on. Last but not least, it ignores the fact that agile methods are very successful in working on complex topics, but highly ineffective with simple or even complicated environments. Here, dogmatism will most probably have a negative impact. Dogmatism may also have positive effects, if the agile transformation is enforced by claiming consequence, discipline or a proper organizational framework. We should not forget that Agile is like performing a somersault. Once you have started the move, you cannot stop it without falling face first.

What is the difference between entitled and unjustified dogmas? There is no clear demarcation line, since agility itself is a complex matter and contradictions and inconsistencies are hard to avoid. Those discussing it will all have different opinions. Agility is a matter of permanent negotiation.

Independent of where dogmatism is coming from, the connected risks demand a minimization strategy. This is especially important within an agile context, due to the required open minded mindset and the necessity to permanently learn from experiments and improvement activities. Dogmatism is quite the opposite.

Beside the negative emotions which result from dogmatism, there are three more aspects to look at:

- Shortening → If only a few aspects are taken into account, the complexity of any context is apparently reduced, but it will be difficult to be innovative and open to discussion.
- Paralyses → In dogmatic environments change is difficult to realize.

- Isolation → Dogmatic persons and groups tend to create borders, and live in a filter bubble.

Tips & Tricks

How should dogmatism be identified and handled? A critical first step is to identify dogmatism as it is. For this, everyone should be self-reflective and ask themselves, what are my behaviors, beliefs, rules, etc.? Do I use words, which could be indicators for dogmatism? Killer arguments, strict statements and so on, may be the result of personal dogmas.

A useful tool for minimizing the risk of dogmatism, is permanent feedback within diverse groups. This enables different views on discussed topics and quite often there is the realization, that there is no right or wrong way, but rather a "yes and …". In agile methods there is clear room for feedback, namely during reviews and retrospectives. When carried out often, this may prevent dogmatism and lead to permanent negotiation (and agreement) of actual common sense.

Another element that helps to minimize dogmatism is the existence of cross-functional teams. Due to different backgrounds and a focus on different aspects of the complex topic worked on, it is harder to maintain dogmatic views. In addition, they tend to have broader life experience and educational backgrounds.

Literature

Glasl F (2004) Konfliktmanagement: Ein Handbuch für Führungskräfte, Beraterinnen und Berater, Verlag Freies Geistesleben

Reference to chapter 3.5 "Principles of Scrum and Kanban Agile Frameworks"

Fuckup "Agility as a fashion"

Why being Agile is not useful for everyone

Description

When something becomes a trend it attracts more people or organizations. They want to label themselves as state of the art and as being first. However, being first is not necessarily being right. And this is even much more true if you fail to evaluate the individual fit for your business. The same is true for Agile. Let's take an example: The German state department is well known for being largely bureaucratic and resistant to change. The Business and IT departments, on the whole, remained true to their own competences and cooperation was rare. Most of this established way of work was due to a stable environment with few changes in service to customers, the citizens. In addition, it was clear to everyone that it was not economic performance and continuous market adaptation that was important, but mainly guaranteeing reliable, timely service with the highest integrity to citizens. It has worked remarkably well over the past few decades. Yet, Agile has been practiced by some of the IT departments and subsequently, management in some areas began to reflect on the idea of establishing user-centred work processes in various parts of the organization. However, implementing Agile in an economic business is different than implementing Agile in a state department. The former targets a market, higher revenue, lower costs. The latter targets customer groups as well as lower costs, but also works under federalist parity and the expectation of reliability. The organization is also much bigger than most companies. Understandably, there was some resistance to being more Agile.

What is true for state departments must also be considered true for any business. The trend of going Agile is very much dependent on careful evaluation of which agile practice is useful, in which part of the organization, and the time frame for implementation and business targets.

Discussion

Agile competes with other trends, such as robotic process automation (RPA), digitalization, AI, etc. If we assume that cost efficiency is a goal of any organisation, RPA can be considered useful for most. Agile, on the other hand, is a multitude of practices for different parts and purposes of an organization. If we look at certain public services and the respective IT infrastructure, Agile only makes limited sense. The registration office for instance, provides basic services around registering new citizens. The target for this service is not to compete in the market, but to provide accuracy, speed and customer service with new service channels in the digital age. So while it is useful to think in use cases and agile testing and piloting, other aspects of Agile may not be useful. Having co-located, interdisciplinary teams who are realizing a project, may get a higher value than those implementing it in day-to-day operation at the front desk or the IT back office. On the other hand, it may be fruitful to consider overall agile governance structures to enhance decision-making. It may also be possible to think about a product oriented, decentralized IT organization, which integrates front desk and back office per product group. In this way, it would be possible to think about cross-functional tribes (as in the Spotify organization model) to enhance knowledge transfer.

Agile production patterns (e.g. Scrum), however, are not quintessential to a registration service as a product, which has remained largely the same for years. In this case, it may be wiser to look at lean production patterns as a way of optimizing repetitive processes.

Tips & Tricks

How to avoid the mistake of implementing a trend? First, be aware that Agile is a set of practices and not one solution. Scrum, for instance, has largely originated from lean production. In its original form it may not be useful to creative companies, although some of its team practices can be adopted.

Second, know your business targets well. This may be obvious for a company as a whole, but needs careful elaboration in the case of particular teams or departments. It is more than common that there is often a great divide due to the differing business targets of the sales departments and project managers. What the sales department promises in order to achieve their sales targets varies greatly from the aims of project managers who are driven by resource availability, scope, quality and budget.

Third, evaluate the scope of your business to estimate how useful it is to become Agile. Even if a multitude of practices are to be implemented, there needs to be a discussion on which department is most suitable to be selected first – the one that is most advanced in terms of Agile, or a selection for political reasons, or a department which needs to undergo significant change. This creates the space for agile tools if they can provide a guidance based on measurements.

Fourth, look at the process. Agile is also process-oriented. When implementing Agile, consider the entire value stream in the respective part of the organization. Otherwise, you will create disconnection, for instance, between front office and back office, which will lead to even more inefficiency.

Fifth, know how to start. Be careful about whether you want to start with a sandboxed pilot. This could include using volunteers from the organization and starting in one team and a project which uses agile practices. If it is part of a larger transformation for a particular value stream or department, then it may be wise to use the situation to implement Agile during the transformation. This will involve a high level of participation by the affected employees and an highly competent transformation management. Lastly, you may also decide to start in a venture company with a cooperation partner who is already agile.

This is only a selection of possible ways to start.

Literature

Agile Alliance (2018) www.agilealliance.org, accessed on 17/10/2018

Reference to chapter 10.1 "Scaled Agile Management 4.0 - new"

Fuckup "External limitations for agility"

How the environment may limit organizations from becoming agile

Description

"We never will agree to this!" The head of the works council has just heard about plans to initiate agile transformation and is extremely annoyed about not being informed earlier. Shortly before the transformation is due to begin and in having leant this informally, he feels that the workers council's rights have been violated. The union agrees with him. The transformation program has to be put on hold for the time being.

A self-organized agile team had prepared and rehearsed the transformation program several times, presented its ideas to management, which agreed to the plans. At that point in time the team realised that they should check labour law regulations and the need to involve the works council. Consultation with Human Resources confirmed that several aspects of the program plan are clearly related to organizational and employee processes, which by law have to be negotiated with the works council. Agreement requires communication and negotiations, which haven't even begun yet. So the program has to be halted until an agreement is reached.

Discussion

Not properly organized, the effects of agile working on existing collective agreements, legal changes limiting the use of freelancers and so on, all create complex restrictions for any organization trying to become Agile. Alongside legal implications, political interests, as well as the resistance of all sorts of officials, have to be considered and there will likely be limitations. Since self-organized agile teams rarely have the appropriate knowledge and experience they often underestimate or even ignore these aspects.

From our point of view it is easy to understand how agile teams and even organizations could ignore such external limitations. Those who fully understood Agile will face many restrictions and resistance from the outside. So sooner or later frustration will occur and the idea of building a cocoon inside the agile filter bubble seems to be an appropriate response. But such behaviour is highly dangerous! Anti-agile legislation, such as restrictions on using external specialists (AÜG-Reform), unions, and state authorities, who have little idea about Agile, for example, are significant blockers. This is normally related to an outdated mindset on how businesses run or should run. It is important to bear in mind that even the most recent articles of the German works constitution act (Betriebsverfassungsgesetz) date from 1972, whereas most date back to the 1950s. At that time no one could have anticipated anything like Agile would surface.

It is essential for anyone who wants to realize a successful agile transformation, to demonstrate a professional attitude and analyse and handle all relevant influences and restrictions. For each and every change, a risk and stakeholder analysis is a must. For this, all external factors need to be weighed independently, to ascertain wheter they are useful or potentially damaging. It is worth involving specialists from different fields, e.g. Human Resources or compliance officers. Their expertise could be your key success factor for transformation to an agile organization.

Tips & Tricks

- Conduct a risk analysis at an early point in your project. This helps gain more time for handling risks and blockers. Keep in mind that many of the traditional processes, like negotiations with a works council, may take significantly more time than projects carried out in an agile manner.
- Use the intense discussions with HR, Finance and other staff as a plausibility check for your plans for becoming more agile. It will increase the accuracy of estimations of time, costs etc. Since most employees have little experience with agile concepts, the discussions will show which aspects have to be addressed in the upcoming process. For those who are agile experienced, it is often surprising to see just how much effort is required to create a basic understanding or even motivation to become more agile. Often the focus will shift from more method oriented thinking to

communication and social processes. This is important for integrating into the transformation process!
- Young colleagues such as apprentices or graduates often are a good indicator for the effort required to create an Agile Mindset. On the one hand they are quick learners, and on the other hand, they have usually not had any contact with Agile and can therefore be seen as absolute beginners. The mindset at schools and universities is very "old school", and far removed from the Agile Mindset we want to build. The time you need to create an Agile Mindset in this group is the minimum time you should estimate for all of the employees in an organization.

Literature

Britta Redmann (2017) Agiles Arbeiten im Unternehmen: Haufe Verlag
http://www.britta-redmann.de/assets/agiles_arbeiten_im_unternehmen_leseprobe4.pdf

Sir Ken Robinson (2017) Do schools kill creativity?:
https://www.ted.com/talks/ken_robinson_says_schools_kill_creativity,
Margret Rasfeld Schule im Aufbruch
https://www.youtube.com/watch?v=e3BOuMsMUCY

Reference to chapter 8 "Reliable and Ultimate Scrum"

Fuckup "Agile stand-alone solutions and the difficulty of scaling"

What works locally, may not necessarily be suitable for an entire organization. Scaling processes do not proceed in a linear fashion. This is a fact that needs recognizing, especially for self-organizing systems which permanently adapt according to changing environmental conditions

Description

Observing the development and the widespread distribution of Scrum in businesses today, it can only be regarded as a success story. Starting 15 years ago in the area of software development, (see Agile Manifesto 2001), this agile technique is now considered a "state of the art" element in multiple areas of project management.

At the beginning of the "agile movement", in traditional enterprises, agile projects were seen as isolated and stand-alone solutions. Very often these projects were exceptional and handled specific ambitious tasks in these organizations, which were governed by top management. In contrast to agile practices in upcoming "start-up companies", it was a challenge to establish agile procedures in "traditional" organizations, because the methodologies were not part of the company culture or the company DNA (also see the topic encapsulation (Pfläging 2018)).

When implementing agile projects in traditionally working organizations, three major challenges were identified:

- First, it was necessary for them to legitimize their way of cooperation with the new products, and different result types against traditional projects and project results. The main objective at this point was to prove that the new products would lead to appropriate project success. (Problem of legitimacy of the methodology)

- Second, at the start, agile projects were an "island of the blessed" that could work within their own dynamics. Everything ran smoothly as long as there was no need to cooperate with different project cultures. But the moment that different approaches were forced to work together, the organization very often faced a "clash of cultures": The inner dynamics of the different teams, the varying type and speed of results, prototypes and products produced, as well as the varied evaluations of these results, lead to a working culture of "two divergent speeds and worlds". At their interfaces you could often trace a high potential of tensions and conflicts. The agile working teams usually suffered more under these circumstances than did their neighboring traditional projects teams (cultural gap problem). These agile projects were seen as a kind of "virus" that the traditional organization was fighting against.

- Third, the growing popularity of agile techniques and the spreading usage of these technologies has prompted many companies today to try, to export or to establish an agile working model in all the departments and branches of the company. In practice this means that a locally successful working model gets expanded – unfortunately, normally without any reference or deeper knowledges of the origin of agile organizational successes. Therefore, what we now observe is a theoretical gap in the market. Most market players are unable to explain their advantages or the innovations they have achieved, using agile self-organizing practices in detail. (theoretical gap problem).

Discussion

Based on the previous discussion, we can conclude that scaling up successful organizational methodologies works perfectly well with isolated projects, but is risky with larger organizational units (although it is still portrayed as a solvable issue (see Computerwoche 2018)). The following need to be kept in mind:

- Although an agile team is the smallest piece of the puzzle in a self-organizing entity, successful cooperation of al team members is not guaranteed. Therefore, successful team performance - for example in applying Scrum methodology – depends on the ability of team members to establish a collective team vision for successfully regulating self-organization processes. (Here we refer to Chapter 3.4 of this book, Self-organization, which describes the parameters of self-organization).
- In addition, it should be stated that scaling up isolated team experiences over an entire and huge organization does not mean that such an organization will be able to progress linearly. On the one hand, the limiting factors are the intrinsic mindset of the employees that normally relies on existing management and governance cultures. On the other hand, scaling is limited by the increased expenditure required for the coordination and planning of scaled up team organizations. Finally, scaling will also be reduced, if all controlling and governance systems, as well as key indicator measurements, remain untouched. (Please also refer to our Fuckup story on controlling and governance systems, with respect to this issue.)

Tips & Tricks

The move to agile working procedures should not regarded as a purely technical change from old procedures to newer or more "fashionable" ones.

Anyone seeking to change an entire organization, will out of necessity have to rethink the entire value, management, governance and controlling system. And it should be taken under consideration or at least must be well approved whether all employees of the whole organization must underlie the new working procedures.

In the end, establishing a "collective mind" is the key factor. This means the introduction of a clear concept of the organizational target vision. Based on this, everyone within the organization will be aware of their role to play in contributing to the organizational success of the business, and know how this is influenced by their actions. If such experiences can be created, the main ingredient for long lasting satisfaction will have been established: This is the intrinsic and sustainable sentiment of "sensing" (Refer to the already described pitfalls here (e.g. in Scrum Academy 2018)).

Literature

Agile Manifesto (2001) agilemanifesto.org, accessed on 17/10/2018

Pfläging N and Hermann S (2018) Komplexithoden, München, 5th edition

Computerwoche (2018) https://www.computerwoche.de/a/scrum-und-co-auch-agile-methoden-lassen-sich-skalieren,3219768, accessed on 17/10/2018

Scrum Academy (2018) https://www.scrumakademie.de/safe/wissen/fuenf-fallen-bei-der-skalierung-von-agilitaet/, accessed on 17/10/2018

Reference to chapter 3.4 "Self-organization"

Fuckup "Inconsequent execution"

An "attempt" to introduce Agile in a bank

Description

The following situation is currently happening, or could happen in a variety of companies:

The Board of a bank faces increasing IT costs every year, and they are confronted with the challenge of limiting or even reducing their IT budget. In addition, feedback on the implementation speed and quality of IT is not very satisfying. Delivery of projects is often late and business goals are only partially met.

A meeting of the CFO and the CIO takes place to discuss this challenge and develop a solution.

The CFO: "*Every year we invest so much in the IT budget, but do not get any real benefit of it. This needs to end. We have to stop this now.*"

The CIO: "*Well IT costs money and if you want a modern IT infrastructure then we need to invest.*"

They both meet up again several times until the CFO states: "*I have heard of something called an **agile approach** that has been implemented in other organizations and they have saved money and created a fast and efficient IT system. Why don't we change over to becoming an agile organization with an agile methodology and maybe this will solve everything?*"

After further discussion the CIO agrees to change to becoming a more agile IT organization

- to leverage efficiencies (carry out the same work in IT but with fewer people) and
- to deliver faster to the market.

A few days after this discussion, the CIO calls in external consultants and internal IT management, to start the process of how to implement Agile. The external consultants propose implementing Scrum as the new project methodology. During the following week the bank:

- reworks the project execution approach in IT
- hires Scrum coaches to teach internal teams the basics starting from management down to developers and
- starts small pilot projects

After four months the first small agile teams report back positively to the CIO and communicate that the agile methodology is working as expected.

The CIO is happy and at the next management committee announces that all IT teams/projects will now be moved to agile mode over the next few months. All teams will now be forced to work with the new approach, including large and complex projects.

Twelve months after the introduction of Agile, there is a situation where:

- there is as yet no visible cost reduction,
- many projects face delivery problems (sprint scope not delivered),
- there are a number of business complaints relating to problems of quality after the software had entered production,
- larger projects in particular are experiencing many dependency challenges (insufficient alignment) and are delayed,
- some internal teams have rejected the Scrum approach, due to the challenges and want to go back to the method they were used to,
- different teams are interpreting the agile approach differently and are subsequently implement different team standards.

In the next steering committee the CFO and CIO reflect on the progress of agility with respect to their goals

- Cost savings
- Efficiency
- Team acceptance

The CFO is disappointed as he cannot see any progress on cost savings. Due to this and low team acceptance and quality problems, the Board decides to go back to the old methodology.

Over the next few months the IT team rolls back everything that was related to Agile and returns to the waterfall model as standard. This causes even more confusion and some frustration within the teams.

Discussion

The introduction of agile methodology is a massive challenge for a company, especially with respect to change management. As a guideline, the success of the implementation of agile methodology is based on Mindset, Governance and Technique with a leverage factor of

- 1000 for the Mindset,
- 100 for the Governance of agile introduction and
- 1 for the Agile Techniques used (e.g. Scrum)

Changing an organization's mindset takes time and effort, perhaps up to several years, especially in deeply entrenched organizations. In particular, the transformation of the mindset of people who have worked using the same "way of thinking" for many years requires a lot of effort.

In the current example of the bank, several key errors were committed:

- Cost reduction should not be the key driver for a move to Agile
- Agile benefits can only be leveraged with long-term commitment and detailed preparation
- The move to Agile creates great challenges within the organization. Only a strong organization with a wider perspective on business (not only for IT) can ensure that these challenges are well managed:
    - Setting the governmental framework,
    - checking the progress and
    - actively lead the transformation

Unfortunately in the example of the bank, the introduction of an agile approach was not implemented with sufficient effort: The governmental framework was not carefully set and the transformation was not well managed. In particular, there was no active guidance with respect to commitment and resistance to Agile.

Tips & Tricks

Upfront:

Build a strategic plan to move to agile over several years containing:

- strong commitment from both top and middle management
- clear goals for the agile approach (speed of projects, time to market, potential cost savings)
- a commitment by all stakeholders especially IT and business
- a solid budget foundation
- strong governance steering the process
- sufficient support from (external) agile experts
- an approach to create agile multipliers within internal teams

Implementation:

- Set up a working feedback process to enable Agile Governance to react to challenges. This process must be pushed forward by activity and create transparency on the progress
- Any serious challenges must be actively discussed within management and commitment to the decision must be regularly renewed

Reference to chapter 4.1 "Principles of Agile Leadership 4.0", **chapter 11** "Agile Transformation 4.0 - new"

Fuckup "Governance and target systems are not aligned"

Organizing agile teams and leaving target systems unchanged, leads to confusion of management and employees

Description

Uncontradicted, corporate culture and its way of management is changing towards a self-organizing system. Yet the old and established governance and controlling systems in most of these organizations still remained untouched. This means that many organizations very often rely on methods developed for the guidance of traditional and hierarchical organized management with a focus on process-orientated organization.

Although organizations should ensure that they align their governance and controlling systems to the new agile requirements, well-established government frameworks continue. Such an approach provokes manifold contradictory effects in the regulation of agile enterprises.

The following examples illustrate such issues:

- **KPIs and business values**
  Agile teams organize their throughput along their product and release cycles.
  Which KPIs will play the role of control parameter in this scenario? Is it capacity utilization or the business value the product increments create?
- **Market flexibility**
  The second challenge for a governance system lies in measurement of organizational ability to respond flexibly to market changes. How does this responsiveness fit into a traditional, but well-organized budget and planning procedures in a business?
- **Earned values as measurement goals**
  Third, it should be questioned whether it is actually realistic that all agile teams should be able to create a profit margin on their

operational output? Such an assumption ignores the fact that many existing tasks in an established organization may remain and therefore should be regarded as support services for other teams. And as suppliers for other teams, they also contribute to the company success, yet as far as accounting are concderned, will they be classed as an overhead cost?

In summary, finding the right balance in the governance and controlling systems of an agile company is a challenging issue that cannot be underestimated.

Discussion

The target and control models that dominate businesses were developed against the background of a working organization that was inspired by Taylorism and the scaling advantages of mass-production. They are almost fundamentally opposite to the current movement towards self-organization.

In particular, the dominance of a budget-oriented target-system has been identified as an impediment for organizational shift. This is due to the inflexibility of a system where targets are fixed and the prospected outcome needs to be defined in advance.

Such fixed rulings counteract the flexibility required today with the movement towards self-organized organizational procedures. This means that without an adopted governance and key indicator system, it will become difficult for both management and employees to create the new organizational model. Experience has shown that a governance change to a policy dominated by self-organizing principles combined with old "command and control" budget governance regulations leads to organizational disorder. Everyone within the organization ends up confused as to which policy is in the "driving seat" and defines the rules.

Tips & Tricks

Apart from a fundamental change in mindset, the establishment of synergetic transformation in a business requires an adopted governance system that supports and measures the success of the organizational change.

The difficulty today is that the existing accounting, budgeting and controlling structures do not contain any tools or means of measurement to support such new organizational concepts. Therefore, a move to synergetic, self-organizing structures needs to be prepared well in advance. With Agile Transformation, management and controlling regulations also need to be coordinated and developed.
All internal organizational changes require adequately developed measuring systems to demonstrate the quality of their results. Governance rules, therefore need to be reshaped to a relative targeting system, as the example proposed by the "Beyond Budgeting" approach (see e.g. Beyond Budgeting 2018 or Pflaeging 2018).

But overall, the focus of the entire controlling system must be redirected in such a way that there is a shift from the dominant cost view, towards a value chain perspective. Value chain accountancy focuses on performance bottlenecks (see also Critical Chain Project Management in chapter 10.2) and on the contribution of agile organizational entities toward value creation (see also Pflaeging 2018).

Challenging and transient targets that allows incremental progress measurement in combination with internal benchmarking of team results, create and contribute a valuable framework for a new Governance system. One such supporting measure might be the evolution and introduction of new technologies like IoT and predictive analysis. Based on these techniques, it is possible to better predict upcoming market changes and have "built-in-flexibility" for Governance monitoring and adaption. Agile companies today most definitely "need to build strategic systems that tune in and respond to data early and often" (Price 2018).

Literature

Beyond Budgeting (2018) https://de.wikipedia.org/wiki/Beyond_Budgeting, accessed on 17/10/2018

Pflaeging N (2018) https://www.controllingportal.de/Fachinfo/Budgetierung/Ziele-und-Leistung-im-Steuerungsmodell-Beyond-Budgeting-eine-Neudefinition.html, accessed on 17/10/2018

Pflaeging N and Hermann S (2018) Komplexithoden, Munich, 5th edition

Price K (2018) https://www.manufacturing.net/article/2018/12/liberate-year-end-planning-outdated-constraints-and-rigid-expectations, accessed on 17/10/2018

Sweet Spot of Agility

Agile Management is the framework used in modern businesses to handle complexity and to help them prosper. The most suitable approach is "probe-sense-respond", which has been proposed from the Cynefin Framework. This is the direction most companies take if they want to become more agile. Initial pilot initiatives – often used to qualify and introduce agile methods – are followed by agile conducted projects and upscaling efforts. This enables a quick start and fast accumulation of knowledge and experience (success and failure). On the other hand, this approach may include opposing impacts or side effects which are unavoidable. The real question is then who will decide under such circumstances what is the right decision?

What can we understand and achieve from our fuckup examples?

We could ask: What are the mutual leverage factors determining success and failure? Looking at it from a helicopter view we ca identify three main factors:

1. Agile Mindset,
2. Agile Governance,
3. Agile Techniques

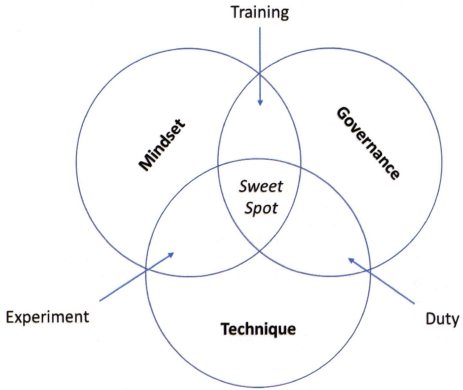

Figure 12-1: Areas of Agility

How should we understand these factors?

1. Mindset: This is the inner attitude, from vision, mission and belongingness to beliefs, values and basic assumptions, to capabilities, behavior and environment. It determines, to very large extent, the way in which agile working is carried out.

2. Governance: A framework of guidelines an organization installs to ensure work is carried out in a proper manner. This framework regulates actions within an organization.

3. Techniques: Methods, tools and instruments (agile or "classical"), as well as interaction and communication approaches and processes.

When looking at the given examples, it becomes obvious that all three factors are required to get into a working agile mode. The area where all three coexist, is what we refer to as the Sweet Spot. However in reality, you will find quite often only one or two dominant areas in an organization.
In such a case, where parts of the three areas - mindset, governance and technique - are overlapping, we describe these areas as follows:

1. Training (Learning) = Mindset + Governance: Agile thinking is transferred (or not) into organizational rules and procedures. Example: Managers are elected by their employees.

2. Experiment = Mindset + Techniques: Agile methods are used (or not) in accordance with an Agile Mindset. Example: In a separate organization (startup, lab,...) agile methods are used, but the company as a whole remains unaffected.

3. Duty = Governance + Techniques: Agile methods are introduced into the organization, supporting (or not) Governance Guidelines. Example: Employees and managers stick to old ways of thinking and working. Agile is ignored or workarounds are established.

To summarize it: An organization needs to ensure that all three areas are implemented in a proper manner:

Management 4.0 = Mindset * Governance * Technique

Our experience shows that the three factors have different relevance for success and failure. Based on our experience, we estimate the leverage relevance as:

Management 4.0 = 1000 Mindset * 100 Governance * 1 Technique

What does this mean for the implementation of agility in an organization?

An organization needs to consider all of the three areas. The key component, with a leverage factor of 1000, is the Agile Mindset within the organization. This is followed by a working Governance (leverage factor of 100), which the organization has to set up carefully. Agile techniques play a comparatively small role with a leverage factor of 1. In addition to these differences in leverage factors, it is essential that all factors are multiplied to create a Sweet Spot.

The Sweet Spot will not exist if one of the factors is "zero", meaning it is not Agile. Most companies use Scrum as a technique, but other techniques or a mix of several methods especially tailored for an organization can also be applied (see Figure 4-7).

Now let us return to the fuckups described earlier and review them with the help of Figure 12-1. Table 12-1 lists the aforementioned fuckups and also indicates why the fuckups occurred and states the area(s) where pitfalls occured during implementation.

Fuckup Identifier	Fuckup title	Possible pitfall	Balancing factor
1	"Social romanticism in agile management"	Mislead mindset (overemphasizing social factors)	Strengthen governance
2	"Agile methods dogmatism"	Focus is mainly on technique	Train Mindset and strengthen governance
3	"Agility as a fashion"	Mislead mindset and lack of seriousness	Strengthen agile understanding through experimenting
4	"External limitations for agility"	Unsuitable governance system (internal or external)	Adapt governance by looking for alternative approaches
5	"Agile stand-alone solutions and the difficulty of scaling"	Scaling of agile method not a linear effort and organizational parameters not appropriate	Ensure proper general conditions and coordination for agile scaling
6	"Inconsequent execution"	Agile mindset and governance falling short	Train mindset and strengthen governance
7	"Governance and target systems are not aligned"	Misfit of principles and measurements	Adjustment of existing and agile mindsets and metric guidelines

Table 12-1: Fuckups and possible pitfalls

Conclusion and Summary

An agile, self-organizing transformation requires an adjusted combination of Mindset, Governance and appropriate Techniques.

In the preceding chapters we presented a selection of specific difficult issues that should be avoided or at least carefully observed, if a transformation of organizations in the direction of agility and self-organization is intended.

Every single aspect of our presented fuckup stories indicates possible pitfalls and refers to frequent and common patterns in which slip-ups can occur if the knowledge and experience of self-organizing processes is lacking.

Our solution space that we described as the "Sweet Spot of agility", is characterized by a combination where mindset plus governance and agile techniques guarantees the expected "performance effect" of an organization. But we concede that this is an unstable and fragile state.

Even more so, we must emphasize that it is a situation in which every organization must evolve individually and which must be adjusted again and again according actual market situations.

Self-organization is a permanent process alongside a permanent cycle of parameter adaptation and aligned responses, respectively. Such continuous change should not be forgotten, because it is the dominant driver of flexibility that is currently required to survive organizationally.

Anyone approaching their tasks with such a level of consciousness, will be well prepared for avoiding the "Fuckups" we presented here, as well as many others already experienced within the agile community. Please bear in mind that continuous learning and development, as well as continuous improvement, are key principles of agility that need applying. So the objective should be to create an organization where the Sweet Spot is maximized. Let's do it!

13 Interaction Patterns for the Digital Transformation - new

Author: Alfred Oswald, Jens Köhler

Summary: We will illustrate that the mindsets of individuals or the prevailing mindset of a population or part of a population are sources of a communication marco-structure. Digitization is a context which modulates this macro-structure, resulting in digitization-specific interaction patterns. For the prevailing mindsets we propose four different Personality Archetypes with different interaction patterns. We outline potential intervention techniques for initiating a successful Digital Transformation.

Key Terms: Digitization, Digital Transformation, Self-organization, Setting Parameter, Control Parameter, Order Parameter, Persona, Personality Archetype, Value-mem, Spiral Dynamics, Learning Level, Micro-tier, Macro-tier, Macro-structure

Introduction

Digitization and Digital Transformation are current buzzwords, but we also feel that digitization will result in a radical transformation of our society.

Obvious examples are social networks, big data and smart data, and artificial intelligence. As everyone knows, all this has significantly changed how we communicate and work together. Data and information have become real assets, more valuable than real estates or machines. For example, the largest taxi company (Uber) based on an App, owns no cars! Data driven companies like Apple, Microsoft, Alphabet inc. (Google) or Amazon, founded just a few decades ago, are extremely highly rated on the stock exchange. In addition, we perceive that with respect to our own lives, that each digitization step will have an immediate impact on our social behaviour: Non-digital companies, such as manufacturers of consumer goods need to become digital or a smart companies to stay competitive.

Management 4.0 has the capability of understanding the key principles of this transformation and can deliver social technologies for the shaping of Digital Transformation. In this chapter we provide the first step in this directon by asking important questions and outlining solutions, by presenting three examples.

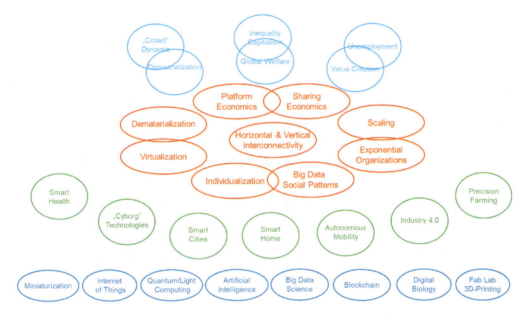

Figure 13-1: The key elements of digitization and Digital Transformation (based on Land 2018, Kucklick 2016, O'Neil 2016)

Key questions with respect to Digital Transformation are: "What is Digital Transformation" and "How will our different individual perspectives on the current status of society influence Digital Transformation?" A subsequent question then follows: "How will this shape the capabilty of an organization or society to cope with Digital Transformation?"

Figure 13-1 summarizes our perspective on digitization and Digital Transformation. We were inspired by the work of Land (Land 2018), Kucklick (Kucklick 2016) and O'Neil (O'Neil 2016).

We are seeing a lot of new basic physical technologies emerging, from miniaturization to 3D printing. This will result in new technology regimes from Smart Health to Smart Home to Precision Farming. And these new technology regimes will eventually trigger the transformation of our society via different forms of interconnectivity, resulting in emergent forms of new complexity: New forms of economies accompanied by new forms of organization are emerging, more and more digital models are shaping our perspective on reality and the physical world. This is likely to result in crowd dynamics and higher inequality which will result in unemployment and the drawbacks of capitalism. But, we can also see a lack of social technologies: Digitization activities, be it in industry or society, are often handled as infrastructure-projects, i.e. it is implicit that the new technology is known and just needs to be implemented without there being any impact on the organization or society. This gap, treating people in the old Tayloristic way, by focusing only on physical technology, will hinder Digital Transformation activities from achieving their full extend and could result in societal disadvantages.

To answer one of our key questions: "How will our different individual perspectives on the current status of our society influence Digital Transformation?", we have divided this into two questions:

"What are the perspectives and impacts of Digital Transformation?" and "How is Digital Transformation preceived by people?"

Adressing the first question, Digital Transformation has the the following perspectives and impacts:

- Individual perspective: Faster and newer competences are always required to handle digital physical technologies (e.g. new basic technologies, new emergent systems) and to handle social technologies for the regulation of complexity (meta-competence).

- Organizational perspective: The faster emergence of new physical technologies that is always required, demands that new social technologies keep pace and regulate organizational complexity (e.g. agile business modelling, agile organizational mindset adaption).
- Societal perspective: New physical and social technologies and their interaction result in macro-structures like platform and sharing economies. These macro-structures need to be regulated by new Governance capabilities.

These perspectives position Digitization as something that is mainly positive and as an enabler of welfare and evolution.

Addressing the second question, we have the following statements and observations to make:

- People see the benefit of Digitization very locally. For example, privately they make use of their smartphones, but as employees resist new corporate tools or data processes when they are introduced.
- Digitization is often seen from the perspective of efficiency, rather than effectiveness. That means that there is no focus on societal opportunities, but only on making things faster (to obtain more money).
- It is unclear as to how Digitization affects jobs. Three effects can be observed: (1) Digitization will eliminate jobs, (2) Digitization will create new jobs, (3) A significant section of society will be unemployed and there will be a dilemma of what should be done in this case? The future situation is totally open and even visionaries like Harari (2017) are unable to describe anything concrete. It is very likely too early for this.
- There is little awareness and competency in required social technologies for VUCA, like Management 4.0: Companies and society see Digitization projects as infrastructure projects without a feedback loop to society itself, just like building a new road.

These perspectives describe aspects of resistance within Digital Transformation.

In the following, we will try and shed some light on these aspects of evolution and resistance by focusing on human interaction patterns (communication patterns). We prefer to derive interaction patterns on the mirco-tier (individual perspective) and to outline resulting emergent phenomena on the macro-tier (organization and society). For an introduction to micro-tier, macro-tier and self-organization, please see chapter 3, chapter 6, in particular, Figure 6-1 and Figure 6-3, and chapter 4.1, especially Figure 4-3.

To help the reader, here is a definition of self-organization in a nutshell: Macro-tier behaviour of any complex (social) system is determined by three parameter sets:

- **Setting parameters**: These parameters charactize "fix" structures or quantities, like space and time conditions, or mindsets of involved people,
- **Control parameters:** These are parameters which can be adjusted and allow the relevant system to "fluctuate", like work in progress or leadership style (e.g. neuroleadership),
- **Order parameters:** This parameter set ensures the emergence of a systemic macro-structure, e.g. the organizational mindset (culture) of an organization or a project team.

We have analyzed and outlined interaction patterns using the Dilts Pyramid, the culture and consciousness Spiral Dyamics model and learning levels (Oswald 2018, Beck 1995, Veit 2018, see also chapter 3.2). For the sake of simplicity we have omitted aspects resulting from additional individual personality characteristics (Oswald 2018).

Our discussion of interaction patterns is based on the assumption that the mindsets of individuals and their learning levels form the systemic interaction patterns. Individual mindsets act like setting parameters in a system (i.e. a team, an organization or a society) and determine systemic control and order parameters in a self-organized way: These control and order parameters then act as a feedback loop and self-consistently build a self-organized interaction pattern "of how people finally work together". Our aim is to adjust setting and control parameters in such a way, that this working mode is value creating.

The rule of thumb is that setting and control parameters determine the potential manifestation space of the order parameters of any complex system. For example, a project solution is only possible if the team-mix fits with the culture of the embedding organization and to the project task. The above cited models of the Dilts Pyramid and Spiral Dynamics help to analyze and adjust the parameters of self-organization accordingly.

When dealing with organizations, details are not the first things that should be considered: Self-organization in social systems is "simple" when focusing on these parameters, like focusing on a compass needle. But time is required to adopt this kind of thinking!

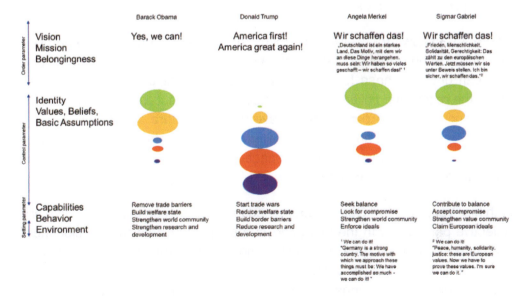

Figure 13-2: Hypothetic Politician mindsets

To illustrate this without focusing on technological aspects, we start by outlining individual order parameters of politicians Barack Obama, Donald Trump, Angela Merkel and Sigmar Gabriel, by looking at the dramatic events that have unfolded in society over the past few years. Whilst doing this, we are also aware that we are only outlining the mindset on the basis of a very small documented excerpt of communication (Wikipedia 2018). So our observations have resulted in a model based on hypothesis, i.e. the above individuals have become part of a model. In addition, we have clearly stated that the intention of this illustration is not to create or influence political opinion, as we are only referring to existing public sources. In addition, we are not passing judgment on the politicians mentioned, be it positive or negative. Our only purpose is to demonstrate how different order parameters can result in different effects.

The value-memes of politicians interact with the respective value-memes of members of a society. Here is another rule of thumb: If a value-meme of a politician fits with (parts of) a society, this is like the attraction of two magnets, or a resonance. If a value-meme violates (parts of) a society, this is like the repulsion of two magnets.

Figure 13-2 shows the well-known focus-forming statements of Obama (Yes, we can!), Trump (America first! America great again!) and Merkel, and Gabriel (We can get it!). These focus-forming statements are order parameter with which the respective politician orders their individual actions, as well as trying to influence and align people to achieve a certain future structure of society. This is why we refer to an order parameter here. The control parameter is given by the (strongest) v-meme of the respective politician and the corresponding distribution of v-memes in the society.

With his "Yes, we can!" Obama addressed the values of an active, creative and collective population. In the language of the Spiral Dynamics consciousness and culture model, we speak of manifestations of the "orange" (active, creative) and "green" (collective, we-oriented) value memes. In Figure 13-1 we indicated this by a value meme mannequin (v-meme mannequin) using large bubbles for the orange and green v-memes and small bubbles for the blue (order), red (power) and purple (mysticism) v-memes.

Trump has given himself another order parameter: "America first! – America great again!". He acts like an agent of disruptive change: Power, provocative leadership using Twitter statements, recklessness, arrogance coupled with a dose of mysticism by introducing "alternative facts" and stylizing America as a promise of salvation. In the language of Spiral Dynamics, we speak of the "purple" (mystical), "red" (power-oriented) and "blue" (order-oriented) value memes.

The German Chancellor Angela Merkel, has also used an order parameter with respect to the issue of refugees: "Wir schaffen das! ('we can do it'!) ". It primarily addresses our need for affection. In the language of Spiral Dynamics, this corresponds to the "green" v-memes (collective, empathic). Looking on the whole statement we guessed a much lower part of orange (activity, creativity), blue (order), a rather big part of red (power) and a small part of purple v-meme (mysticism).

The former German minister of foreign affairs also used "We can do it!". But examining the full statement, we can derive a different v-meme mannequin (see Figure 13-2). The message here is that a closer examination of the context of a statement such as "We can do it!" may result in a rather different value meme structure. And this different v-meme structure (v-meme mannequin) will result in different behavior patterns.

In Figure 4-5 in chapter 4.1 "Principles of Agile Leadership 4.0" we outlined the four basic human needs: need for self-appreciation and self-protection, need for orientation and control, need for pleasure and pain-prevention and need for affection. Oswald et al. (Oswald 2018) have linked the red v-memes to the need for self-appreciation and self-protection, the blue v-memes to the need for orientation and control, the orange v-memes to the need for pleasure and pain-prevention and the green v-memes to the need for affection. So value memes represent our basic needs and motives. These four v-memes can be referred to as the first tier of consciousness. Spiral Dynamics identifies a so-called second tier of consciousness, which currently includes two levels: yellow (integrates all perspectives in a meshwork) and turquoise (perceives the world as a holistic whole). We have not outlined these levels in Figure 13-2, because we did not find any indication of these v-memes in the order parameter statements of the politicians.

The presence or absence of v-memes are strong indicators of personal consciousness with respect to attentiveness, mindfulness, awareness and wisdom (Oswald 2018). For an organizational mindset the v-memes are indicators of organizational maturity (Laloux 2014).

Here the key issues are:

- **Key issue 1**: Personal setting, control and order parameter greatly influence our behavior.
- **Key issue 2**: With a communicated order parameter and related v-memes (control parameter), only a certain type of people are addressed (by e.g. a politician, a leader), namely those who have a similar v-meme structure (please refer to the magnet metaphor above).
- **Key issue 3**: The v-meme structure (especially second tier maturity) determines the ability of a leader to integrate the mindset of people and lead them.
- **Key issue 4**: The v-meme structure determines the ability of learning (Learning Level I-IV) to a great extent. The v-meme structure of an organization or society determines the learning level of a community and therefore how an Agile Transformation should be designed and led (see chapter 11). It is unlikely that a v-meme transformation will incorporate more than one v-meme leap (e.g. the activation of orange v-memes starting with blue v-memes may be possible, but not the activation of green v-memes).

With his order parameter, Obama addresses different people and v-memes to Trump. Obama addresses people with a v-meme preference of green and orange; Trump addresses people with a v-meme preference of blue, red and purple. These preferences are actually represented as approximately 50%:50% in the American population.

If value memes are missing, this also has consequences: With repsect to the refugee issue, the orange and blue memes were missing to some extent – resulting in the corresponding results that we are all aware of. Sometimes the lack of value memes or the selective use of value memes has an amazing effect: In the case of Trump's confrontation with the Korean dictator Kim, Trump beat him at his own game, because the value memes of both of these individuals have strongly similar characteristics. On the other hand, Obama failed to have any impact on Kim's value memes. It is also worth considering if the values memes with which the EU is currently trying to effectively communicate with Trump will have any success.

But it would be fatal to play different sets of values against one another or to suggest that one value constellation is "more valuable" than another. Instead, it is the task of leadership to take into account the different v-meme structures in a population or organization. If a leader is not capable of integrating everyone in a population (team, organization or society), social groups with different v-meme structures will seek their own way via self-organization. Self-organization is not good per se, as it can lead to disaster. We hear this almost daily in media reports. It is crucial that leaders are aware that their behavior contributes significantly to such developments. This happens if a leader's communication violates - objectively or emotionally - the prevailing v-memes of a population or a social group. Brexit and the emergence of right-wing populism, in addition to recent violent eruptions have the same fundamental causes: In their leaders' actions, the affected population perceives, either consciously or unconsciously, v-memes which do not support their interests and objectives.

In chapter 4.1 we emphasized that leadership in a complex world requires fewer "small-scale" micro-management activities and more leadership through Governance. Governance means the conscious design and continuous adaption of setting, control and order parameters.

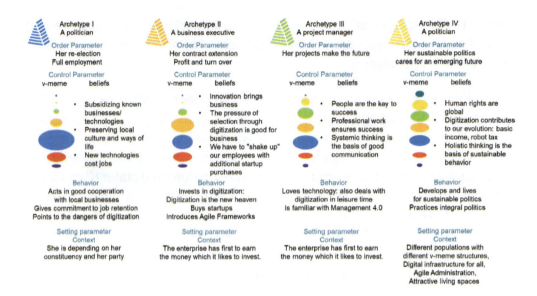

Figure 13-3: Personality Archetypes by Learning Levels

As stated above, the ability to lead a system (team, organization or society) is to a large extent, determined by the "completeness and balance" of the v-meme structure and the related emergent learning level. Figure 13-3 outlines examples of four Personality Archetypes for the four learning levels (see also Table 3-2). The learning levels are developmental stages of a personality and are a "measure" of meta-competence. We have chosen persona (two politicians, a business executive, a project manager) to illustrate these archetypes. Each Archetype is represented by a coloured Dilts Pyramid. The colour of the Dilts Pyramid represents the highest dominant v-meme.

Archetype I is the persona of someone who likes to live traditionally and to act in accordance with current system structures and processes, accepting innovations if the degree of innovation is not to high. This Archetype is represented by the "blue" v-meme (order, structure).

Archetype II is the persona of someone who believes in herself and is open to new things, especially if it brings in money and is good for both her personally and the welfare of the system. Learning is not really essential, power, status and success are the key motives. The implications of innovations are not really perceived. This Archetype is represented by the "orange" v-meme (entrepreneurship, success).

Archetype III is the persona of someone who believes in people, is aware of an ubiquitous meshwork of natural, societal and technical interrelations. She loves innovations and perceives implications and can cope with the paradigmen shift related to Management 4.0. This Archetype is represented by the "green" v-meme (affection, collective acting).

Archetype IV is the persona of someone with a balanced v-meme structure, aware of the meshwork of complexity, she practices holistic thinking and behavior. This results in integral and sustainable theory and practice. This Archetype is represented by the "yellow" v-meme (integral meshwork, collective mind).

Based on these archetypes we have outlined interaction patterns and the above listed key issues for three examples: A project, an organization and a society.

Example: A digitization project for the fictitious company "IceMachine"

Let us assume that the CEO of the company IceMachine SE, which is a manufacturer of white goods, would like to benefit from digitization and has initiated a "digital transformation" project to manufacture and sell smart white goods. The CEO is really keen to lead her company into a new age. She has already found a project leader who likes innovation and has a feeling for people (see Figure 13-4 Archetype III); the CEO utilises the project leader's order and control parameter (key issue 1).

Archetype II
CEO

promoter

Archetype III
Project manager

supporter

Archetype I
A local politician

 endurer
opponent

Archetype IV
A federal politician

 supporter
endurer

Figure 13-4: The stakeholder interaction patterns

The project leader starts the "digital transformation" project enthusiasticly with her team, taking care to observe all learned Management 4.0 issues. For example, creating a target hierarchy with her team (see Figure 13-5). The CEO is very happy with this creativity, but is aware that "digital transformation" will probably result in a great deal of resistance from employees, especially as new technological know-how is required and other know-how will lose importance.

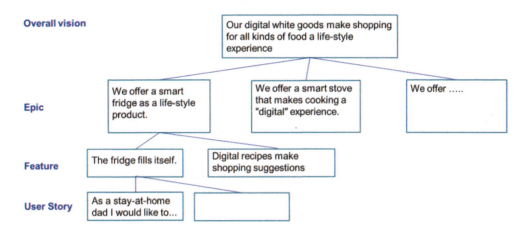

Figure 13-5: Target hierarchy of IceMachine as a story map

Presumably, this will bring about employee redundancies. Therefore the CEO contacts a local politician to enlist support for her enterprise: She tells the politician that she would like to enter into the new digital age by creating new jobs; the CEO is utilising the local politician's order parameter (key issue 1). She asks for government structural support; she addresses the blue v-memes control parameter of the local politician (order and structure). In addition, the local politician's order parameter is activated, because she hopes for new jobs in her election district. She in turn asks for support from federal government, especially from the newly created position of "Digital Transformation Ambassador". The Digital Transformation Ambassador is happy to support her colleague and IceMachine: A first meeting between these four key stakeholders is agreed.

Based on her long-term management experience, the CEO was able to utilize the personality preferences (here control and order parameters) of the stakeholders' 'project manager' and 'local politican'. So the meeting between the four stakeholders starts off with a good atmosphere, but after a while this quickly changes.

The local politiciain asks for a workplace guarantee and the CEO wriggles uncomfortably, unable to make a concrete statement. The project manager sees parallels with other projects where she feels that the CEO is not really interested in changing the way she thinks (key issue 4): The project manager considers that the CEO's behaviour lacks a sustainable, more human oriented aspect and feels that the CEO is only interested in making money.

The federal politician, the Digital Transformation Ambassador, recognizes the systemic structure: The local politician and the CEO are quite strictly driven by their v-meme structure and are presently incapable of seeing an integral perspective. The project leader does not have sufficient influence to open up the discussion and initiate a learning process with both. The Digital Transformation Ambassador knows that she will have to accept the different archetype preferences (key issue 3).

She outlines the new political direction for the Digital Transformation of the Federal Government (see the example below: A hypothetical scenario of a successful German Digital Transformation). The key issue of this new political orientation is that politicains have to embrace and to respect the as-is v-meme structure of society. A transformation can not be enforced, but politicians are tasked with designing learning spaces for different sectors of society. This gives the different sectors of society time to transform the v-meme structure in an appropriately balanced way.

She therefore proposes that IceMachine is transformed using a Fab Lab Hub (Gershenfeld (2017)): Fab Labs transform bits in atoms using digital models of products or parts of products to create (personalized) customer products. Many people believe that Fab Labs are the third Digital Revolution. 3D printing is one of the new physical technologies used in a Fab Lab.

The Digital Transformation Ambassador is aware that the IceMachine Digital Transformation requires balance and the integration of current machine and material know-how and future digital engineering know-how. Current know-how needs to be embraced and respected and then new know-how will be welcomed. IceMachine has the engineering and material know-how, which will combine with digital engineering know-how. The Digital Transformation Ambassador emphasizes that to be sustainably successful in the market, the introduction of appropriate social technologies will need to accompany physical technologies. She therefore suggests that the Federal Government supports the Digital Transformation of IceMachine financially and with trainers for Management 4.0 social technologies (key issue 4).

If we assume that IceMachine has a v-meme structure similar to the hypothetical v-meme structure of Germany (please see below): A I (60%), A II (30%), A III (9%), A IV (1%), this opens up the way for IceMachine to achieve a sustainable Digital Transformation: The v-meme structure will probably change to a more balanced one: A I (30%), A II (30%), A III (20%), A IV (10%). But this need time and it is impossible to say how long the transformation will last. To design the transformation, similar steps to those in Chapter 11 Agile Transformation 4.0 are required. We mention here also a very big "dog chasing its tail" - problem: In our example, the Digital Transformation Ambassador is an external person who is delivering an integral perspective and leading the stakeholders out of a deadlock situation: If there are no stakeholders with an integral perspective, the Digital Transformation can not start. In particular, this means that if a society has no critical mass of political influencers with an integral perspective, or an organization has no critical mass of leaders (C-level, middle management) Digital Transformation - as we have described it – can not start (key issue 4).

We have assumed for our example that in the meeting, all of the stakeholders are extremely surprised about this transformation, but they have the feeling that the suggestion is possible: The local politician has received an assurance that the people in her election district will not lose out, the CEO has the feeling that there is really a big opportunity for designing the company's future, and the project manager feels that "real" sustainability will find its way into the company.

Example: Making FAIR Data - Governance

Before transforming any company into a digital company, the first hurdle needs to be crossed: Consistent data needs to be used throughout the company. In this example we show a typical pattern, which arises in many companies.

We will discuss a fictious mid-sized company, TheWashMachine GmbH, who manufacture washing machines. Due to market pressure, these machines need to support smart homes in the future. One feature requested by customers is the connection of a machine to the user's smartphone. The user can then track the number of minutes the machine needs to run and whether there are any problems like loss of water etc. Another feature amongst many others is the ability to connect the machine to the manufacturer to report defects or attrition, to help improve the design for future machines. In case of attrition, the user will be notified by smartphone and a maintenance date will be offered, including a precise estimation of costs.

The company itself is proud of their products and in particular of the precison mechanics used in their washing machines. They are aware of digitization, but it is nevertheless, new terrain. The employees are aware that digitization opens up new business opportunities, but they are unaware that this also requires new data-related behavior: Data need to be processed throughout the company. This same data also needs to be understood by the user's smartphone as well as by the IT systems that produce the components of the machines. The CEO (Archetype II) identifies a suitable project leader for this topic. The project leader suggests introducing the FAIR data format, since it can be exchanged both inside and outside the company: FAIR stands for **F**indable, **A**cccessible, **I**nteroperable and **R**eusable (FAIR 2018).

The FAIR format requires strict discipline when creating, processing and using data. It also requires the introduction of additional IT systems, such as Master and Meta Data Management, and the management of unique identifiers. All this will affect the whole organization. The CEO is a promoter of Digital Transformation and therefore also of all necessary sub-tasks like introduction of the FAIR data format.

The project leader in charge of implementing the FAIR format is of course, also a supporter (Archetype III) and drives these activities with passion. Middle management and their co-workers prefer to work according to their old habits (Archetype I) and see this transformation as additional effort without any reimbursement. They prefer to store data locally, e.g. in Excel or local IT systems and still focus on the design and manufacturing of precise components for the machines. When using data from other departments, which does not often happen, they are prepared manually. Funnily enough, this is one of the biggest hurdles for transforming the company into one producing smart products. The project leader is still enthusiastic and provides data templates for entering new data using the FAIR format. He also introduces projects for simultaneously changing all (local) IT systems to be able to adapt this format. The CEO is convinced that FAIR appears to be user-friendly and intuitive so that employees will easily adopt any changes related to FAIR. Everything looks fine so far.

After a while, the project leader starts to experience resistance in the organization and feels trapped: The CEO continues to push the transformation, whilst sections of middle management and some of the co-workers resist. Pressure on the project leader dramatically increases, as do complaints about him (key issue 2): Finally, there is the danger of a complete mental block. On the micro-tier, local data management dominates and on the macro-tier, the company is still far from being transformed and capable of producing smart washing machines. The CEO hires a consultant (a digital evangelist) who acts as a supporter (Archetype IV). The supporter has the task of connecting with the co-workers and convincing them of the advantages of digitization. After several workshops, the co-workers still remain sceptical. The generic message from the CEO that "digital transformation will create new opportunities and will bring more efficiency" is not perceived in connection to a concrete product, the smart washing machine (key issue 3). In the end, resistance increases and a lot more energy will be required to convince the co-workers.

During the workshops with the co-workers, the consultant comes to the conclusion that the only chance for progress is to create cases studies demonstrating that FAIR data will bring the necessary benefits. He and the project leader develop a transformation model (key issues 1-4). They came to the conclusion that the co-workers' control parameters are determined by the local culture of focusing on precise components for the machines (blue v-meme) and neglecting the power of FAIR data.

The consultant and the project leader identify early adopters with dominant green value-memes (Archetype III), who are also well respected by their colleagues. These early adopters will support the creation of the case studies. Once they have demonstrated the benefits of the case studies, other colleagues will likely follow their lead (key issue 2, 3).

This is a detour, which carries extra costs, but it is necessary to address the dominant "blue" value-meme which dominates the local structures and culture. Having these case studies in place provides an opportunity to challenge the as-is situation of manual data handling and demonstrate the value of the FAIR concept to middle management and co-workers. At this stage, the micro-tier still consists of isolated case studies, each benefit-generating, but without any chance of connecting data throughout the company. The manual data curation problem still exists, even if some co-workers and middle management have now been convinced of the FAIR data concept.

The consultant then takes the next step (key issue 1): The introduction of a governance structure to enable the emergence of a target macro-structure supporting FAIR data throughout the company. The governance structure consist of guidelines and a monitoring concept of the effectivenesss of the guidelines. The case studies gave hints as to what the guidelines should look like. During creation of the case studies by the co-workers, the project leader and the consultant very carefully and transparently looked for suitable setting and control parameters from which to build guidelines.

In addition, the concept of having a guideline also allows departments to retain some of their habits, since the guidelines will be developed in "local" SOPs (see also Oswald (2018)). It is also essential to establish the governance **after** having implemented the case studies, since the company culture is very practice oriented with little meta-competency. The stakeholders involved are now able to see the benefit of having a governance and the implementation step can be carried out successfully. A discussion about governance at an earlier stage without the use of case studies, would most likely have resulted in resistance (key issue 3).

A new order parameter using FAIR data can now emerge throughout the company (key issue 3): Local data handling can be changed in a coherent way, determined by the guidelines: Master and Meta Data will be introduced and stored centrally. Along with unique identifiers for naming entities and data domains. Because the case studies which were used recently (for local data management) are also transformed, resistance will still be present but below a critical threshold. Once the first prototypes of the new washing machine have been produced and after playing around with them, the co-workers begin to like the concept of FAIR data, because they see the advantages of having smart washing machines. Now the organization is in a self-enforcing mode: Governance is one control parameter and positive experience with FAIR data is the other main control parameter. Both parameters have been created by connecting the individual experiences of the co-workers to the FAIR data concept via the "positive feedback-loop in small steps" control parameter.

What is the difference between the first chosen approach (unsuccessful) and the second (successful) approach: The first approach, which is clearly the CEO's favourite (orange v-meme), since it retains the high speed of the transformation by bearing no extra costs, will end up in a mental block, since the blue v-meme is dominantly in the group of co-workers and middle management. This subsequently requires the second approach of respecting the local culture and habits (blue v-meme). From the CEO's perspective, this approach is a cost intensive detour. The consultant should be able to convince the CEO that the costs will finally produce pay back. In addition, the co-workers have learned to appreciate the advantage of having FAIR data. If this behavior is used for a certain time and shows sustainable benefits for individuals, as well as for the organization as a whole, behavior will result in a transformation of the organizational culture. This will probably result in a transformation which includes blue and orange v-memes. The dominance of blue v-memes is reduced and the orange v-meme can come into play. In the same step, a leap to a transformation, which includes green v-memes is rather unlikely (key issue 4). The early adopters with dominant green value-memes (Archetype III) will be able to help start the next transformation cycle to implement green v-meme elements (please see chapter 11 Agile Tranformation). This transformation needs to include the transformation of the CEO's v-memes, too.

Example: A hypothetical scenario of a successful German Digital Transformation

Let us assume that we can hypothetically model German Society using the following Archetype percentage shares: A I (60%), A II (30%), A III (9%), A IV (1%). The question is: "Could there be a successful Digital Transformation with these setting conditions?".

The first step in answering this question is to look at the average behavior of each member of this population in the context of digitization (key issue 1). This means looking at the micro-tier of the different populations and the resulting macro-structure (below indicated by bold letters). For different populations, different intervention techniques (below indicated by green letters) are necessary to make the Digital Transformation successful (key issue 2 and 3):

A I (60%)

- No pro-active behavior, has a limited understanding of what digitization is, sees more risks than advantages.
- Believes that small enhancements and improvments in the current structure will make the future liveable: Digitization means the improvement of digital infrastructure (Giga-bit cables, laptops for schools, etc.).
- **This population determines the overall flexibility of society resulting in limited agility.**
- Give this population safety, structure and order with the following key measures:

- Regulate capitalism and exponential organizations and introduce a basic income,
- Support a paradigm shift of work: total income = basic income + work income,
- Initiate a paradigm shift of the education system to cope with complexity (this is also valid for the other sections of the population),
- Much more appreciation for a range of professions.

A II (30%)

- Very pro-active behavior, see the next chance to make money. Focus on the lowest two digitization levels of Figure 13-1, because these levels bring new opportunities to make money and money is the basis of welfare.
- **A lot of startups are founded, but with low sustainability.**
- Establish transparency, foster technology exchange as well as monitor and regulate self-organization.

A III (9%)

- Promotes digitization, because it will help make the world a better place.
- **Encouraging people and therefore it is necessary to invest in a mindset shift and open mindsets by teaching an understanding of complexity.**
- The politics should give an ear to this population and build together with them social platforms of consciousness and culture development.

A IV (1%)

- Promotes digitization, because it is the key to the next step of evolution.
- **Looks for understanding of the emergent new structure, to monitor these and to develop relevant Governance and social intervention technologies.**

- This intervention technique is identical to that in A III (9%): Give an ear to this population and build social platforms of consciousness and culture.

It is likely that at first, the resulting population macro-structure is not very different than the as-is structure, but this does not results in a limited agility of the whole society, but opens up the way to social consciousness and culture development (key issue 4).

The above mentioned hypothetical structure and related proposed cross-grained interventions are societal setting and control parameters. Together with a 'by the society for the society' worked out Digital Transformation vision (order parameter), these will induce an unknown dynamic. But, we have the hope that this dynamic will induce a new, more appropriate v-meme structure. This will only happen, if society pays attention to the following key principles:

- Digital Transformation has to be sustainable and holistic: A Digital Transformation is a transformation where social technologies are at least as essential as physical technologies.
- Digital Transformation has to remove a massive deadlock: An Archetype III/IV meta-competence is required to effectively design the Digital Transformation. But the majority of society does not (currently) see this need, so that Archetype III/IV (currently) does not play an essential role in the design of future society. And to be able to see this, it is necessary to have some aspects of an Archetype III/IV persona.
- Digital Transformation requires organizational and political leaders that lead by a Governance which permits self-organization and learning to thrive.

Literature

Beck DE, Cowan CC (1995) Spiral Dynamics: Mastering Values, Leadership and Change, Gb

FAIR (2018) https://www.force11.org/fairprinciples, accessed on 28/12/2018

Gershenfeld Neil, Gershenfeld Alan and Cutcher-Gershenfeld Joel (2017) Designing Reality – How to Survive and Thrive in the Third Digital Revolution, BASIC BOOKS, New York

Harari, Yuval (2017) Homo Deus: A Brief history of tomorrow, Harper

Kucklick Christoph (2016) Die granulare Gesellschaft: Wie das Digitale unsere Wirklichkeit auflöst, Ullstein Taschenbuch, Kindle edition

Laloux F (2014) Reinventing Organizations: A Guide to Creating Organizations Inspired by the Next Stage of Human Consciousness, Nelson Parker

Land Karl-Heinz (2018) Erde 5.0: Die Zukunft Provozieren, futurevisionpress e.K., Kindle edition

O'Neil Cathy (2016) Weapons of Math Destruction: How Big Data Increases Inequality and Threatens Democracy, Allen Lane, Kindle edition

Oswald Alfred, Köhler Jens and Schmitt Roland (2018) Project Management at the Edge of Chaos, Springer Heidelberg

Veit Heiko (2018) Praxishandbuch Integrale Organisationsentwicklung – Grundlagen für zukunftsfähige Organisationen, Wiley-VCH Verlag, Weinheim

Wikipedia (2108) Wir schaffen das, https://de.wikipedia.org/wiki/Wir_schaffen_das, accessed on 28/12/2018

Notes